Bringing Up Race

How to Raise a Kind Child
in a Prejudiced World

Uju Asika

First published in Great Britain in 2020 by Yellow Kite
An imprint of Hodder & Stoughton
An Hachette UK company

1

A CIP catalogue record for this title is available from the British Library

Hardback ISBN 978 1 529 36872 7
eBook ISBN 978 1 529 37170 3
Audio Download ISBN 978 1 529 37319 6

Typeset in Baskerville by Hewer Text UK Ltd, Edinburgh
Printed and bound in Great Britain by Clays Ltd, Elcograf S.p.A.

Hodder & Stoughton policy is to use papers that are natural, renewable and recyclable products and made from wood grown in sustainable forests. The logging and manufacturing processes are expected to conform to the environmental regulations of the country of origin.

Yellow Kite
Hodder & Stoughton Ltd
Carmelite House
50 Victoria Embankment
London EC4Y 0DZ

www.yellowkitebooks.co.uk

To my parents, who made me. And to Abiye, Ezra and Jed who make me want to be a better human.

Contents

Author's Note

The path to publication for a Black author in Britain is not always easy. In an industry that is nearly 90 per cent White, you wonder if there's space for someone who looks and sounds like you. On June 15, 2020, energised by global Black Lives Matter protests, the newly formed Black Writers' Guild put out an open letter to the publishing industry calling for sweeping changes. I was proud to add my signature to a list of incredible writers including Afua Hirsch, David Olusoga, Candice Carty-Williams, Malorie Blackman, Sir Lenny Henry, Benjamin Zephaniah and Bernadine Evaristo.

There is a lot to do but I'm hopeful that changes will happen. If you are a Black or Brown or marginalised writer who's never had the confidence to pitch your work before, I hope you will seize this moment. The world is waiting for your story.

I am so grateful to the many writers and mentors who have supported my journey to becoming a published author (see Acknowledgements p.307). However, I would like to credit my cousin here. She was aware of my blog and my experiences as a Black mother, and she insisted I should write a book on the subject. When initially I hesitated, my cousin sent an email to agents asking if they would like to read a book proposal from me. I am not sure I would have written this book without her persistence.

Preface

When I was pregnant with Ezra, like any first-time mother, my number-one concern was bringing him into this world alive and healthy. I remember the panic of a slow-kick day, when I'd move around vigorously just to shake my belly awake. Then there were the sleepless nights when Ezra wouldn't stop scoring 'top bins' in my womb.

From the minute I learned I was pregnant (several cocktails too late), I knew I was having a boy. I knew he would have fat cheeks, like his half-brother, Isaac, and soft hair, like mine. I imagined him running into his father's arms, squealing with delight. Curling up on my chest to fall asleep.

The one thing I didn't think too much about was how racism might affect him. I'm a Black Nigerian woman who grew up in Britain, so I'm no stranger to prejudice. But most of my mental space was taken up with browsing baby catalogues, dreaming about eating soft cheese or counting heartbeats on a monitor. All I wanted was a healthy, happy baby.

Just before Ezra was born, my husband, Abiye, and I moved back to London after two years living in Lagos. I had my first taste of being treated like the Other again. While Abiye and I were going through prenatal classes, the hospital demanded we provide 'proof' that we were staying in the country. That we weren't planning to drop sprog and run. We knew that, in spite of our British passports, our Nigerian names had flagged us up as potential health tourists. The hospital threatened us with a large bill if we didn't offer evidence right away.

There was some heated back and forth, culminating in my husband firing off a letter outlining his disgust at their treatment of us, and inviting them to look us up in a year's time. But they never bothered. And we were here to stay.

Both my sons, now 9 and 13, have grown up in London since birth. They are the smart-mouthed, fun-loving stars of my blog, 'Babes about Town', all about raising cool kids in the capital. We find parent-friendly things to do around town, and I share with my audience around the world the cute conversations we have, as well as funny and insightful tales of family life.

One story I shared with my Facebook followers happened after an Arsenal match. The babes are keen footballers and we'd seen an image of striker Pierre Aubameyang standing tall and strong, over a banana skin that had been chucked at him from the stands.

'What does that even mean?' my boys wanted to know.

I sighed. I told them about the use of bananas as a racist symbol directed at Black people. Why some idiots call us monkeys, and how many footballers have had to endure bananas and worse over the years. They were outraged for a moment and then, as kids do, they moved on to something else. But it broke my heart a little.

We are proud to live in London, one of the most diverse and integrated places on earth. However, even in London, you can't escape the many shades of racism.

Professor Beverly Tatum, an author and clinical psychologist, describes the effects of racism as 'smog in the air'.[1] You can't avoid it, because it's everywhere. In the looks my kids get in certain spaces. The manner in which some people speak to them. The stuff that goes over their heads. And the stuff that makes them cry, even when they don't know why.

How do you bring up your kids to be cool, kind and happy when there is so much out there trying to break them down?

This book is my attempt not necessarily to answer this question definitively, but to consider it with the weight and attention it deserves. For it's a question that affects us all.

Introduction

A little girl sat on a playing field, her bottom damp with early-morning dew. Behind her, a tall stone building, the entrance to one of England's top boarding schools. Beyond her, more grass and trees and farmland, as far as the eye could see. It struck her that no matter how long she walked, she would be the only Black girl for miles. The little girl hugged her knees to her chest. She had never felt so far away from home.

Then a voice inside her whispered: 'That's ok. You will never be one of the crowd. And that makes you special. You can choose who you want to be. That means you're free.'

Growing up Black

Growing up between Britain and Nigeria in the '80s, I had a shifting sense of identity. Nowadays, there's a term for it: 'third-culture kid'. It was disorienting at times, but also liberating. I realised early on that I didn't have to be one thing or the other. Straddling two cultures added a depth and richness to my life, and an openness to new experiences.

My early encounters with racism were minor compared to what my older sister went through. As the first Black girl at our boarding school, she was once tied to a chair by fellow pupils hurling racial insults at her. She was six years old.

By the time I joined the school, I was one of at least four other Black kids, including my two older siblings. Still, my difference marked me out for jokes like: 'Smile, otherwise we can't see you,' after the lights went out. Sometimes I wonder if my overtly smiley personality came as a response to comments like these. Toothy grin, lips stretched wide, just wishing to be seen.

Actually, I've always been a happy-go-lucky kind of girl. Old photographs, and scratchy video footage from early childhood, reveal my giggly nature, or what my sister fondly calls me to this day, a 'laughing jackass'.

My memories of growing up are overwhelmingly happy ones. Ours was a tight-knit school where I made many friends. We'd roll down hills, climb swing ropes, play Stuck-in-the-Mud and whisper secrets in the dark. I had my first long-term romance with an English boy. We 'dated' for two years, between the ages of 9 and 11.

Holidays in Nigeria meant endless cousins for sleepovers, afternoons spent devouring the contents of my parents' bookshelves, or playing cowboys outside, climbing trees for fruit, watching *The Sound of Music* on repeat.

Yet, I also remember the helplessness of walking down a London street and someone shouting 'Nigger' from a car window. Being called a 'blot on the landscape' by a girl who would later call me her best friend. A toddler reaching out and trying to rub the brown off my skin. Cracks about Africa and monkeys and mud huts.

I remember my best friend at age nine pulling me in for a tight embrace and then looking at me with sorrow (or pity?) in her eyes.

'I wish you were White,' she said, before running off.

I can still feel the visceral shock of having the word 'Nigger' spat at me by a boy in my class. I didn't know what I'd done, if anything at all, to offend or provoke him. Several friends leaped to my defence, but I had no words, and that was part of my shame. Words were my allies, my armour, but they had let me down.

I smiled and I carried on.

I could imagine a future, though, when things would be different. I wanted my kids to grow up in a world where nobody could make them feel less than they were, just because of the tone of their skin or the tightness of their curls. I wanted a life in which insults like 'Nigger' would never have the power to leave me speechless.

I had it all planned out. I would be worldly, wealthy and magnanimous. I'd adopt a rainbow tribe of babies from every corner of the planet, like Josephine Baker (or Angelina Jolie, as it happened). Of course, by that time, grand-scale poverty, disease and famine, nuclear disarmament and peace in the Middle East would be sorted too. Yes, I too had a dream.

It's 2020 and I'm no longer dreaming. As a woman of colour in today's Brexit and Trump climate, you have to stay woke.

Things didn't turn out as I'd imagined, although we've certainly come a long way.

I live in one of the most cosmopolitan cities on earth. London is one of the few places where I get to feel like me. Not solely a Black woman or a Nigerian or an African, but just another mum going about her day. I've lived in America, where – even in New York – I 'felt Black' every time I stepped out of my front door. In Nigeria, my birth country, I can be singled out for the way I talk, how I dress, what my kids look like. In London, I feel free. I can choose who I want to be.

Yet it's hardly Utopia. People of colour in Britain overwhelmingly face social barriers. Class barriers. Stop-and-search barriers. Prison barriers. Employment barriers. Professional barriers. Media barriers. Economic barriers. School-exclusion barriers. Knife-crime barriers. Policing barriers.

'Babes About Town'

In 2010, I launched a popular blog about raising cool kids in one of the coolest cities in the world. By 2011, London was on fire. The riots turned neighbourhoods over and burned to ashes any notions of the UK as a 'prim, proper and post-racial' society.

We were watching news images of people looting and buildings set aflame, and my then five-year-old Ezra turned to me, solemnly.

'Mummy,' he said, 'the youths are going crazy.'

I couldn't help chuckling at his turn of phrase, but my heart felt heavy. How could I begin to explain to a small child what was happening? I could hardly understand it myself. But I knew there was a lot more to the picture than the misplaced anger of displaced youths. The riots were sparked by the death of Mark Duggan, a young Black man who was killed in a police shooting.

At what age would I have to have 'the talk' with my boys about how to keep yourself safe in a world that often sees young Black men as a threat?

I carried on blogging. I wanted to take back the city I call home. I wanted to showcase the best of what I love about London, and to encourage other families to seek more fun, wonder and adventure in the everyday.

When my cousin suggested I should write a book, inspired by my blog, on the experience of raising happy Black boys in a prejudiced world, I struggled at first. That's not what my blog is about, I told her. I write often about my heritage, featuring photos of our family life and highlighting activities around town that are multicultural. But I've deliberately steered away from making our Blackness a 'thing'.

However, the more I thought about it, the more it made sense. A big part of my blog is giving my kids an immersive cultural education in London and beyond. I take my boys everywhere – not just to street parties and family festivals, but to traditionally 'White' venues like theatres, the opera, ballet, the National Gallery, classical concerts. I am fully aware that we are helping to change the narrative of how Black people engage, create and consume the culture at large. We flip the script, simply by being visible in those spaces.

My audience is mostly UK-based, but I have readers all over the world. By inviting them to be part of our journey, we are changing the way many of them see Black people too. And our presence encourages more people from Black/ethnic backgrounds to follow in our steps. It's important to show that these spaces are not just for a certain 'type' of Londoner, but for every one of us.

A simple but powerful message.

On a deeper level, showing happy Black boys thriving in the face of negativity and low expectations is in many ways a radical act. We were living #Blackboyjoy before it became a trending hashtag.

'Babes about Town' is ostensibly a blog for parents in London (and beyond) who want to find fun things to do with their kids, recover their cool and rediscover their city through new eyes. But the true story is that of a modern Black multicultural family out there, living our best life, in spite of the haters.

It is a story I've been writing my whole life.

So why this book? Because we have so much work to do, collectively. Parenting is hard, for sure. Racism and bigotry might be the last thing you want to think about when you're just trying to keep a tiny human alive.

But there's nothing more urgent than bringing up our kids to think globally, fairly and with empathy for their fellow human. We need to be responsible for raising a generation of people who are more open, more tolerant, less afraid. We need to challenge the Boogie Monster of the world and cut it down to size.

Happy Lives Matter

Sometimes it feels like we're living through an increasingly dark and disturbing period in global history. It's not always easy holding your head up and encouraging your children to keep theirs up too. But we can all be part of a quiet revolution. Choose joy over fear. Choose love over division. Choose education over discord. Every single day.

Mark Williamson, director of Action for Happiness, has interviewed hundreds of parents over the years. He says the number-one thing they say about their kids is, 'I really just want them to be happy'.

Happiness matters. And the wonderful thing about happiness is that it's contagious. An extensive study published in the *British Medical Journal* in 2008 identified that our individual happiness can affect others by 'three degrees of separation'.[1] In other words, our happiness makes our friends happier, and our friends' friends happier, in turn.

How do we raise happy kids? For a start, we raise them strong. Studies about Danish people, who regularly top global happiness scores, reveal an interesting factor. The Danes are masters at reframing – looking at things that happen from a broader point of view. Apparently, this is one of the keys to happiness. The ability to see any situation from a new angle, to focus on the more positive aspects and to bounce back, no matter what life throws at you.

I'm blessed with two exceptionally bouncy boys and, as they grow older, I am trying to empower them with a strong sense of self, rooted in that playful spirit. I tell them possessions aren't important, but they should keep their cool, their sense of humour and their sense of perspective. When faced with a challenge, I encourage them to think, take a step back and look at the bigger picture.

In this book, you'll hear from a range of professionals and influencers, friends, family and colleagues who have been directly touched by the issues raised. I'll share personal stories and conversations I've had with my kids too.

When my youngest, Jed, was around four years old, he took my face between his chubby little hands:

'Do you know why I love you so much, Mummy?' he asked. 'It's because you're brown.'

Such a sweet, innocent, surprisingly moving statement. An affirmation for my brownness, for seeing himself in me, for loving me as he sees me. Not wishing I was something entirely different. Not switching the lights out on my identity.

Fat, tall, wide, small, pink or brown . . . all any of us wants is to be seen and appreciated for exactly who we are. This is the essence of love. In my native Igbo language, when we say 'I love you', it translates as, 'I see you with my eyes'.

To the blond woman being asked if her Brown child is her son/daughter when she is picking them up from school, I see you. For the little girl watching wide-eyed as her dad gets roughed up by police, I see you. For the couple trying to comfort their son after he's called 'Darkie' in the playground, I see you. For the mixed-heritage Londoner holding back another sigh after that familiar question, 'So, where are you actually from?', I see you. This book is for you.

And this book is for that little girl inside me, still smiling her heart out. I see you too.

A caveat: I am not a parenting expert. In truth, I'm not sure such a person exists. I consider myself an expert in parenting my own kids, and even then, I'm learning as I go. In writing this book, my goal is not to have the last word, but to encourage you to have these conversations within your own homes and beyond, and to keep them going. Every voice matters.

Please note also, this is not a how-to manual in the typical sense. It will include insights and tips from experts and others. And each chapter will end with some talking points, based on discussions I've had with members of my community. But what you'll hear most of all are stories. As a storyteller, I believe we don't need more 'strategies'; we need more stories. Not just stories of woe, but stories of joy, enlightenment and transformation. After all is said and done, it is our stories that save us.

CHAPTER 1

Whose Child Is That?

There is no such thing as other people's children.

Russian proverb

I was walking through Abuja airport, sweating under the weight of baggage and baby. Nine-month-old Ezra balanced precariously on a hip-seat buckled awkwardly around my waist. A nappy bag, crammed to bursting, was slung low across my body, knocking my right thigh repeatedly.

I'm an anxious flyer at the best of times, and this was my first experience travelling solo with an infant. The journey itself had been relatively smooth. Yet my nerves were jangling after trying to breastfeed discreetly on a flying vehicle packed with strangers, changing nappies in the pop-up cot and being on red alert for six hours and counting.

Despite the combo of exhaustion and discomfort, I was bubbly with anticipation. It was my first visit home since becoming a mother. The first time I would present my newborn to his

11

grandmother, who was waiting with open arms and full table at her home in Maitama.

I was born in Nigeria, and although the greater portion of my life has been spent abroad, when I talk of 'home', it's still the first place that springs to mind. I consider myself a Londoner through and through, and of course, that is home too. It's where I live, how I express myself, the city where my kids were born. But nothing compares to the feeling of stepping on native soil, taking in the familiar clash of scents, my skin shocked by the heat. Shocked but happy. Yes, my heart whispers, welcome back.

As I walked through the airport, I was increasingly aware of stares. Eyes snapping wide at the sight of dark-skinned me, proudly lumbering along with what could be described as a chubby Samoan baby on my hip.

When Ezra was born, he had straight, jet-black hair, almond eyes and pale skin. As the weeks went on, his cheeks and frame filled out and he took on the appearance of a jolly Buddha. I would sometimes entertain his dad by dressing Ezra up in a skull cap and waving his arms along to the lyrics of Fat Joe. He looked a lot like the Latino rapper and it cracked us up.

So there I was, Fat Joe bouncing along on my hip, heading blithely towards passport control.

The Nigerian character is the antithesis of subtle. As a nation, we are loud and in your face. Back in England, even if passers-by wondered about us, few would dare to remark on our difference. Here, in my homeland, the staring was audible. An airport official marched over.

'*Na your pikin be dis*?'

From Pidgin English, this translates as 'Is this your child?'

It was my turn to stare. What was this person asking me? How should I respond?

A part of me wanted to quip, 'No, actually I picked him up at Heathrow'. But you don't joke with Nigerian airport officials. Not unless you're safely through customs or have several crisp notes to shake hands with if the laughter stops.

The stares and questions followed me not just through the airport but throughout our trip. People would ask how I got this *oyinbo* (White) baby, where his father was, if I was really his mum . . .

My responses veered from irritation to amusement. I got used to dishing out flat, forthright answers that rarely seemed to satisfy. Or making up stories. Like the one about Ezra's father, the Sumo wrestler, who was stuck in Japan at a tournament.

Is That Kid Yours?

When your child is placed in your arms for the first time, the world comes sharply into focus. Nothing matters more.

I remember stepping out of the hospital, a brand-new Ezra in my arms, feeling like I'd been unplugged from the matrix. Every sense was tingling. I could hear, see and smell the city and all its dangers, but I was ready. Now I understood why I had been born – to be a warrior for my baby. I would slay dragons, tear whole armies apart with my teeth, if anybody tried to harm a hair on his head.

Yet with one question, a complete stranger could throw me off balance.

'Is that kid yours?'

I didn't know whether to laugh or scream. Yes, I carried that baby for nearly ten months. I cut out alcohol. I had sciatica and restless legs, crazy dreams and a belly that will never, ever spring back. Are you effing kidding me right now?

Maybe it's not the question itself, but everything it implies: you don't look like the mother, so you can't possibly be the mother. Your child is approximately White, with that good hair and, well, look at you . . . How did you get to have such adorable kids – I mean you're attractive and all, but still . . . Where's the daddy? Is he White? Chinese? Why isn't he around? Did he abandon you? Couldn't you find any decent men of your own kind to procreate with? I wish I had cute kids like yours, I'd prefer them to be light-skinned, I'm thinking of getting a White man myself . . .

For most mums, being told you don't belong with your child is like the ultimate slap in the face. My inner 'Nigerian Big Madam' swells up like, 'Do you know who I am?'

My friend Nomita Vaish-Taylor, owner of the blog Your 'DIYFamily.com', feels my pain. She talks about going home to Mumbai with her daughter, Anya, whose father is White. 'People literally follow us in the street, and you can see them wondering about us. Like, where did she get her from? As if I stole her. It's only when Richard is with us that we make any kind of sense. I shrug it off, but it's pretty annoying.'

You don't have to be of a different ethnic background from your baby to be probed in this manner. Mothers I've spoken to have faced intrusive comments for appearing older (grandma?), having multiples (IVF?) or if one child stands out from the rest (milkman?). For White mums of dark-skinned children, strangers often assume they've fostered them or adopted from overseas.

On parenting forums, mums share snappy comebacks to the very rude query: 'Where did you get that baby from?'

'From my vagina,' is a personal favourite.

Who Does Baby Look Like?

One of the weird things about motherhood is how everybody and their mama (and she should definitely know better) has an opinion about you and your child.

From midwives to the man on the street, the first thing people will tell you is who your baby looks like. I've heard folks become adamant, almost rabid, about this.

'He's the spit of his father. He looks *nothing* like you.'

I spent 15 hours in induced labour with Ezra. From the first waves of pain, I was Bruce-Lee stoic on the outside, bawling on the inside. Doing my best to ignore my husband beside me, as he puffed on my gas and air for fun and asked helpful questions like, 'What's wrong? Are you in pain?'

Then came the emergency C-section in which I could feel the surgeon's first cuts, after I'd peaked on pain meds. All this and, within moments of Ezra's birth, nurses were tripping over themselves to tell me how 'he looks just like his father'.

I didn't mind at first. I thought he looked like Abiye too. But soon it started to get old. Sure, the resemblance was strong. But I did all the hard work – shouldn't I get some credit?

For parents, claiming whose genes 'won' can become a competitive hobby. Maria Jose Ovalle is a Chilean American blogger and actress who says her three kids look just like her.

'I personally love it,' she says. 'My husband gets a little jealous but admits they are my mini mes. Right down to their bossiness!'

Londoner and political activist Laura Vogel says she and her husband josh about who 'owns' whom, though her kids are a 'good hybrid'. What she loves is seeing the ancestors echoing down the lines. 'Just a glimpse of family resemblance makes you start thinking about how your kids connect the past and the future.'

I remember once lying on a bed beside my aunt, when she suddenly exclaimed, 'Look at that!', raising her foot up and inviting me to do the same. It was uncanny. Mine was pale, hers several tones darker, but otherwise they were almost identical. Right down to the shrivelled bulbs that were our baby toes. It set us off giggling. We get it from my grandmother, she told me.

There is a rare delight in seeing your ancestry passed down through you, to your offspring. So it's one thing being told your child looks like his father (the handsome man that you chose to procreate with) and another to be told your baby looks *nothing* like you. I'd shrug it off, but sometimes I felt like a kid with my hand up at the back of class, watching the teacher erase my family tree from the board.

There's a theory that all newborns look like their fathers, at least for the first six months. It's a sort of evolutionary paternity test – a way of making sure Papa sticks around. For some animal species, it stops Daddy from snacking on his own children.[1]

However, the shuffling of up to 100,000 genes among 46 chromosomes – 23 from each parent – is complex, throwing up wild cards. People are often curious that my husband isn't fully White, since our kids are so fair. But the 'light' gene also runs in my family.

My Auntie Obii gave birth to a very light-skinned daughter with hazel eyes, and she remembers people shouting through the village: 'Come see wetin Pax wife don born o!' (Come and see what Pax's wife has given birth to.)

After she had two more children, similarly fair-skinned, tongues stopped wagging. Her third child was born in London. The maternity nurse who'd taken over duty from the night before came into the ward, carrying baby Daibi. Her cheeks flushed pink, as she held him forward.

'I think this is your baby,' she said, nervously.

'It's ok, he's mine,' my auntie said, laughing, as she claimed her White-skinned, blue-eyed boy.

Another of my mother's sisters, Auntie Ngozi, told me about being mistaken for a nanny as she pushed her 'White' baby around Baltimore in the early '70s. She said adults would bend down and speak directly to her daughter, cooing at the child, while ignoring her mother as if she was just the help.

Not the Nanny

In a public library, I was flicking through *Grazia* magazine, while keeping an idle eye on Ezra roaming through the bookshelves. Jed was asleep in his pushchair. A voice piped up beside me.

'These boys are so cute. Are you the nanny?'

Record scratch.

It wasn't the first time someone had assumed I was the childminder. I thought about the many hours I'd studied to get a postgraduate degree. I thought about the barriers I'd faced, as well as the choices I'd made, that had led to being a work-from-home mum. I caught a glimpse of my reflection in the library window, in jeans and headscarf, and wondered if I'd have assumed the same thing too in another person's shoes.

In 2017, Professor Robert E. Kelly was caught being 'video bombed' by his kids during a Skype interview on BBC's *Newsnight*.[2] The sight of Prof Kelly trying to maintain a straight face while his toddler and baby bopped into frame is pure gold. It hits peak hilarity when his wife, Jung-a Kim, slides in, grabs the kids and bolts. The world screeched with laughter, the video went viral and Prof Kelly and family became Insta-celebrities.

But the story took an ugly turn when some mainstream press and social-media commenters described Jung-a Kim as the nanny. While some people claimed it was an honest mistake ('look how she was dressed'), others said it played into racist stereotypes. Like the one about Asian women in subservient roles. Or the idea that an esteemed White professor couldn't possibly hook up for life with a Korean native. Some people went on to insist that she couldn't be the mother because she just didn't look like her kids.

In response, mothers from all over the world hit social media and shared their own stories of being mistaken for someone other than their child's parent. #NottheNanny became a trending hashtag. Some of the stories were funny, but many brimmed with indignation, anger or deep hurt.

'Being challenged over my connection to my children strikes me on such a personal level, I can't even explain it,' says Justine (name changed). 'It's almost like I'm not worthy to be their mum. Worse, I've imagined maybe I'll be separated from them in some way, by people who've decided we don't belong together.'

'Are you the nanny?'

The lady asking me this question in the library that day was a Black woman herself, who was nanny to the two White children in her charge. She was just trying to make conversation, as it turns out.

I smiled and explained who I was, and that was the end of it. But my first instinct was to look over at Ezra, to see whether he'd overheard. I'm not always bothered by intrusive, lazy, dumb or flat-out racist speculation. However, it bothers me when it happens in front of our kids. Because children absorb, they take notice and, frankly, they deserve better than our ignorance.

Since my kids have got older, the questions about their parentage are not so frequent. As often happens with Black babies, their skin got a little darker over time, their hair bloomed into glorious Afro locks. Their features are a happy combination of mine and their father's, and many people think they look just like me.

I still face curious glances at airports, but mostly because we use different surnames. I've learned not to attempt leaving the country without a letter of paternal consent. It's a safeguard to prevent children from being kidnapped or taken out of the country against another parent's wishes. Although for many mothers, it grates on a visceral level. Another slap in the face.

Belonging

I'm no longer fussed about whether people think I look like my boys. Instead, I worry about raising Black boys in a world that sees colour first. A world that has been putting a price on their skin tone since they were born.

'What am I?'

It's a question that raises my hackles, as innocent as it sounds. A question that is typically asked of people whose racial mixture isn't quite clear-cut. One that threatens to dehumanise. What even are you?

Ezra is waiting for my response. 'What am I, Mum? I mean, what race am I?'

His father answers sharply, 'The human race'.

We all know the answer is much more layered, and political too. When I'm faced with the form requesting I check a box for my kids, I usually check Black African. That's the bulk of their heritage (through me) and at first glance, that's how they will move through the world. No matter if they're seen as having fairer skin and 'good hair', for all intents and purposes they're Black boys.

'But am I mixed race?' Ezra wants to know. Jed smirks and Ezra shoots him a look. 'If I'm mixed race, that means you are too, by the way.'

Jed's eyebrows go up.

Ezra is the lightest-skinned person in our family, and he's told me that when he was younger, in primary school, some of his friends thought he was White. It amuses me, as there's nothing about his features other than his complexion that would suggest it. Yet, his nana is White and so, by definition, he's mixed heritage. It's clouded by the fact that in this country, mixed heritage usually means one of your parents is White.

'You're Black and biracial,' I tell him, which is as close as we can get to a straight answer. We talk more about the political implications of choosing 'mixed' over 'Black'. The complexities of checking boxes or leaving them unchecked entirely. The fact that ultimately, you don't have to clip your wings with someone else's labels or string out your identity in a series of hyphens.

You are Nigerian, and so am I. You are British, and so am I. You are a Londoner, and so am I. You are Kalabari and Sierra Leonean, like your grandfather. You are Scottish and New

Zealander, like your grandmother. You are Owerri and Onitsha, like your mother. You are Black and White, like your father. When we watch sports, we support Britain and Nigeria. We also support France, because your older brother is half-French, and your auntie has lived there most of her adult life. You are Arsenal through and through.

We are all a compendium of the genes we inherit, the places we visit, the people we move with, the ones we fall in love with and the ones we give birth to. There is no single story to the way we look, sound or interact.

There is no single story to how we make a family. If your child worries about people who are different or questions where they fit and how, reassure them with this simple truth. Belonging is more than skin deep.

Fifteen years ago, my mother adopted a baby girl in Nigeria who now could pass for my blood sister.

'It's weird,' my older sister tells me. 'She looks just like you.'

Whose child is that?

Na my pikin. Na your pikin. They belong to all of us. Let's act accordingly.

• Talking Points

Q. What do I tell my child to say when someone asks where they're from?
A. Teach them to state clearly and with confidence where they were born, or where they live, if that's how they identify

culturally. Also, they should follow up with: 'And where are you from?' It doesn't matter if the person they're talking to is White, Black, Asian, Muslim, mixed ethnicity or of ambiguous origin. They can treat it like a conversation starter, rather than an interrogation. If the person pushes for more information ('Where are your parents from?' for example) they are welcome to answer if they choose or say, 'Why do you want to know?' Once again, encourage them to turn the question on the person asking. The point is that your child should not be made to feel like a stranger in their own country, simply because they look different or their parents were born overseas.

Q. How can I talk to my child about our lack of family resemblance?
A. It can be tough when your baby looks nothing like you. Especially if they appear to have different ethnic origins. This can be tricky as your child grows and wonders why they look so different from Mum or Dad. I find it's helpful to track through your lineage, look at old family photos together; often you'll find someone that resembles your child. A great-grandmother, a distant uncle. You can also look for stand-out features you and your child might have in common, such as size and stature, hair colouring, shape of ears/nose/fingers. If there's no visible resemblance or your child is adopted, you can talk about shared personality traits, interests and passions. Look for other things that connect you. Also celebrate your child's unique qualities, how each of us is as individual as our

fingerprints. Don't forget children's faces change throughout their lives. All my childhood and early adulthood, I was told I was the spit of my father and my paternal grandmother. But as I grow older, I see more of my mother too. My smile, the shape of my mouth, how I tilt my head sometimes. I've always had her long fingers. These features comfort me now she's gone.

Q. If my child is curious about someone's family background, how can they ask without appearing rude or racist?

A. They could wait until they've got to know that person better, so that it's a natural conversation. As they become friendlier or more intimate with somebody, it's normal to share personal details such as family heritage. What's not ok is asking questions like 'What are you?' Encourage them to share their own family background, with the hope (but not the expectation) that the other person volunteers that information too. Depending on the relationship, approaching the topic with 'I hope you don't mind me asking/I hope I'm not being rude/please feel free to tell me to go away', etc. can also take the sting out of the feeling of being 'othered'. Try to manage their curiosity, and teach them this simple rule of thumb: always question yourself (and your intentions) before you question someone else.

CHAPTER 2

How Kids See Colour

It is time for parents to teach young people early on that in diversity there is beauty and there is strength.

Maya Angelou

In the kitchen getting lunch ready, I heard yelling from next door. I ran into the living room to find my four-year-old hurling himself around. A football match roared on TV.

'What happened?'

'The blacks just scored!' Ezra said, still trying to fist bump the ceiling. 'The whites are on top, but I want the blacks to win.'

'Cool,' I said. 'Try not to break the sofa, ok?'

I went back to the kitchen.

Now, I can sense some eyebrows arching. Maybe a few eyeballs popping. Some of you are wondering if my child was being a little bit . . . you know . . . racist?

What if I told you he was talking about football shirts, not footballers? You see, when my boys were very little, they were far more likely to group people by the colour of their clothing than the colour of their skin. It would be at least a year before Ezra understood people could be Black and White too. Probably another year before he claimed 'Blackness' as his identity.

Are Kids Colour Blind?

Every now and then, I come across a story about kids of different ethnicities who are closer than siblings. The adorable buddies who toddle into each other's arms like brothers from another mother. Or the best mates who got the same haircut to fool their teacher, so she couldn't tell them apart. The fact that one boy was White and the other African American didn't seem to faze them.

These kids are super cute and readers can't get enough. Their stories attract hundreds of comments on social media from people of all ethnicities, praising the children (and their parents) for being exemplary to us all.

'Children are beautiful because they don't know racism.'

'Love doesn't see colour.'

'We are all one race; if only adults could remember this.'

These tales tug at our heartstrings because they hint at a different world. A post-racial Utopia in which it really doesn't matter if your skin doesn't match. If only we could all stay as innocent as the children . . .

But as any parent will tell you, kids aren't always so innocent. Sure, they can be big-hearted and pure-minded, but they can also be little Shitlers. You only have to watch a mum trying to feed a fussy toddler to learn the meaning of picky, separatist and dictatorial.

A small child can abandon a plate because the food isn't all white. They can scream for hours because their hair clips don't match their dress. They can decide you're not their friend based on the colour of your shoes.

What's more, study after study shows children aren't colour blind when it comes to race.

Shanthi Annan, daughter-in-law to former UN Secretary General, the late Kofi Annan, was only five years old when she learned this first-hand. Now a mother of three and a busy entrepreneur, Shanthi describes herself as equal parts Ghanaian, Nigerian, English and Indian. With some amusement, she recalls an incident in kindergarten:

The first time I was conscious of my race was in conversation with another little girl at assembly. I had a flesh cut on my leg and she said, 'Ew, you're brown on the outside and white on the inside'. Realising she was entirely ignorant, I retorted, 'Well . . . it's better than being white on the outside and black on the inside.' I freaked her out, but I felt empowered.

Rachel Ezekwugo, a former journalist, lives with her husband and two daughters in a leafy suburb of south-west London. She says her girls are proudly Nigerian (with a Welsh great-grandma), although both were born and raised in the UK. When her eldest started in reception, some kids made mean comments about her skin colour: 'The teachers would tell me "somebody said her skin was the colour of poo". Luckily, the school had a zero-tolerance approach to bullying and hopefully much of it went over her head.'

When I was seven, I had a bestie named Tamsin. Her mum was friends with my mum and had been in a relationship with my uncle. In our eyes, we were practically family.

Tamsin and I told kids at school we were related. At first, we said we were sisters. Then we called ourselves twins. We would walk around arm in arm and shout down anybody who told us we were making it up. That's despite the obvious. I had deep brown skin, darkened by the Enugu sun; my hair had been cropped close to my skull and slicked into Jheri curls (don't laugh, it was the '80s). Tamsin was a Lincolnshire lass, pale-skinned with white-blond hair and light blue eyes. We looked like a walking Benetton ad.

I wasn't colour blind and neither was she, but that was part of the fun. Soon enough, schoolmates stopped questioning us. Kids have short attention spans and our 'sisters-of-another-skin' story fizzled out in a matter of weeks. I made new buddies, some almost like siblings. Yet none of that protected me from feeling like a misfit or from some of the casual racism I endured as a young girl. Like being called Poo, an actual nickname from some of my closest friends.

But I Don't See Colour . . .

Maybe you're one of those people who pride themselves on not noticing ethnic heritage. After all, we're all human, we all bleed red – what does it matter if you or your ancestors came from somewhere else? You might even say things like: 'I treat everybody the same; it doesn't matter to me if you're black, white, yellow, purple, blue or orange with green spots.' You describe yourself as colour blind and you're raising your kids that way too.

The problem with a colour-blind approach is that it silences any meaningful conversation around race. It leaves some of us tongue-tied and the rest of us feeling invisible. When you teach your child that everyone is equal, you minimise the struggles of minorities and disadvantaged people all over the world. When you tell your child that we are all the same, regardless of skin or background or heritage, you erase an important part of my identity.

American-born Nigerian Ebele Okobi is raising three gorgeous kids, twins and an older sister, in south-west London. She is married to an African American and works at Facebook as Public Policy director for Africa, Middle East and Turkey. The family live in an area that she describes as:

. . . incredibly, incredibly White. It is so White that most of the children are blond. There are more redheads than Black people. The issue is that the children are noticing and feeling like the onlies. The school is an Ofsted Outstanding school, but there is extremely little teaching about cultures other than White European. The school refused to celebrate Black History Month, because 'children don't see race'.

Italian Londoner Monica Costa, editor and publisher of *London Mums* magazine, told me she never saw colour, only 'people with their personalities' and that's how she brought up her son, who is now 12 years old. However, she's starting to understand that this is a limited perspective:

I never made a point about race. But I was once criticised for this because I wasn't aware of all the deep reasons behind Black History Month. Now I appreciate why celebrating racial differences is important, especially because we live in a society (not just Britain but everywhere in the world) in which we are all mixed up. Celebrating differences is important to keep the various traditions and identities alive.

Author Angie Thomas sums it up in her bestselling novel, *The Hate U Give*: 'If you don't see my Blackness, then you can't see me.'

As a child, I could see colour every time the school photographs revealed me, the only patch of brown among a wash of pale faces. Every time the lights went off and someone would joke 'Where did Uju go?' or feel around for me in the dark. Every time a parent's smile tightened at the sight of the friend their daughter wanted to bring home.

Yet I came across many adults who 'didn't see colour'. Like the ones who congratulated me on my British accent, saying you couldn't tell I was a foreigner if you spoke to me over the phone. Before I joined them at school in England, my sister and brother tried to give me voice coaching. They wanted me to shake off my strong Igbo accent. They thought I would embarrass them with how I pronounced words like three (te-ree) and first (fust). Who knew my accent would change flavour almost overnight, from beans and dodo to tea and crumpet?

I would always ease into my Nigerian accent at home and with other Nigerians. Our parents never spoke Igbo to us, so English was our first tongue. However, Nigerian (or Naija) English is a language on its own. It delights me when my kids, born and raised London boys, use pure Naija expressions. I also enjoy tracing Africa in people's voices, no matter whether the accent is from Trinidad or Cuba, Portugal or Pasadena. A certain rhythm, a timbre, a turn of phrase.

Africa flows through my veins, springs up from my scalp, coils itself tightly in my DNA. I am proudly and visibly Black. Yet I've had people tell me I wasn't 'really Black' – as in, not like 'Africa Black'. I've met adults so hesitant to acknowledge skin colour, they twist their tongues into knots to avoid mentioning it.

'Do you know that man over there, you know the one in the blue shirt?'

'Which man, exactly?'

'He has quite, um, funky hair?'

'Oh, you mean the Black guy.'

Blushes. 'Yeah, him.'

It reminds me of a story Oprah Winfrey told on her show about a conversation she had with her White neighbour: 'He said to me:

"Oh, you're not Black, you're just a neighbour". I go, "I most certainly am Black". But that was his way of saying – you're not like what I think other Black people are.'

I guess it's meant to be a badge of honour. The implication that you're no longer Black, because you're better than that. I can name celebrities like Oprah, Sidney Poitier, Trevor McDonald and Will Smith among this exclusive club. So successful, so beloved by the mainstream, they're practically neutral. They are post-Black.

Aside from being the ultimate backhanded compliment, it's nonsensical. For as I'm about to show you, even a three-month-old baby can tell the difference between Will Smith and Will Ferrell.

When We Start Seeing Race

Do you play peekaboo with babies? I do it all the time – on buses, in the supermarket, at the doctors' office. It's such a universal icebreaker. I love how making your face vanish and reappear can amuse and surprise infants from Alaska to Zanzibar.

What is it about peekaboo that tickles them so? Apparently, it's all about their developing sense of how the world fits together. Swiss psychologist Jean Piaget called it object permanence. When they figure out that even if you can't see something, it still exists. Babies can take up to two years to understand this concept fully. (My kids still haven't worked this out, judging by the state of their laundry baskets.)

Another theory about peekaboo is that it tricks young kids into thinking they are invisible. Researchers at the University of Cambridge set up an exercise with three- and four-year-olds, giving them mirrored goggles that hid their eyes yet let them see.[1] The kids who believed nobody could see their eyes also imagined nobody could see them at all.

Think back and you might remember this from your own childhood. Hands over your eyes like an invisibility cloak. Isn't it sweet that babies can get this from a game of peekaboo? I've noticed with babies of another ethnicity sometimes I work harder to connect. It's as if the baby spends a little longer on my face, taking in all my features, before they're ready to offer up a smile. Peekaboo, I see you. Can you see me too?

This is not all in my head. A study from the Department of Psychology at the University of Sheffield tested babies at three months old to see if they could tell different ethnicities apart.[2] By showing the babies images of people from various racial groups, researchers found the babies were more drawn to faces that matched their own race. This was in contrast to an earlier test with newborns, who showed no preference for any ethnicity.

By nine months old (prime time for peekaboo), babies begin to react to ethnic differences. That's around the age when they start developing 'stranger anxiety' and their hearts actually beat faster when they come into contact with people they don't recognise. If that stranger has markedly different skin, hair and features from Mum or Dad, their little hearts might thump harder with apprehension.

Wait a minute. Does this mean we're born racist? Not at all. The research simply shows we have an instinct for familiarity. It's a primal impulse, feeling safer among your clan, that starts as soon as you form attachments to your first caregivers.

You see, up until a few months of age, babies don't realise they are separate beings from their mothers. After all, their limited existence so far has taught them: you breathe, therefore I breathe. You feed, therefore I feed. I suck, therefore we are. But as the weeks and months go by, babies start to form their own identities and that feeling of separation kicks in. It's an unsettling time, realising you don't actually control that person you thought was an extension of yourself.

Now let's say the face you see leaning down over your cot every morning has deep brown skin. That is all you know of the world around you. One day, here comes another living, breathing being with creamy pink skin. Why wouldn't you stare, maybe shrink back or even bawl for help?

Making Friends With Difference

Let me clarify again that nobody is born a bigot. Young babies don't react to racial difference when they first notice it. The 'Uh oh, who dis?' shift happens around nine months. A team at the

University of Massachusetts Amherst studied 48 White babies who'd had little or zero contact with Black people. In a series of experiments monitoring brain activity, they found babies at five months were easily able to tell any face apart, irrespective of race.[3]

But by nine months, the babies were better at being able to differentiate between two White faces. Also, when gauging whether facial expressions were 'happy' or 'sad', the five-month-old babies processed information for all racial groups in the same area of their brain. But the nine-month-olds' brains switched the processing of this information from one brain region to another, and again were more accurate with their own race.

Psychology researcher Lisa Scott, who was part of the study group, compared the results to how children learn language. Babies in multilingual households can discriminate sounds in multiple languages, but babies who grow up in single-language environments do not have this ability. Similarly, she explained, infants exposed to a wide mix of people of different ethnicities will maintain the ability to distinguish those people, regardless of race.

In other words, diversity matters. Exposing your kids to other ethnic groups from an early age makes a difference. Babies aren't born to hate; they're born inquisitive. It's good to mix up a little more, so that our naturally curious infants get to explore, discover and learn and to familiarise themselves with all types of people. Think of curiosity as a muscle. Let it grow and we can raise children who are kinder, more open, more sensitive to other cultures. Everybody gets stronger. Let it wane, however, and it can shrink into apathy, fear, ignorance.

If you live in an area where everybody looks the same, maybe it's time to step out of your comfort zone. Diversify the media you consume, the shows you watch, the books you read. Be intentional about whom you hang with and whom your kids play with too. You have to be proactive because, whether you like it or not, kids are learning about race all the time from the world around them.

Numerous studies show that by age two, children have started sorting themselves into groups, showing a preference for people who are more like them. By age three, they show signs of unconscious bias against other ethnicities.

I'll say that again for the people in the back. Your child, at the tender age of three, is already conditioned to be biased against people of a different race.

It's shocking but there are ways to counter this. An international study at the Ontario Institute for Studies in Education at the University of Toronto explored the impact of using a touch-screen app to help reduce implicit bias in young kids.[4] They invited four-, five- and six-year-old children to play with this app for 20-minute sessions. The app's goal was to teach children to identify people using names and personal attributes, rather than blanket traits like 'the Black boy'.

They tested the app with 95 preschool kids in China who'd had zero interaction with people of African descent. They found the kids automatically associated Black people with negative emotions and Chinese people with positive ones. Yet just two sessions on the app for 20 minutes reduced racial bias against Black people significantly. And the effects lasted up to 60 days.

It saddens me a little to imagine young Chinese kids needing an app to help them think better of me as a Black person. On the other hand, isn't this a variation of the games we play with babies? Peekaboo, I see you. Can you see me too? I am helping you make a connection. I am teaching you about the world. I am showing you that I am fun, I am safe. I am just another human like you.

How We Interpret Colour

When speaking about skin colour, young kids take things quite literally. It's not often you'll hear a small child describe another human being in black or white. They go by what they see. And let's be real, nobody is actually white like alabaster or black like coal. So a child might talk about being 'creamy' or 'peachy', 'chocolate' or 'caramel'. Parents might encourage their little ones to use such sweet, easily digestible terms. However, this can cause some sticky situations.

Mercy Osei-Poku, a civil servant and Ghanaian mother of three, told me about an unpleasant experience one of her sons had in Turkey. 'While living in Istanbul, there was this time when a girl licked Jordan's arm on public transport because the Turkish call Black people "chocolata". I guess she took that literally. The kids refused to get on public transport after that incident.'

Anti-racism educators say it's important for children to learn to name and frame Whiteness, Blackness and other ethnic identities without sugarcoating. It's kind of like teaching young kids to use the correct terms for their genitals. Cute pseudonyms like Miss NooNoo or Mr Pickle are funny but can put children at risk. It can dissociate them from their own bodies, making them feel these areas are unmentionable. This can leave them more vulnerable to sexual predators.

As early as possible, we need to help kids find the language to describe who they are and how they fit in the world. What's tricky is that racism is coded into language itself. Think of all the words in the English language that pit blackness against whiteness and leave the former coming up short. Why would a small child want to describe themselves as 'black' when it's associated with everything bad?

I used to love the story *Black Beauty*. I wasn't exactly mad about horses, but a small part of me relished hearing those words together. Black and beauty. It made a welcome change from black as dirty, black as murky, black as night, black as funereal, black as evil.

These ideas play on your subconscious, even when you're too young to really get what's happening. White is light, soft, clean, innocent, pure, aspirational. The good witch. The most beautiful girl in the land. In 2019, a cartoon uploaded on YouTube's My Pingu TV featured an angel who is cursed to lose her beauty and turns Black. When her dark skin and curls disappear, her beauty magically returns. Viewers freaked out and 400,000 views later, the video was taken down. But I can't help thinking about all the children who watched it and absorbed its message like a dirty secret.

It's the same message written into books and magazines and billboards and TV shows and our universal subconscious. Our kids are growing up in a world where almost everything we see, hear and say is filtered through a prism of 'Whiteness rules'. The spoken-word poet Guante famously described White supremacy as the water, not the shark. In other words, it's not just the skinhead with swastika tattoos or the men in hoods burning crosses on a front lawn. It's the environment that surrounds us, that we swim in, bathe in, drink and even pee in. It affects everybody in one way or another. Yet, like water, it can appear neutral, transparent. Almost as if it's not there.

Perhaps the concept of White supremacy is too complex for little people. So let's talk about something all kids, even the ones who can't speak yet, can get a grip on. Crayons.

The Colour of Skin

Some time in 2019, a box of crayons became a trending story. Grown folk were raving about Crayola's range of colours for diverse skin tones. 'These crayons have made this Black girl very happy,' wrote Buzzfeed blogger Ehis Osifo. 'Can't wait to use them in my adult colouring book.'

These ravers were a little late to the party. Crayola Multicultural crayons have been around since the '90s. The

39

range was launched in 1992 in response to calls from parents and schools. Teachers said they were tired of kids drawing the Rev. Dr Martin Luther King Jr in black crayon. (Mind you, this was a whole 30 years after Crayola rebranded its original 'flesh'-colour crayon as 'peach', under pressure from the Civil Rights movement.)

Crayola Multicultural's eight colours are meant to represent skin tones from around the globe: apricot, burnt sienna, mahogany, peach, sepia, tan, black and white (the latter two are included for toning and shading). Cynics say Crayola is only making money off diversity. Fox News commentators called it 'pandering to liberals'. However, a quick look at the online reviews shows how kids, parents and teachers have embraced this product.

'All of the children use them, to draw pictures of themselves, friends, teachers, family or just folks they see on TV. No child should be without the colour of their skin or someone they know.'

'This was a great collection of skin tones,' another writes. 'I am old enough to remember when my crayons only had the color FLESH. Bravo Crayola for adding these multicultural colors.'

A reviewer called Maya adds: 'I remember when I got these as a kid and wanting to cry for joy. Gone were the days of pure white, yellow and orange people.'

If you are a person of colour raised in the West, you have grown up with the idea that White skin is 'flesh' coloured and the rest of us are something else. This message has been pushed by brands for decades. It has coloured our crayons, our make-up, even our underwear.

I remember being given 'nude' tights for ballet and gym class at school and feeling even more awkward about my legs, which already stood out for being stockier than my classmates'. It never occurred to me that pink ballet shoes were also meant to create the illusion of flesh. For years, Black ballerinas had to 'pancake' their shoes with make-up to match their skin tones. Finally, in 2016, in response to an Instagram rant by ballet dancer Eric Underwood that went viral, Bloch released the first ballet shoe for dancers of colour. Three years later, top ballet-shoe company Freed launched their own range for darker skin.

Afrozina Abaraonye, a 12-year-old student at Ballet Black in London, snapped hers up instantly. She told the *Guardian*: 'Because I've been wearing pink since I was little, I've got used to it. But there was always that weird thing when I was standing next to my friends and the pink ballet tights and shoes always looked better on them.'[5]

This is more than a #firstworldproblem. In Japan, the word for skin colour, '*hada-iro*', is seen as pale peach by up to 79 per cent of the population. In India, a second-year law student filed a suit against Hindustan Pencils for pushing a peach-coloured crayon as 'skin'-toned. Chirayu Jain accused the company of promoting light skin as preferable, in a country where most citizens are darker shades of brown.

The Hate You Give

True story. A little Black girl goes to a predominantly White school in the Western Cape of South Africa. She is in Grade 3, around age seven, and she's asked to draw a picture of herself. When drawing her self-portrait, she colours herself White.

Neeske Alexander, the teacher sitting in on her class, is dismayed. Especially as she finds other brown-skinned children in the class – the Black kids, the Asian kids, the mixed-heritage kids, officially labelled as 'Coloureds' – are doing the same thing.

When she looks into it, the teacher discovers something that cuts to the core of a system built on a hierarchy of race. She learns that the kids are using a crayon called 'skin' or 'flesh' in English or *menskleur* in Afrikaans.

Menskleur. It means 'human colour'.

Now picture that little Black girl, sitting carefully in her chair, art supplies spread around her. She has taken time to draw the outline of her body, to give her face some personality. Round eyes, hair in bunches, big smile. Now she is shading herself in, brow furrowed with concentration, tongue sticking out slightly with effort. She colours herself *menskleur*. A girl sitting next to her leans across and pulls the crayon out of her hand.

'That one's not for you.' She tosses a brown crayon at her. 'Use this instead.'

The Black girl stares at the brown crayon, knowing that it's the closest colour to her skin. Knowing also that it is anything but 'human colour'.

Human colour. The legacy of White supremacy, apartheid and colonialism captured in a single crayon. Is it any wonder the Black and Brown kids were colouring themselves *menskleur*? Who wants to be subhuman? You could view the darker children colouring themselves *menskleur* as an act of rebellion: if you insist on naming one colour as human, we will damn well colour ourselves that too.

In her 2016 thesis for Stellenbosch University, Alexander noted that, when given a range of paint tones to create their self-portraits, all the kids chose the lightest colours available.[6] She records one Coloured child who was offended by another child suggesting they mix in some black paint:

'Teacher, he thinks I'm black—'

'No, teacher, she's a person, *jis* I didn't say she's a black person—'

This is how racism takes hold in our children: one cartoon, one pair of ballet shoes, one crayon at a time.

What happens when a generation grows up to believe their skin is not ok, that it doesn't fit in, that it is less than human? To paraphrase the rapper Tupac, the hate you give little infants colours everybody. It is a stain on all of us.

What We Teach Kids About Race

The irony about colour blindness is that it doesn't mean seeing no colour. It simply means you are unable to distinguish between specific colours – usually reds and greens or blues and yellows.

From what we understand about our eyesight, most of us are only seeing the world in part. What we think of as colour is how our brains interpret light hitting an object and being reflected back. When we look at the sky, we see blue only because molecules in the air scatter blue light from the sun more than they scatter red light. The sun itself is white, yet sunlight contains a rainbow spectrum of colours, and again, it's molecules in the atmosphere that make the sun appear yellow. The true spectrum of colours in a rainbow is so vast (up to 1 million) that we don't have the language to describe it. If we could see the world in all her radiance, it would leave us speechless.

Human skin is not black or white, much more than 'flesh' and 'other'. The Fitzpatrick scale, a recognised standard for dermatology, measures skin tones along a spectrum of six colours that are not based on race or ethnicity. The scale from Type 1 (very light, burns in direct sunlight and never tans) to Type VI (deep pigmented brown or black, never burns) is based on how skin reacts to ultraviolet light.

You can have different skin types along the scale within the same ethnic group, even within the same family. In fact, you can find pretty much every skin colour on the planet in Africa, where all human life began. From the light beige-skinned San of South Africa to the blue-black Dinka of South Sudan. As evolutionary geneticist Sarah Tishkoff, lead author of a ground-breaking study on gene variants in skin colour, told *Science* magazine: 'There is so much diversity in Africans that there is no such thing as an African race.'[7]

There is no such thing as race, full stop. Ask any scientist worth their salt. The biological evidence for distinct human races doesn't exist. What we think of as race is made up – it's a social construct. What we think of as colour is a trick of the light.

However, we can't turn a blind eye to the world around us. Race is a fiction, but it is also a fact of life. It affects us from birth and even babies can tell ethnic groups apart. Colour is illusory, but that doesn't mean we don't see it. It is the wonder of a rainbow. It is the polar bear and the brown bear and the panda. It is the difference between you and me.

We teach children to distinguish between red and green, so they know when to stop and when to go. We need to talk to our children openly and positively about racial difference too. Encourage them to recognise and respect all skin tones. To look for the beauty in every kind of face. Most of all, give them space to ask questions and prepare yourself for some difficult but necessary conversations. Are you ready? Because what we teach kids about race can change everything.

• Talking Points

Q. I grew up in an era when people of African descent were called Coloured, and now the term is 'Black', but I still find it awkward when my kids use it. Are you sure it's not a problem?
A. The term 'Coloured' fell out of fashion in the US after the Civil Rights movement, and in the UK around the early '70s. It

was a specific racial category under South Africa's apartheid laws and is still used there to describe people of mixed Black and White ethnicity. Once Black people in the US and UK had taken ownership of their Blackness, as a political and cultural statement, 'Coloured' became outdated and derogatory. As a child, I hated it because it sounds like you're supposed to be White but someone has coloured you in. Black is a catch-all that speaks to many people of African descent, whether they were born in Africa or in the diaspora. In more recent times, the phrase 'people of colour' is used generally to refer to anybody non-White – including Black, Asian, Latino and indigenous people. You can teach your child that the best thing to do is call someone what they like to be called, so if in doubt, ask.

Q. What should I do when my child argues with me about their skin colour – for example, 'I'm Brown' (when they're Black) or 'I'm Creamy' (when they're White)? Can't we just leave it at that?
A. Children don't understand the political implications of skin colour descriptions until they're a little older. Even then, it doesn't really make sense. Still, it's important to put things in the right context as early as possible. If your child is really small, you don't have to insist upon them calling their skin 'Black' or 'White'. However, you can start to explain the differences between ethnic groups and how society defines them. As they get older, you can continue to discuss these issues and teach them what these labels mean – culturally, politically and historically.

Q. If I don't raise my child to be colour blind, won't they focus too much on race and isn't that racist in itself?

A. As I've outlined in this chapter, kids who are taught the opposite of 'colour blindness' when it comes to race are usually less likely to display racist behaviour. Teaching your child 'not to see colour' creates cognitive dissonance, where your kid can visualise difference but feels unable to articulate it. It can also make other children feel unseen, and their struggles seem unimportant. When you celebrate people as individuals, including all their ethnic features, your child learns to appreciate diversity from an early age.

CHAPTER 3

Conversations About Race

Mummy, what's the N-word?

Jed, age eight

Sometimes parenting a tiny human is like living with a walking question mark. Or a toddling time bomb. A small child can knock you sideways with their observations. Leave you cringing with their total disregard for boundaries. Often in public. Who am I kidding? Especially in public.

'Daddy, why is that man brown all over?'

'What's that woman wearing a sheet for?'

Your first instinct might be to shush your child and keep it moving. After all, you don't want to offend anybody. So you squash it and make a dash for the nearest hole in the ground. But those questions don't disappear. They nag away under the skin, until eventually, they burst through like gremlins, greedy for answers.

'Why do they have such funny hats and beards?'

'Is her skin dirty, Mama?'

No matter how tricky the question, silence is never the right response. Not where a kid is concerned. If you say nothing, that wild little imagination will fill in the gaps. And if you hush a child who asks about something race-related, they get the message it's a rude, taboo, even dirty topic. The little girl carries on staring at the 'brown man', feeling she's touched a sore point. Maybe there's something bad about brown skin, otherwise why can't she mention it?

We need to talk to our children about race long before they start making up their own stories. We need to tell them before the world whispers too many lies in their ears. Remember those studies in the previous chapter about implicit bias and how it sets in by age three (see p. 36)? Your three-year-old is already assessing and judging people (and themselves) based on how they look, how you interact with them and what society tells them.

Facebook executive Ebele found this out the hard way: she says:

We originally started by being very deliberate about not talking about racism, only talking about the joy of being an African/African-American child. Then, when he was three years old, my son got called a 'stupid little Black boy' by a teacher in nursery. He acted out for weeks (including starting to talk about how he wished he was White so his hair 'could flip like this, Mama!') before he told me. At that point, our pretend world where we could wait to talk about racism came to an end. Now we talk about race ALL THE TIME.

49

Bringing Up Race

Dion is a sweet, chubby-faced Black boy with special abilities. You might call him gifted, although that doesn't impress his white head teacher. One day, Dion gets into a spat with Jordan, a classmate. Jordan started it, but when the head teacher catches the boys fighting, he threatens to exclude Dion. Dion's mum, Nicole, tries to intervene with the help of a teacher (also Black), but the head continues to pick on Dion. The whole thing smacks of racism.

When Nicole tells her sister about the incident, her sister says it's time she told Dion what was really going on. Nicole's response is, 'But he's only seven!' Her sister insists he needs to know. With a heavy heart, Nicole sits Dion down and explains that the head teacher wasn't just being mean. She tells him there are people out there who don't like him and will treat him differently because of the colour of his skin. Yes, even despite the hard work of Dr Martin Luther King. It's a difficult conversation, but Nicole doesn't fake it or act like she has all the answers.

If you've watched the Netflix series *Raising Dion* (do see it, it's awesome), you'll remember this scene. It's particularly affecting because Dion is so young. I felt an ache inside watching it, because I've had to sit with my sons and face hard truths about race too. Much sooner than I wished.

For people of colour, talking to kids about who they are and what that means to the world outside is usually not optional. Patrick is an engineer of African-American heritage and father to Noah, now in his teens. Patrick's partner, Mali, is from

Thailand and they live in west London (names changed here). Patrick says:

As a Black parent, there comes a time when you have to have that conversation about race with your child. We've always raised Noah to embrace both sides of his heritage, African American and Thai. He speaks Thai and last year we visited Thailand for the first time. It was pretty deep, going to the 400-year-old temple and knowing it was where his family has worshipped for generations. Today, he's fully confident and secure in his identity as both Black and Thai. Still, I had to tell him about what to look out for as a Black boy living in London. I told him there's a certain attitude you have where it's like drawing a line in the sand nobody can cross.

Former journalist Rachel from south-west London says she speaks words of love and positivity to her daughters daily to counter the racist stereotyping pushed by the media:

For me, as a Black parent, I think you just have to be constantly on it. Because there is so much BS out there. My 12-year-old has started reading *Vogue*. All I can say is thank the Lord for Edward Enninful! I tell my girls every day how proud I am of them. I guess it's confidence building. You do try and shield them to some extent because I want them to have their childhood intact and not constantly be thinking about being different.

If you are a visible minority, most likely you have a suitcase of stories to unpack. Stories of feeling unseen or singled out, of being mistreated or misunderstood, of pain, shame, frustration.

Vicki Broadbent, author of *Mumboss* and co-founder of the Working Mother's Academy, says as a British-born mum of Greek Cypriot heritage, sometimes she feels like an 'invisible' minority:

I've had people diminish my experience, saying, 'You're White so you won't have suffered racism'. I'm what is known as olive-skinned. I'm an ethnic minority and proud of that fact. My parents were incredibly candid to me about their own struggles as immigrants to the UK. My mother was ignored at antenatal classes by fellow mothers, deemed a foreigner or constantly referred to as 'exotic'. People mimicked her accent and were shocked to find she was university educated. My father, who had a dark black beard and hair in those times, struggled to find employment, despite being highly educated.

Vicki recalls being told to 'go back to her own country' by a boy in her class when she was seven years old:

'I was baffled! I spoke to my family, who explained people can say cruel things, but must be ignored. They assured me this was my home, but I was lucky as Cyprus was where my roots "grew from".'

Have You Had 'The Talk'?

One of the hardest things to do as a parent is to prepare your child for a world of hurt you know is coming their way, sooner or later. For many Black families in America, facing up to racism isn't a question. It's a matter of life and death.

As other parents um and ah over the facts of life, African-American parents steel themselves for a much tougher conversation. 'The Talk' is about what it means to grow up Black, especially a Black male in America, and how this marks you as a target. Parents teach their wide-eyed children how to stay on the right side of the authorities. Keep your hands where everybody can see them. Don't make any sudden moves. Don't argue. Don't turn the tension up. Whatever you do, try to stay alive.

A pivotal moment in the movie adaptation of *The Hate U Give* shows 16-year-old Starr sitting quietly with her siblings while her father gives them 'The Talk'. He's training them on how to handle themselves in a police encounter. This talk doesn't stop Starr from witnessing a killing, but it might just save her from being shot herself. Author Angie Thomas told fans on Twitter the scene was based on real life: 'Fact: the talk Starr and Seven were given is based on the talk I was given by a cousin. Who was a cop.'

I took Ezra at 13 to watch *The Hate U Give* at the cinema. By then, he had already read the book. And we'd had numerous conversations about race over the years. 'The Talk' is not a British tradition in that sense, but I have to keep it real with my kids. In the UK, racism is less in your face, but I can't pretend we live in a fair and equal society. Black boys in Britain are 70 per cent more likely to be excluded from school; 12 times more likely to be stopped and searched by police; three times more likely to be arrested or tasered; nine times more likely to wind up in jail; four times more likely to be caught in a knife or gun attack; twice as likely to be unemployed as their White peers.[1]

If your daughter is in a hijab, she is more likely to be verbally abused, spat at, even physically assaulted. If your son speaks with a foreign accent, he is more likely to be mocked by peers or treated like a simpleton by adults who should know better.

We need to give children the language to frame their experiences and the ability to speak for themselves and call out racism wherever they see it. The way forward is to start having more open, honest conversations about race with our children and with each other.

Are You Sitting Uncomfortably? Now Let's Begin

All right, let's talk about race. You go first.

I get it. It can be awkward, no matter your background. The thing is, while Black, Asian and minority ethnic parents might fumble their way through, for many White families it might never come up. This one-way silence on race creates a wall far bigger than anything Humpty Trumpty could conceive.

In a frank and lively discussion at Northwestern University, comedian and author Trevor Noah (*The Daily Show*) emphasised the need for people to start talking:

And when I say talk about it, I'm speaking to White people predominantly. It's a frightening conversation to have, but it's a conversation that needs to be had, and that conversation is race. That conversation is understanding the very fibre of the country you are living in. Those conversations need to be had with your friends and family. It seems like it's impossible, it seems like it's a mountain that can never be climbed, but I do believe we can make inroads. I do believe that as people we can move a conversation forward.

In the book *White Fragility: Why It's So Hard for White People to Talk about Racism*, Robin DiAngelo shines a spotlight on why so many White parents skip over this topic. For some, it comes back to being raised 'colour blind' and believing in vague, blanket statements like 'everyone is equal'. Others, she says, are stuck in 'fragile mode'. Any mention of racism or White supremacy makes them ultra-defensive, as if their very essence is under attack. DiAngelo says it's important to free yourself from the good/bad binary in which 'good' people aren't racist because everyone knows racists are evil. When you understand that you have been conditioned into a White supremacist worldview, it shifts the focus to 'how – rather than if – our racism is manifest'. It's no longer about blame but about personal accountability and recognising thought and behavioural patterns that need to change.

In other words, stop pointing fingers at those racists over there. Remember we are all drinking and swimming and bathing in the same water. Think about how White supremacy shows up in everyday life and how you can disrupt it. How you can teach your kids to disrupt it too. Stop seeing racism as a 'Black problem' or a 'White problem'. It is everybody's problem and we all have work to do.

Don't assume because your child is growing up in a racially diverse environment, they aren't picking up coded messages about who matters more in society. Don't assume because your child plays with mine, they are exempt from racism.

I've made that mistake myself.

A Wake-Up Call in Chinatown

When Ezra was five years old, I took the boys out to a restaurant in Chinatown. The waiter came to take our order and as he walked off, Ezra used his fingers to pull his eyes towards his ears.

'I'm Chinese!'

He burst out laughing.

I was gobsmacked.

'Stop that!' I said in that hoarse shouty-whisper mums use

when they're trying to tell their kids off without anyone hearing. 'What do you think you're doing?'

I couldn't believe it. Ezra's best friend, Adam, was Chinese!

Ezra's shoulders drooped, his big eyes round with confusion.

'It's funny,' he said, uncertainly.

'No, it's not! Who told you that?'

'John [not his real name] was doing it at school.'

'Listen, we don't make fun of people, and we especially don't make fun of people for where they come from or how they look. Imagine if Adam saw you doing that? Don't you think he'd be hurt? Or what about all the people who work here? Don't do it again, Ezra!'

He apologised in a small voice and I ruffled his hair. Our food came and he quickly got stuck into his egg-fried rice. He never pulled his eyes like that again.

Looking back on it, I wish I hadn't spoken so harshly to Ezra. He was only five, after all, and hadn't meant anything by it. I was just so thrown; I forgot to take a breath, count to five or use any other strategy to avoid Mamageddon.

All I wanted was to raise my boy as a cool, kind individual. This was a stark reminder there were conversations we needed to have and keep on having. I couldn't rely on his diverse friend-ship circle – far less his education in the playground – to teach him a better way.

Talking to Our Sons

Over the years, we've had frequent talks about race. Nowadays, it's often more light-hearted. Ezra's in secondary school – half-boy, half-banter. I can keep up with the kids as much as any 40-something still rocking her Nikes (but craving afternoon naps). When their jokes and backchat cross a line, I check them right away.

Every now and then, one of them tells me a story that cuts me to the core. Like when Ezra spoke about being glared at on public transport:

You know one thing I really hate? It's when I'm sitting on the bus, just minding my own business, and I look up and see some person – usually an old White person, if I'm honest – just eyeing me as if I'm going to mug him or something. It's totally based on what I'm wearing as well. If I'm in my uniform or shirt and jeans, then I'll only get a couple of looks. But if I'm coming back from training and I'm wearing a tracksuit or I've got my hood pulled up, they'll be giving me these evil stares, like I'm a criminal. I mean, I understand when I'm with a group of my friends and we're talking bare loud and I can see how that can be a bit annoying or whatever. But it annoys me if I'm just sitting looking at my phone, not doing anything to anybody, and I get those looks. It's so unfair.

It's so unfair. At first, I was at a loss for what to say beyond platitudes of 'rise above it'. I told him sadly this was a symptom of how much of society views Black youths. Research shows

Black boys and girls are more likely to be treated older than their age.[2] At 14, Ezra is one of the shortest in his class. He is on the cusp of manhood, but still very much a kid. It hurts to know strangers already see him as somebody to fear. Then I thought about Tamir Rice, the African-American boy who, on 22 November 2014, was shot by police while holding a toy gun. Tamir was 12 years old.

What's a mother to do? I feel like walking in front of Ezra carrying a banner that says: please see my son. See him in all his sweetness and his softness and his roughness and his boyishness. He's the same lad you used to stop me in the street about to tell me how clever he sounded for a toddler. The exact same kid whose dance moves had you cheering at that festival. The same sweet little thing whose pushchair you once helped me lift onto the bus. When my baby blew a kiss at you, you blew a kiss right back.

Please see our sons. Really look at them, beneath the top fades and hunched shoulders, the cocky smiles and watchful eyes. They are still our babies. All we pray for them is happiness and safe passage as they move through life. Can you be a kind face in the crowd for my child? I will be a kind face for yours too.

When to Start a Conversation

There are people who believe the world would be a much fairer, happier place if people didn't keep bringing up race. They think talking about racism creates more division.

'Leave it alone,' they insist. 'You're stirring up things that don't need stirring.'

However, a pot still stews, even if you don't stir it. And one of the biggest contributors to the stew of racial hatred is ignorance. When ideas and attitudes remain unspoken, untested and unchallenged, they can turn dangerous. In a world becoming more and more polarised, talking to our children about race might be our saving grace.

So when is the right time to bring up such a sensitive topic? Sooner than you think. By the time your child asks you that embarrassing question, it is already late. Never *too* late, however.

Now is a good time to begin. You can even start with a baby bump or a newborn. Some experts recommend talking with your baby before they can talk back. Sounds a bit cuckoo, but it's pretty smart, because you can talk without fear of judgment. You can practise saying things out loud that you might feel awkward saying in adult company. Sachi Ferris runs the excellent online resource Raising Race Conscious Children. She blogs about reading the board book *Baby Faces* with her newborn when he was five days old and pointing out each baby's ethnic differences. During Raising Race Conscious Children's workshops, she asks participants to pretend they're talking to a baby.

If you've been babbling away with a baby, you'll be more prepared for those toddler and preschooler interrogations. At this stage, kids might be super curious about visual differences between themselves and their friends. They might also have picked up on disparities in who lives where, who works in what job and who is in your social circle. Be ready to answer as openly as you can.

Entrepreneur and mother of three Shanthi says:

I'm very open and factual about race. My son asked me why there aren't many Black people at school and I told him we are in Europe, which means geographically there are more White people here. I also reminded him that when he is in Ghana there are mostly Black people there and he got it. A friend told me about a conversation her son had with mine when they were four. Her son asked my son why he is brown and my son answered, 'Because people are different colours' and they happily went about their day. I was very pleased to know he had an empowering first experience on this subject.

If you get stuck, you can meet a question with another question. 'I'm curious, why did you ask me that?' Or you can turn the answer into a treasure hunt. 'Hmm, I'm not sure about that, shall we find out together?' There's no shame in admitting you don't have all the answers. Kids appreciate that you are on a learning journey too.

Books make excellent teachers and conversation starters. Stuck on what to tell a child about why hair is frizzy or straight, why noses are pointed or curvy, why skin is pale or freckled or earthy or patchwork? Somebody else has said it before you, probably with illustrations to match. You can find books for every age and stage to help your child learn about diversity, kindness, self-appreciation and cultural respect (see Further Reading, p. 297).

Beyond books, my best tip for handling the race chat comes back to the birds and bees. According to sex-education experts (and common sense), you can't rely on one big awkward talk with your kids. You need to have several as they grow older. The same approach works for conversations about race. The trick is to start young and take it at your child's pace, using age-appropriate language. Drip feed rather than drench them with information. You want to educate and empower them, not freak them out!

Going Deeper

As your child gets older, you can have deeper, more layered conversations with them. Broaden their horizons with a variety of multicultural resources from books to TV and film, news media and websites. Take them to museums or plays that create opportunities for further discussion. When you visit a different country or neighbourhood, explore what other people eat, how they dress, what language they speak. After her son's early brush with racism, Ebele and her husband Richard took a proactive approach:

We doubled down on talking about their culture. We started taking them to a different country in Africa every summer. We talk about colonisation, slavery, White supremacy, inequity. Memorable conversations include talking about theft at the British Museum and why it's theft if some people do it and conservation if others do the same thing. We started a weekend liberation school with other Black children to connect them to each other, create community and instil cultural pride and the ability to question and think critically.

Sometimes you learn as much from listening to your kid as from your own investigations. It helps that children will say things that crack you up. I've been keeping notes of funny things my boys have said since they started talking. Author/illustrator Mira Jacob turned her conversations with her son (and other family members) about race, politics and identity into the graphic memoir *Good Talk*. In a series of refreshingly open, sweet and funny chats with her boy, she discusses everything from skin-colour prejudice to why Brown kids get a raw deal in the media.

Author, podcaster and relationships expert Natalie Lue, host of the popular *Baggage Reclaim* podcast, has two daughters with her partner from Sierra Leone. She says:

We've always had open conversations about race, but upped the conversations from around age six/seven when they were hearing and reading things at school like, wait for it, 'All Black people were slaves'. From the outset, we encouraged them to know and love their hair, to play with, read and watch things where they could see themselves. The conversation that stands out to me was when they both came to me at around ages five and six and asked me why they rarely saw Black people in advertisements on TV. 'Don't Black people buy things?' They're hilarious and so on point. Now, they think it's hilarious the placement of Black and Brown folk in adverts is so formulaic.

Growing up Jamaican Chinese in Dublin, Natalie often felt like an outsider, but found it hard to share with her mum. However, a funny slip-up at dinner turned into an unexpected icebreaker.

When I was eight, I called my brother the C-word at the dinner table. We were living in Zambia at the time (we spent two years there after my mum married my stepdad). They went into shock when I said it, and then my mum asked, 'What do you think that means?' I replied, 'A black clown.' That sparked a rare funny discussion about race.

Keep Talking

It's ok to have funny, messy, rambling, vulnerable conversations. Be open about what you can't explain or don't fully understand. You might feel stumped trying to break down concepts like White privilege, police brutality, intersectionality. Maybe you don't fully understand the issues yourself. The best approach is to start with what you know, meet children at their level and use words everyone can understand.

Race is a big topic and talking about racism can feel over-whelming. But you need to push past your own resistance. Your discomfort is a good sign – it means that it matters.

We have to keep talking, not only with our kids but with our elders and our peers too. We have to normalise the conversation around race. Even if you have had no direct experience of racism, you are called to do your part.

Living in a mostly White, middle-class suburb, Rachel expresses some of the frustration she's felt trying to talk about race with fellow mums.

I know you're not racist, but please don't Whitesplain my experience. If I'm having conversations with my kids that I would rather not have had until they were in their teens, then you also have to engage. And please just ask me if you're not sure about something, I won't take offence. We've known each other since our kids were in nursery. We should be able to have these conversations, even if it makes you feel a little awkward.

Remember, we are all accountable. We can't leave it to those who suffer to shoulder the burden. Together we must bear the weight of racism, feel its sharp and ugly edges, the parts that dig into our skin. If we carry it together, maybe we can lighten the load. Maybe one day we can finally let go.

It is time for you, dear reader, to lean in to the conversation. Invite friends round for a meal or a cuppa and get chatting. Ask your kids what they think, know and appreciate about people who look different from them. Ask them what they understand about racism, if they've had any times they felt unwelcome, or how they feel about their friends coming from different backgrounds. Talk to your Black friends, your White friends, your Jewish friends, your Asian friends, your Muslim friends, your friends whose parents came from elsewhere.

Here's a simple conversation opener: 'How do you talk to your children about race? Have you had any interesting conversations? Did you ever talk to your parents about this stuff? What kind of things came up? If there was one thing you could teach your child about race, what would it be?'

It's a scary thought, but one day our little people will be in charge. They will be the ones making decisions, voting leaders into office, teaching in schools. The ones in hospitals holding people's lives in their hands. We can't control the future, but we can do our best to raise a braver, kinder generation. It is never too early, or too late.

• Talking Points

Q. My child asked me why Black people were so hated and I was tongue-tied. How do I explain anti-Blackness without making him feel upset (since it upsets me too)?

A. The answer to this depends on your child's age, but broadly speaking, first, you can explain that the opposite of love isn't hate, it's fear. You can talk about the connection between fear and hate and why Black people are not so much hated as feared by racists. Tell them fear usually comes from what you don't know, like when you switch off a light and start to wonder what's out there. But the more you know, the less you fear. If they're slightly older, it can help to put this in a historical context, using books and movies to help keep the conversation going. Explain how a drive for power, wealth and control had colonialists plundering Africa for its resources – land, minerals and, worst of all, people. The drive to keep this system in place is what has kept anti-Blackness going for centuries.

You can also remind them that, in spite of racism, people of African descent are some of the most influential, resourceful and resilient humans on the planet and that every single human has a genetic link back to Africa. Give examples of Black people who are doing amazing things and are adored by the public. Remind your child that nobody who knows them personally could ever hate them.

For very little children, you can keep it simple by explaining that only very silly people hate others because of their skin. There are people who think badly of Black people but that's because nobody taught them any better. There are people who think badly of other ethnicities too and it's all wrong. Tell them they are loved and appreciated by everybody who counts and that as they grow older, they can take action to change things for the better.

Q. My daughter asked me why White people were so mean to other races and I didn't know what to say.

How do I talk about this without making her feel ashamed of her own ethnic background?
A. It can be extremely painful confronting modern-day racism, as well as the history of colonialism and slavery. It's especially painful trying to talk about it with your children. However, these conversations are necessary to create understanding and build bridges between past and present, as well as between races. Remember to keep the discussion age-appropriate as you don't want to frighten or overwhelm younger ones. You can show her examples of the many White people who have been great friends, wonderful helpers and powerful campaigners for civil rights.

This is an opportunity to talk specifically about the lie of White supremacy. How it was created through slavery and colonisation to hold onto money and power, and why it's still affecting societies at every level. Be sure to emphasise that being White isn't bad, it's the system that's wrong.

Sit with your child in their feelings of discomfort or shame and admit that sometimes you feel ashamed too. But the best way forward is to choose to do better. To speak up when it counts, to keep learning and growing, and to be open and embracing of people no matter where they come from.

Q. My child asked why their grandfather always says rude things about people of other ethnicities. How can I handle this?
A. Tell your child that what their grandfather says might come from ignorance, or because of the time in which he grew up,

but that there's no excuse. It is mean, it is racist and it is wrong. It's important also to stand your ground when you visit their grandfather. State loudly and firmly, 'That's racist, can you not say anything like that in front of me or the kids please?' or 'That's a very offensive comment. Have you thought about what it is you're actually saying?' If he's not listening/responding, you can address your children in his presence: 'What Grandpa just said was racist. We don't talk about people as if they are less than us. If Grandpa wants to carry on like that, then we can't stop him. But I want you to remember it's wrong.' If it's really bad, you can even choose not to visit at all and let Grandpa know why. The important thing is not to act like it's not happening. Remember that little eyes are watching and learning from everything, including your silence.

CHAPTER 4

The First Time

Stand before the people you fear and speak your mind – even if your voice shakes. When you least expect it, someone may actually listen to what you have to say.

Maggie Kuhn, American activist

Parenthood is filled with exciting milestones. The first smile, the first steps, those adorable first words. But for parents of colour, or indeed anybody parenting a child perceived as 'different', there is another first. The first time bigotry comes for your kid.

I will never forget being called a nigger for the first time. The memory of it lives in my skin. What I don't remember is my earliest experience of racism. It was my mother who told me about it when I was much older. She had put me in a local kindergarten in London when my brother and sister started boarding school. I was only three, and my time there was short-lived because I was subject to racial bullying.

'There was this little Indian boy who made your life a misery,' my mum said. 'You would come home crying every day. We had to pull you out.'

70

We returned to Nigeria and I wound up at Lilian's Day Nursery in my birth town, Enugu, under the leadership of Mrs Udozo. I have precious memories of those early years, standing in line singing nursery rhymes, playing dress-up and attending classmates' birthdays in my frilliest dress and shiniest shoes. My London nursery days and the bully that drove me away are little more than an anecdote.

Sometimes I wonder about that boy and where he is now. Whether he thinks about the little African girl he used to make fun of and how he feels about it; or has he forgotten too? We were practically babies, after all.

Maybe he grew up to be a bully in the boardroom, the bedroom, his marriage. Maybe he was being bullied himself and I was a deeper shade of different, so he took his hurt out on me. Maybe he had a secret crush on me. Like a boy at school who tormented my sister Nkiru for years, slinging racial abuse at her whenever they crossed paths. 'If I saw him walking down the corridor towards me, my blood would run cold. I'd think, Oh no, what's he going to do now?' she said.

The teasing went on until they both left for secondary school. Then, one day, she got a letter from him telling her he was sorry for the bullying. He confessed he had been in love with her all that time.

When I asked if he was one of the kids who had tied my sister up and hurled racial insults at her, she reminded me there was more to that story. 'They didn't just call me names. They whipped me like a slave.'

My mouth fell open. How come I hadn't remembered this detail?

'It wasn't physically painful, they were fake whipping, using stuff like jewellery chains. Apparently, it was a game. I mean, they were my friends, supposedly. I guess for them it was fun. But I didn't really appreciate it.'

The Stories Beneath Our Skin

I'd been married to my husband for more than a decade before he told me about a nightmarish experience he'd had in his boyhood. We were visiting Cambridge on a nostalgic trip back to the area where he grew up. Abiye was born in London, but raised in Cambridge, where his dad attended King's College and his mum trained and worked as a psychotherapist. Abiye went to a local primary school and one weekend, he took me and the boys on a mini tour.

As we walked behind the school, he told me about what happened to him after a screening of the TV series *Roots*. Apparently, the show inspired Abiye's classmates to act like slave masters. 'They started chasing after me, with sticks and stuff, shouting at me as if I was a runaway slave. I ran all the way down here, all the way back home. It was pretty intense. It felt like I was running for my life.'

As adults, we tend to romanticise childhood. But we've all been there. We know kids can be beastly sometimes, especially when mob mentality takes over.

I wasn't a model child myself. I could be cliquey and catty. Sometimes I laughed when I should have spoken out. I might not have been the instigator of teasing children who were over-weight, but I didn't always intervene. It's easy to dismiss what happens in the playground as kids being kids. Grow a pair, toughen up, give as good as you get. But bullying can wreck lives.

In 2018, I read about McKenzie Adams, a sweet-faced little girl who lived in Linden, Alabama. She loved going to the beach, riding her bike, making silly videos with her cousins. She wanted to be a scientist when she grew up. On 3 December, her grandmother found McKenzie's body in her bedroom. She had taken her own life. McKenzie was nine years old.

Her mother, Jasmine, said she had been the victim of racist bullying at school. Many of the taunts centred around McKenzie's friendship with a White boy. The school wrapped up an internal investigation, concluding there was no evidence of bullying to support Jasmine's case.

I couldn't stop crying when I read McKenzie's story. She was the same age as Jed at the time. How alone she must have felt, how utterly hopeless. The Monday after her death, McKenzie's mother put up a heartbreaking note on Facebook: 'My world is gone . . . my first love.'

I try to imagine what it's like being a schoolgirl in the climate of Trump. A Black schoolgirl growing up in the American Deep South. I remember driving through Alabama in my teens, dropping off relatives one summer. We stopped off at a gas station and entered the shop.

The woman behind the counter was a stereotypical redneck, heavyset, buffalo arms and eyes like bullets. She glared at us as we wandered through her shop. When I paid for my wares, she snatched her hand away as if she couldn't stand to touch me. I kept expecting her to whip out a rifle from under her counter and tell us 'negroes' to 'get to steppin'. I've never been so glad to get out of a shop in my life.

When It Happens To Our Kids

Those of us who bear the scars of racism can be quick to anger when it happens to our kids. The first time it happened to my boys, my head lit up like a struck match.

Ezra and Jed had come home from primary school, the little one close to tears. A boy in the year above Ezra (four years older than Jed) had been calling them names. A football game near school had got heated. The boy started swearing at them, mocking them for having 'fat lips'. My boys didn't fully understand the racial implications, but it wasn't lost on the eyewitnesses who reported it to me and, later, to the head teacher.

When the head called a meeting with parents to try to resolve our issues, one of the major points of contention was the comment about 'fat lips' and whether it was racist.

'My boy doesn't have a racist bone in his body,' his mum said, quivering with anger.

She was furious I had played the race card, when (according to her son) it was my eldest who started everything. The head teacher was quick to point out it wasn't me but another parent, a White mum, who had witnessed the incident and complained about the racist taunts.

What is it about being accused of racism that gets people so worked up? It's like you're tarring them with a brush dipped in Nazi ink. Anyone would think it was more offensive than racism itself. Actually, I would hesitate to call any child a racist. Generally, kids churn out what they've learned. Whether you like it or not, the world will spoon-feed your child ideas of what skin colour is best, which gender rules, who is worth more. If you don't intervene as a parent, their chances of growing up without prejudice are slim.

I would love to say the incident at school was a teachable moment. Unfortunately, the mum left our meeting angrier than when she arrived. The boy got into tangles with other kids until he went to secondary school, where he was bullied himself. But at least our school took decisive action. Following our meeting, they held a couple of extra workshops for students on bullying and discrimination. Ultimately, I was glad my children's first direct hit of racial abuse was comparatively minor. Flesh wounds, not soul injuries.

Ghanaian mum Mercy lives in a suburban market town in the UK with her two younger boys (both of mixed heritage). Her eldest, Jordan, faced relentless abuse when they first moved to the area.

One child was told off by his parents for being friends with my son. Another kid stole Jordan's trainers, so the school called his parents to discuss. The parents failed to show up at the meeting but sent a message via their son that they wouldn't attend because a nigger shouldn't be able to afford those shoes. Jordan moved out from the area as soon as he turned 18 and went off to university. He never returned, still hates it here.

Mercy has stark memories of her own first experience of racism as a child:

It was in Amsterdam of all places! I was travelling from Slotermeer to Centrum on border bus 21. As I attempted to sit next to this White lady, she quickly placed her dog on the seat to stop me sitting there. When I told my mum about it, she told me I should be grateful that the lady was overtly racist and not a hypocrite like others. At least I knew what I was up against. I was young, but I understood the point she was trying to make. My mum was very resilient and she raised me the same way. That's what I want to pass on to my kids. Be resilient and challenge racism wherever you see it.

How to Keep Your Cool in the Face of Haters

So how do you teach your children to stand up against racist bullying? It's natural to feel shocked, upset, enraged. However, don't let anger consume your focus. Stay clear and cool.

If you've already started having conversations with your kids about race and racism, you'll be in a much better position to handle any incident. And they will be more likely to share it with you if anything comes up.

Be present for your child. Give them your full attention and your undiluted support. Let them tell you their story in their own words. Studies show people who can put painful experiences into narrative are more likely to get through without long-term trauma. Listen to your child speaking their truth, without interruption. Ask questions where appropriate, but mostly recognise their feelings, without trying either to minimise or catastrophise the situation.

Take time to acknowledge your own feelings of anger, guilt, frustration, pain too. What our kids go through can be a powerful trigger for us as parents, especially if we suffered similar abuse. It's ok to share some of what you're feeling with your child, but it can terrify them to see you fall apart. So if you need to rant and rage, try to do it away from little eyes.

Tell your own stories. When you are open about your experiences, it can help kids feel less alone. It offers them a point of reference on how to deal with future incidents. Tell stories about people you know, people in the news, people in the Civil Rights movement to help your child understand the greater context of racism and how their response ties in to a tradition of fighting for equality.

Empower your child to feel more confident and assertive in who they are. Knowledge is power and educating them about their heritage is essential. You might consider self-defence or martial-arts classes to give their confidence a boost. Even a drama, sports or creative writing class can enhance their self-esteem. Point them towards role models they can respect, both in the public eye and in their everyday lives. Depending on the severity of the abuse, professional counselling could be a big help.

Take action against racism. Take it up with the school or parent in question (if it happens outside school). Keep a record of everything your child said about the incident, as well as any eyewitness reports. Insist on some accountability for the bully as well as a more proactive strategy of training and conversation. When dealing with her son's case, Mercy not only worked with the school, but also reported the bullying to the county council.

'The last thing I wanted was to be labelled "angry Black woman",' she says, 'so I took the "diplomatic" approach. I made sure all incidents were correctly logged by the school, which they hated because it affected their reputation.'

If you can't get any further with a specific case, then take it to your community. Racial bullying is a hate crime, so you are within your rights to make a complaint to the police. If you feel the issue needs wider coverage, see if you can get your story in the media.

After McKenzie Adams' suicide, her school refused to take responsibility. However, her mother persisted with getting her story in the news and gained tons of public support. By November 2019, nearly 80,000 people all over the world had signed a petition demanding justice for McKenzie and her family. And in January 2020, McKenzie's family filed a federal lawsuit against her school, US Jones Elementary Demopolis.

The lawsuit claims: '(The defendants) exhibited deliberate and blatant indifference to the wrongful persistent bullying and harassment, rife with racial and gender-based slurs, imparted upon McKenzie by a boy who was her classmate.' The school denies the claim and we await the outcome of the litigation.

What If Your Child Is the Bully?

I teach my boys that there is a hurt child inside every bully. This doesn't excuse the behaviour (Donald Trump's 'hurt child' can take a running jump). But it can be helpful to remember childhood bullies are usually going through difficulties themselves. Often, it's a child who doesn't know how to cope with their own feelings – whether that's anger, fear, insecurity, a sense of otherness or even attraction (as in the case of my sister's primary-school tormentor).

Make sure you get the full picture. Boys are often seen as being more physical and rough than girls, even if there's evidence to the contrary. Black parents are more likely to find their sons labelled as aggressors, which in itself is a racist stereotype. A playground skirmish might result in the Black kid being blamed, as with Dion in the Netflix series, *Raising Dion*.

This happened to Patrick's son Noah when he was ten years old:

He came home from school one day and told us one of his classmates had called him a nigger. He was at a predominantly White school. Noah faced this boy down and they got into an altercation. A teacher came along and pulled them apart and Noah got put in detention, while nothing happened to the other boy.

Patrick says their first instinct as parents was to go straight to the school, but Noah wanted to deal with the situation himself. He wrote a letter to the headmaster, outlining what had really happened.

The headmaster called the teacher in and the end result was that the teacher had to apologise to Noah and the boy admitted what he'd done. It turned out the boy had also said racist things to one of the only other students of colour in the school, but that pupil had been too intimidated to make a complaint at the time.

If your child is pulled up for bullying, try to get to the root of the problem. Listen to what they say provoked the attack. Get as much information as you can from the school, what they believe happened and how they intend to handle it. Arm yourself with all the facts before you take any kind of action.

Keep your cool. Don't go on the defensive or on the attack. Take private time to acknowledge your feelings and save any ranting for a trusted friend or partner. You can express your disappointment to your child and get them to acknowledge that what they did was unacceptable. Also, try to get a sense of their state of mind. Has anything upset them lately, causing them to lash out at others? Have there been any recent changes like trouble at school, a big move, divorce or bereavement that have left them feeling out of sorts?

If your child is accused of racist bullying, try not to freak out. What your child did was bad, but that doesn't mean your child is a bad seed. They've learned something wrong and it can be unlearned. The two most important things are for your child to own what they did fully, without excuses, and to put themselves in their victim's shoes. One powerful exercise is to get them to write a letter in the other child's voice, so they can try to see what happened through another pair of eyes.

Make sure they understand just how serious racism is and that in the UK, racist bullying is the only type of bullying that schools must keep a record of.[1] In most countries, racism is a crime and depending on what they did, they might feel the full force of the law.

Whatever you do, don't sweep it under the carpet or assume you have no part to play in this. Children are picking up messages all the time and it is your job to keep talking and teaching your child about race and racism. It's a good opportunity to (re)educate yourself too.

Racism and Mental Health

Racist bullying is on the rise. In 2018, a *Guardian* analysis recorded a sharp increase in numbers of children excluded for racist bullying.[2] The jump to 4,590 cases (up from 4,085 the year before) was the highest leap in a decade and it is said to be rising at a faster rate than student population growth. Children's charity the NSPCC reported a jump in hate crimes against under-18s around the time of the 2016 EU referendum and again after the 2017 terror attacks in London and Manchester; the UK's head of counterterrorism policing, Neil Basu, acknowledged in January 2019 that a spike in hate crime since the referendum had 'never really receded'.[3]

Racism has been shown to be one of the leading causes of anxiety, depression and low self-esteem in young people. Children of colour growing up in a prejudiced world are more likely to suffer from mental-health complications.

British-Bangladeshi baker Nadiya Hussain, winner of *The Great British Bake Off* in 2015, attributes her panic attacks to a racist experience she had at school when she was seven. She was bullied for having dark skin and once, some boys held her up against a chalkboard and smothered chalk dust all over her face. She told *Loose Women* viewers she believes it's what triggered her anxiety disorder: every time she feels her panic rising, it reels her right back to that assault in front of the chalkboard.

I had never linked my own struggles with anxiety to growing up as an outsider. I had enough personal trauma to pin it on: from the quiet sorrow of miscarriage to the private horrors of #metoo experiences. And I still carry the grief of losing my father in successive blows. The first stroke at 58 that paralysed half his body. Then, five years later, another stroke that stole his speech and faculties. The final stroke that killed him at 68. Five years since her death, I'm still haunted by my mother passing away suddenly in her sleep.

Then I think back to my childhood, when I learned to hide so much to hold myself together. Those early days of feeling walled in with children whose faces and voices and family experiences were so alien to me. The food I couldn't stomach for weeks. The looks and stares and fingers on my hair and skin. Black people caricatured in fiction and films and history books. My name a sound nobody could pronounce.

No wonder my senses remained on alert. No matter how chill and smiley my personality, there's a girl inside who walks a high wire. A small part of me that easily panics about what if, what's wrong, what's next?

Michelle Chai, owner of popular blog 'Daisybutter', recalls the stress of growing up as an outsider in Hertfordshire, England. Kids at school would call her 'Chinky' and make fun of her family's takeaway restaurant. When she was 17, she was working at the restaurant when 'suddenly a brick came flying through our window, narrowly missing our brand-new touch-screen order machine, and my head'.

Michelle says she suffers racially induced anxiety, particularly since Brexit:

I stay at home a lot to avoid encounters because racism is on the rise in my area. I feel truly helpless because it is nothing short of terrifying to know you're almost powerless if you're alone. I suffer from regular panic attacks, particularly around the fear of a racially provoked attack where I might be pushed in front of a train. A few of these stories hit the news a few months ago and now it has indelibly impacted my life.

In 2019, the American Academy of Pediatrics released its first major policy statement on the impact of racism on children's mental, social and physical health.[4] The results were clear. Racism harms people on multiple levels. It creates anxiety, which, in turn, causes a variety of ailments. The report links the impact of racism to birth disparities, mental-health problems in children and adolescents and inflammatory reactions leading to chronic disorders, caused by prolonged exposure to stress hormones like cortisol.

Maria Trent, who co-authored the report, talked about racism as 'a socially transmitted disease', something we pass on to our children.

And you don't have to experience racism directly to feel its negative effects. This type of violence hurts everyone in its path, from oppressors to victims to witnesses. The report states that young adults who were simply bystanders to racism experienced physiological and psychological effects when asked to remember such events that can be compared to what first responders experience after a major disaster.

The Bully of the World

When I told my children I was writing a book about kids and race, I asked if they had any title ideas. I particularly liked Ezra's suggestion, 'Kids v Racism: Beating the Biggest Bully of Them All'.

Racism is the bully of the world. It comes in many forms. It can shape-shift into anti-Semitism, tribalism, fascism,

Islamophobia, misogyny. It wants you to believe we are enemies, that some people are less and deserve less, that there can never be enough for all of us. It can snipe you from a rooftop. Or sneak up like a drive-by shooter.

Indian mum and blogger Nomita recalls walking down the road when a car drove up beside her:

There was a boy in the passenger seat. He leaned out the window and shouted, 'Fucking Paki'. He couldn't have been more than eight or nine. What got me was that his dad was driving and he didn't say anything to his son. He didn't even look at me. He just carried on driving.

Sometimes the bully speaks in the voice of a child. But it is not that child. It is the grown-up in the driving seat who doesn't say a word. You see, racism doesn't live in our children. It lives in our silence. It is all the tiny, daily acts of hate, mistrust and fear happening under the surface. The face that looks the other way as the car keeps driving, even as the wheels come off.

• Talking Points

Q. My daughter's best friend told her that her skin was dirty. What do I say to comfort her?
A. Hug your daughter tightly and tell her that her skin is absolutely beautiful. Tell her she is blessed to have skin that protects her from direct sunlight and that resembles so many

olours like trees and earth. Give her words to

her skin that will make her face light up with pleasure: like chocolate, cocoa, shea butter, mahogany, coffee, brown sugar. Talk to your daughter about the many gorgeous skin tones not only around the world but in your immediate family.

Next, tell her to inform her friend that what she said wasn't just hurtful, it was racist – and that not only is racism a form of ignorance, it's a hate crime and she could get in a lot of trouble if she carries on like that. She should tell her friend to educate herself on why people have different skin colours and how none is any better than the other; they are all simply part of God and nature's rich palette. If your daughter is really young, she can simply say something along the lines of 'That was very rude, but my skin's not dirty, so even though I was sad when you said it, I'm not sad any more. My skin is just like the skin of [insert favourite person] and I love it. If you say mean things, I won't play with you again. I'll find somebody nicer to be my friend.'

This might also be a good time to have a conversation with the girl's parents about what ideas and attitudes she might be picking up.

Q. I caught my nephew cracking jokes about Indian people, using an accent and stuff, and I was appalled. Should I say something to his mother?
A. Yes, please say something to his mother. And as his auntie, you are also within your rights to intervene on the spot – call it what it is and tell him you don't appreciate that kind of

mimicry. Try not to fly off the handle about it though; remember, kids are kids and say a lot of stuff they don't mean. Keep the conversation light if you can, but make sure he understands that what he's doing is not acceptable. If he says it was just a joke, tell him that people have been harassed, put down, tormented and even driven out of their homes, based on similar, narrow ideas. Tell him it might be funnier to make fun of his own quirks and characteristics than to pick on anybody else. And if he hears his friends sharing such ideas in the name of 'banter' he should challenge it where he can and choose not to participate.

Q. My son was accused of racist bullying at school, but I know it can't be true. We never raised him to be racist; he doesn't even know the meaning of the word!
A. It might shock you to hear racist slurs or ideas coming out of your little one. Especially if you consider yourselves to be a non-racist, liberal family. But nobody plans to raise a racist (unless you are a racist by ideology). However, all of us are being raised in a system of White supremacy that affects so much of how we see, act and relate to each other. You don't have to be actively feeding your child racist or bigoted ideas for him to pick them up. He might have got them from school, media, family members, even unconsciously from you and how you relate (or don't relate?) to people of other ethnicities.

What's important is that you don't just shut your son down with a punishment. Try to go a little deeper. Ask where he thinks he learned those ideas, and what he thought he would achieve by bullying a child in that way. Ask him to put himself in that child's shoes (see p. 81). Tell him you hope he didn't intend to be racist and that you are going to do some work, as a family, to understand more about race, how it shapes us and what you can do to challenge prejudice. This is not a time for hand-wringing; it's a time to act positively and equip yourselves with the tools and resources that will serve you all for a lifetime.

CHAPTER 5

Under the Skin

You cannot fix what you will not face.

James Baldwin, African-American author

Racism doesn't always throw a brick through your window or shout hate speech at you from a passing car. For the most part, it's more subtle. An offhand comment, a narrowing of the eyes. A look that says you aren't worthy, you shouldn't be here, you don't belong. This type of racism is almost imperceptible, like a chill entering the room when the door's slightly ajar. You might shiver, but you're not always sure if it's happening or if it's all in your head.

A few years back, I was with my children in a small gift shop in north London. I was paying at the counter while the boys browsed toys on the shelf. After I'd paid, I found them both looking annoyed.

Jed was first to report: 'Mum, that woman over there just told me, "Move yourself!"'

Ezra chipped in: 'We didn't even know she was behind us.'

He glared in her direction. 'If she comes by us again, I'm going to stand in her way deliberately. And if she tells me, "Move yourself!" I'm going to say, "What's the magic word?" '

As an African raised with African values, I'm big on respect for your elders. But I also teach my children that respect is a two-way street (you'd be amazed at how some people deal with children when nobody's looking) and since they were little, I've encouraged them to call out bad behaviour, even if it's coming from a grown-up.

'Use your big voice and speak up for yourself. Talk about how they made you feel,' I tell them. 'Be polite; never let anyone accuse you of being ill-mannered. But speak up for your rights.'

The lady in question was White, elderly, well-to-do. Maybe it wasn't about race. Maybe she was just rude. After all, plenty of Black and Brown adults talk down to younger ones or treat them like they have no rights. However, I can sense when people are judging my kids for having wilder hair, darker skin and a louder presence than others in the vicinity.

At the time, I was mostly amused by Ezra's response. 'What's the magic word?' But what strikes me now is the way the woman spoke to my son. 'Move yourself!' I don't think she would have spoken that way to a stranger's dog.

Every Day I'm Muffling

There's a name for everyday bigotry, the mini assaults that chip away at your sense of self. The word 'microaggression' has trickled down into popular culture from the field of psychology. American psychiatrist Chester M. Pierce coined the term in the 1970s. More recently, it's become a buzzword in debates around race, gender and identity.

If you've ever been on the wrong side of a power imbalance, most likely you've experienced microaggressions. For a woman, it can come in the form of wolf-whistles and leers as you walk down the street. Or the indignity of your boss (aka former UK prime minister David Cameron) telling you to 'Calm down, dear' in a political debate.

The insidious thing about microaggressions is that they happen in a sort of grey area. Often, the person doing the hurting has no idea. Social psychologists Jack Dovidio, Ph.D. (Yale University) and Samuel L. Gaertner, Ph.D. (University of Delaware) have done several studies examining the unconscious racism of well-intentioned White people.[1] Their findings reveal that in experimental interviews, for instance, White potential employers favour White over Black candidates when their qualifications are interchangeable. These are White people who consciously advocate for racial justice and equality, yet under different circumstances, their unconscious bias kicks in.

And what's troubling is you can't always spot it and you certainly can't talk about it – at least not without being accused of playing the victim. Was that lady in the shop with my boys naturally short-tempered, having a bad day, generally impatient with kids, or was there definitely a racial element? You find yourself doubting and second-guessing such interactions.

Columbia University psychologist Derald Wing Sue has studied microaggressions and their impact. He wrote about an experience he had travelling with an African-American colleague. They boarded a small plane and sat at the front. Three White men boarded last and sat in front of them. Next thing, the flight attendant asked Sue and his colleague to move to the back of the plane, to distribute weight more evenly. Feeling unfairly singled out, and his blood pressure rising as a result, Sue decided to question the flight attendant for asking two passengers of colour to move to the back of the 'bus'. The flight attendant was indignant, claiming she 'didn't see colour' and was only trying to give them more space and privacy. Sue points out that if it hadn't been for his colleague validating his feelings, he might have wondered if he'd made a fuss over nothing.

In a paper titled 'Racial Microaggressions in Everyday Life – Implications for Clinical Practice',[2] Sue identified three types of racial microaggressions:

microassaults are deliberate verbal or non-verbal attacks like name-calling and other discriminatory actions.

Microinsults are subtle, often covert snubs that demean a person's heritage or identity.

Microinvalidations are communications that exclude, negate or nullify your experiential reality as a person of colour.

For example: a Black man walks into a lift and the White woman inside moves away and clutches her handbag (a microinsult with the hidden meaning: Black men are criminals); or a British-born woman in a hijab is asked when she arrived in this country (a microinvalidation with the subtext that Muslims can't be truly British).

British Chinese blogger Michelle is all too familiar with microaggressions:

How it feels for people to stare at you and whisper to their neighbours in the doctors' waiting room. How it feels when an elderly White person asks you where you're really from. How it feels to have somebody painfully enunciate something to you when you're a native English speaker with a First-Class degree in journalism.

I'm Not Being Racist but . . .

Did you ever have a friend who started sentences with 'I'm not trying to be mean, but . . . '? And you'd brace yourself, because you knew she was about to hit you with one of the meanest comments yet? Was that friend you?

If you want to understand how microaggressions work, picture that mean girl. She's not trying to be mean but she's brutal. She doesn't intend to hurt you, at least not consciously. Or maybe she's hurting you deliberately, while hoping to get herself off the hook with a disclaimer. Either way, the effect is the same. She drops her bomb, then carries on with her day and you're left reeling from the impact.

Psychologists say any time you insert the word 'but' into a comment or an argument, you immediately cancel whatever came before it. In other words, 'I'm not being racist but . . . here's the incredibly racist thing I have to say.'

In some circles, microaggressions are a bit of a joke. You'll find right-wing tabloid articles mocking university students as 'snowflakes' for their overuse of terms like 'microaggression' and 'triggered'.

However, those of us who experience these everyday acts of 'othering' know how unsettling it can feel. As actor and producer Samuel L. Jackson said: 'People know about the Klan and the overt racism, but the killing of one's soul little by little, day after day, is a lot worse than someone coming in your house and lynching you.' Some call microaggressions 'death by a thousand cuts'.

A series of studies published in the journal *Personality and Social Psychology Bulletin* by Dr Keon West blew away the 'snowflake theory'.[3] He tested 500 participants including White, Black and Brown people to see how they respond to microaggressions. He found that (shock, horror) nobody likes being treated like they're alien or inferior, even if it's subtle. And how badly you react to microaggressions has nothing to do with race. It's just that White people don't experience them as frequently as people of colour.

Countless studies have proven the cumulative impact of microaggressions on performance and achievement. In his groundbreaking work on stereotype threat, Stanford University psychology professor Claude Steele, Ph.D. showed that if you tell a girl that females are bad at STEM subjects, it actually affects her ability to pass a maths or science test.[4] Similarly, when children of colour have to cope with racial slights and microaggressions, it stops them from being able to complete regular tasks successfully. Over time, these small knocks can make a big dent in their academic attainment levels.

As novelist Toni Morrison said, the main function of racism is to distract you from doing your work.[5] It keeps you in a constant state of having to prove your worth or justify your reason for being. British playwright Inua Ellams has talked about being Black in a majority White society as always being 'under pressure', and it's a feeling many people of colour can relate to. The sense that, any day now, someone can pull the ground out from under your feet.

Some parents try to teach their children to keep a low profile: don't stick your head up and you won't get mud in your face. However, this can do more harm than good.

Michelle recalls coming home upset after schoolkids called her racist names. She said her parents answered in 'classic first-generation Chinese immigrant manner':

Mum would tell me that they were being rude, but they were probably just not educated about why it was rude. I genuinely can't recall them using the word 'racist' when I was growing up. My parents taught me to be unheard, not to provoke anything and 'they don't do anything to you', and basically to try and fit in (with the White British majority).

Every person of colour I spoke to for this book has felt the pressure of exceptionality. How their parents taught them they would have to work twice as hard and be three times as excellent as their White peers to get a look-in. We see this across every sphere of Western society: from the overqualified immigrants working multiple jobs to make ends meet, to the Obamas being held to ridiculously high standards compared to any other First Family. It's a familiar verse in the song of assimilation. Be outstanding but keep your head down, don't challenge the status quo, do whatever you can to fit in.

Author, podcaster and relationships expert Natalie Lue recalls her childhood in Dublin, where she was the only Black girl in an otherwise all-White Catholic school:

We were taught from an early age about what was and wasn't ok for White people to see us doing. Don't eat bananas in front of them, don't be loud, don't talk about your business, be careful when you're in their homes because if something breaks or goes missing, you will be blamed. Lots of stuff about being clean because Black people were seen as 'dirty' apparently.

One damaging side effect of all this home training, Natalie observes, was that she was inadvertently taught about shame:

Black children are often taught to check themselves, to be guarded, to 'know your place'. It's not that White girls didn't have issues, but their appearance is 'the norm' and they're not carrying around a whole load of baggage about their wrongness or 'exoticness' when they walk into spaces. It's tough growing up with people touching you, asking weird questions, and yeah, sometimes coming out with stuff that left you feeling humiliated and small. I found it's exhausting to deal with situations where people are denying the more covert stuff.

Like many of her peers, Natalie is determined to break the cycle and plays a different tune for her own children. One of less pressure, more hope: 'We're having open conversations about race, but we're also encouraging them not to limit themselves. We're not teaching them something that I was taught: that you have to work a thousand times harder when you're Black.'

All Eyes on Me

You might wonder what all this has to do with you as a parent. Why would you want to explain microaggressions to someone not old enough to spell the word?

I'm not trying to explain the term here, I'm trying to explain the feeling. Because this isn't about social studies or intellectual theorising; this is about real human feelings. Something even a small child can understand. It's about what's fair, what's right, what hurts. You don't need to know what microaggressions are or have learned about racism to feel when something's wrong. A young person can sense racism even if you don't name it.

Former journalist Rachel told me about her earliest experience of racism, which she didn't fully understand at the time. Up until age 12, she lived and was schooled in Nigeria and said she felt 'cocooned' against it for the most part:

I used to come to the UK for Christmas holidays from about age five, always Christmas because we loved the snow. I was about eight or nine, and I remember going into Boots [pharmacy] with my mum and the security guard was basically stalking us. I remember telling my mum: 'Why's that man just following us around?' We were well presented, not particularly scruffy or overdressed. Bless my mum, she ignored it, but that's the first time I was aware 'What's wrong here?' It didn't cross my mind that it was a race thing. Now I know that we were being profiled.

I've lost count of the number of times I've entered a shop and instantly felt the security guard clocking me. Sometimes I offer a nod or a half-smile, a sort of 'I'm-cool-no-worries' look, but I can feel his eyes on me. If I'm dressed a bit more 'expensive', I might get a shop assistant harassing me for whether I need help. But I've been followed around by security and I've seen my children followed too.

I remember yelling at my boys when they acted out in public because of that extra pressure – being judged by the shade of your skin. Sometimes I wish I could turn back time on those episodes. I cringe at the image of a crazy Black woman shouting at her little roughnecks in the street. Then I realise I'm humming that same old song of shame. For why should I be so hard on myself? Like so many mamas, I was doing the work of a village on my own.

I imagine every parent knows that feeling. The sensation of all eyes on you, judging you, judging your children. The covert glances and the tuts. The shame and frustration and isolation. That is just a glimpse of what it can feel like to be the Other in society.

Get Out

In Jordan Peele's brilliant, hilarious and terrifying movie *Get Out*, that sense of othering takes on horrific proportions. The main character, Chris (played by Daniel Kaluuya), visits his White girlfriend's parents for the weekend and tension builds as we slowly realise things aren't what they seem. Every interaction between Chris, the solo Black person (aside from serving staff) and his girlfriend's family and friends highlights the difference between them. At first it's funny but it starts to affect his mental state. Of course, he wonders if he's imagining things, especially since his girlfriend can't see anything wrong. Eventually, Chris is trapped in a living nightmare and has to use every ounce of willpower to break free.

Get Out is a clever, creepy twist on microaggressions and how they get to you. It's about the racism that lives under the skin of polite society. It shows how something as simple as someone touching your hair or commenting on your name can set your teeth on edge. What's so smart about *Get Out* is that it centres a Black man as the hero (unlike other horror movies where he'd be the first to die). It allows every viewer to look through Chris's eyes and see, perhaps for the first time, what this type of racism is really like.

Jordan Peele describes the movie as 'a documentary'. Already studied on several college courses, *Get Out* is a useful conversation starter to discuss race with teens and young adults. It works on many layers, it's highly entertaining and it will scare the crap out of you.

Do Kenyans Have Internet?

Jed comes home from school, dumps his book bag on the chair. 'Mum when I told my class I was going to Nigeria, some of the kids told me I was going to catch ebola. I told them ebola wasn't in Nigeria, but they were all really worried for me.'

Heavy sigh. This is ignorance dressed up as concern and it's a microaggression. You can't blame the kids – they're only reporting back what they hear. But Nigeria was the first West African country to declare itself free of ebola in 2014, and yet years later, Jed's classmates were fretting (or teasing?) about a disease that claimed 19 victims and 7 deaths in a population of more than 170 million. As I edit this chapter, East Asians around the world are reporting horrific racist abuse based on misconceptions about COVID-19. The epidemic here isn't ebola or a coronavirus. It's what author Chimamanda Adichie calls the 'danger of a single story'.

Every African I know who went to school abroad in the '70s or '80s had to field similar questions: did you live in mud huts, did you swing through trees, did you travel here by canoe? Do you know it's Christmas?

My cousin Uche told me about her schooldays in Wales when fellow students tried to communicate with her in sign language, even though she was responding to them in perfect English.

Just last year (in 2019, for the love of Tarzan) someone posted the question 'Does Kenya have Internet?' on Quora. The comebacks from Kenyans make highly entertaining reading. I encourage you to Google it.

My friend Ike Anya, a Nigerian doctor and writer, shared a hilarious account on Facebook of a racist encounter he had while travelling back from a conference. Ike says he arrived in his first-class seat, sweaty and dishevelled from rushing to catch the train. A young man pushing the catering trolley eyed him suspiciously and demanded to see his ticket. 'I've done this trip often,' Ike writes, 'catering staff don't check tickets.'

Nonetheless, Ike smiled and showed his ticket. As the trolley steward moved on, Ike called out: 'Are you going to check the tickets of everyone in this carriage?' The young man stammered 'Yes', and then had to ask the businessman in the next aisle for his ticket. Ike kept his eyes on him throughout, forcing the red-faced trolley steward to keep up with his charade, to the confusion of other passengers. Ike rounded off: 'Young man has not seen anything. He wants to be ticket inspector abi? His catering work is not enough to occupy him, eh? He will inspect tickets at every single destination until I get off this train. He has just appointed me his supervisor. Nonsense and ingredients.'

I'm still chuckling at the image. However, racially based ignorance is no laughing matter – because it speaks to a deeper ailment in society. Microaggressions harm on multiple levels: first, they hit you at the core of who you are. But they also reinforce structural inequality. It's about putting you in your place.

Weed It Out

Ok, so here's the challenge. If this type of bigotry is so insidious – when even adults struggle to recognise it – how on earth do you raise a child to do better?

The first step is to teach children to distinguish regular mean behaviour from microaggressions. In an essay for the Southern Poverty Law Center on schooling first-graders about microaggressions, California teacher Bret Turner explains that not all unkindness is the same. All kids say mean things sometimes. We have to teach children that it becomes discrimination if you target something that a person cannot change, like their race, gender or religious background. When your comments or actions are extra hurtful because the underlying message is about who holds the power in society.

Turner describes a classic teacher activity known as 'the wrinkled heart', where a large paper heart is passed between students. As they share moments when their own hearts were hurt, they crumple a piece of the heart until it's a small wad of paper. Then they share moments that made their hearts happy and the paper heart is unfurled. But every student can see the crumpled lines are still there. Those little wounds never go away.

When does a child know if what they're doing hurts? If what they're saying crosses the line? Encourage them to pay attention to what people are trying to communicate, even when they don't say a word. You can develop this skill by reading books and watching films together and asking deeper questions, like what's really happening under the surface? How is this character feeling and why? What is the story beneath the story? The more your child understands about subtext, the more heightened their sense of empathy will be.

You can also remind your child to stop, look and listen in any encounter, just as they would before they cross the road. Teach your child to be mindful of the words they use. If they're about to crack a joke or make an observation that might be hurtful to somebody, they need to consider if it's the kind thing to do. What do they gain by saying it and what would they lose by choosing to keep quiet? How would they feel if somebody said something similar about them?

When you create a safe, honest space for your child to talk openly about race and other tricky subjects, you are building a trust relationship that lasts a lifetime. More importantly, you are teaching them to trust their own sense of right and wrong.

Now, I'm not suggesting we all float around like sensitive flowers (or snowflakes, God help us). If there's one thing being a Black woman and sharing stories with other people of colour has taught me, it's that we're resilient. I never want to lose that quality and I'm glad it's showing up in my kids. I'm glad they have a sense of humour and that they're quick with a comeback. When it's right, I'll be quick to back them up. What's the magic word? Yeah, lady, he said what he said.

The trouble is, while humour can be a secret weapon, it can also blow up in your face. And most of us are tired of laughing things off. We can't let everyday racism slip by unnoticed, unseen, unspoken. We have to start calling it out and teaching our children to do the same. Remind them to separate intent from impact, and also to challenge the behaviour rather than the human being. Offer them a template to stand up to microaggressions, however they surface. They might say things like:

'I'm not sure you realise it, but what you said was racist. Here's why . . .'

'I don't appreciate that joke; it makes people feel like they don't belong here.'

'I'm sure you weren't planning to sound like an asshole just now but . . .' (Ok, maybe save this one for when they're much older!)

Or just keep it simple. That's not funny. That's not kind. That's not true. That's not ok. That's racist.

Chet Ellis, a student at Staples High School in Westport, USA, won the town's teen diversity essay contest writing about the racism he'd faced as a Black student.[6] At first, he stayed silent but that only made him more of a target. Finally, he came to understand that racist, sexist and homophobic ideas are 'like weeds' that need to be yanked out from the root. Otherwise they can turn into 'vast fields of hate and bigotry'.

It's tiresome to pluck those weeds out but we have to keep at it. Remember, pluck is another word for courage. So raise kind kids, but raise them plucky too. Raise a child who can use their big voice, be polite but clear, talk about their feelings, point out what isn't fair. A child who can make someone accountable, even if that person is a grown-up.

• Talking Points

Q. After reading about microaggressions, I took the implicit bias test online and it came out badly. I'm worried about what I might be passing on to my own kids, unintentionally. What steps can I take to change things?

A. First, you should realise that nobody ever 'passes' an implicit bias test. We all hold various unconscious biases, preconceptions and negative assumptions that we need to confront. If you were shocked by what the test revealed about how you think about the world, this is your opportunity to try something new. Diversify your bookshelf, mix up your social circle, start open conversations with people who are different from you. Recognise that you are a learner in this just like your child, so you can go on this journey together. Stay open, keep learning.

Q. I tried to take a group of my son's friends, all Black and Asian, to a restaurant but the manager said it was full, even though we could see empty tables inside. Another White family was seated while we waited. I'm still shaking with anger and upset. Is there anything we can do to make this right?

A. It saddens and disgusts me to know this kind of behaviour is still happening in the 2020s. Yet yours is far from the only case I've heard. You should certainly make a formal complaint, in writing, to the restaurant owner. But don't leave things there, especially if they are reluctant to issue a formal apology. Sometimes sharing your experience via social media, tagging the restaurant in question, can create a powerful viral call to action. You could even get some mainstream media coverage.

The main thing is not to brush this off, as it shows a systemic problem at the restaurant that could affect others. It also highlights the ongoing impact of racism in society that is too often swept under the carpet. I believe it's important for your son and his friends to see you taking a stand and to make their voices heard too. One suggestion would be for the kids to write as individuals or in a joint letter, sharing their experience in their own words. They should write from the heart about what it feels like as a child to be excluded from a restaurant because of the colour of their skin. If you are so inclined, you could even start a petition via a forum like Change.org to make sure your story is shared widely. The more we speak out against incidents like this, the closer we will get to stamping out hate in all its forms.

Q. My child is never invited to birthday parties and I know it's because of her race. How do I bring this up without sounding like an angry Black mother?

A. Have you spoken with your daughter about what's going on at school? You don't want to make this about race if there's another issue (e.g. friends falling out, girls being cliquey, etc.). However, if your gut tells you it's a race matter, you could talk to some of the other mums. Approach them one on one (rather than via a WhatsApp group, for instance) and share what your child is going through, discussing any steps you can take as a school community so that no kid feels left out. You might follow up with a teacher – or even the head – about what they teach on diversity, cultural appreciation and inclusivity. Has your daughter invited these same children to her own parties – and do they come or always make excuses? If it's the latter, the racial bias might run deeper and it might be worth taking this up with the school's board of governors. Also, look for opportunities for your daughter to make friends outside school, whether in community clubs, with extended family or neighbours.

CHAPTER 6

Mixed

I am not a lack of anything; rather I am a whole of many things.

C. JoyBell C., American author
and philosophical essayist

My other half has a theory that in the future everyone on earth will look like him. He says this with a twinkle in his eye, like he thinks he might have it in him to populate the planet. I roll my eyes at what sounds like a *Boys from Brazil* super-cloning fantasy. But Abiye's theory is closer to fact than science fiction. What he's alluding to is that more and more children are being born from interracial partnerships. In Britain, people who identify as mixed are the fastest-growing ethnic group. One out of every seven kids in America is 'biracial', according to a Pew Research Center Poll.[1] Almost every parent I spoke to for this book was in a multicultural relationship. In a *Sliding Doors* alternate reality, I might have been mixed too.

Before he met my mother, my dad was married to a White American woman, a linguistics expert named Karen. She was a fellow student at UCLA and they were together for three years. After Dad passed, my brother reached out to Karen and we began writing to each other. I loved getting letters and old photographs from her, insights into a life before our father dreamed of having us.

Their relationship caused grievances on both sides. Apparently, my dad's brother had written to let him know their mother had said she didn't want any 'khaki-coloured' grand-kids. Karen's mum wasn't keen on Black grandkids either, and when, after the wedding, she suffered a stroke, Karen got blamed for it. She wrote, 'Of course, it was really her pack-a-day cigarette smoking and her very stressful job, or a weak blood vessel in her brain, or all three! But I believed it was my fault at the time.'

Karen and I have stayed in touch over the years. I consider her my 'almost' stepmother, a member of my extended family. She was amused when I told her I'd wound up with so-called 'khaki-coloured' kids myself.

Brown Baby Boom

When you walk around modern multicultural London, it seems bizarre to imagine that less than two generations ago, it was taboo to mate with someone of a different complexion.

In 1950s Britain, more than 2,000 mixed-heritage babies were abandoned to care homes. Dubbed 'Brown Babies' by the American media, they were the offspring of White mums and Black GIs who weren't legally able to take them back to the US.

Anti-miscegenation laws prevented sexual or marital relations between Whites and African Americans. It wasn't until 1967, in the case of Loving v. Virginia (following African American Mildred Jeter and White American Richard Loving's conviction for being a married couple by Virginia authorities), that the US Supreme Court ended state laws banning interracial marriages. In South Africa, the very first apartheid law was the Prohibition of Mixed Marriages Act in 1949. Mixed-heritage people got classified as 'Coloureds' and the government did checks to make sure you weren't trying to sneak your Blackness past them.[2] These included the pencil test (see p. 174), assessing your buttocks or jaw line or pinching people to see what language they said 'ouch' in.

Cut to the present day and while even countries like South Africa are becoming more integrated, interracial families around the world still face a number of challenges. For instance, how do you raise a mixed-heritage child to be secure in their identity in a society at odds with itself?

You'll notice throughout this book I've chosen to use the term 'mixed heritage'. It's a little clunky, but it feels more inclusive. When we say mixed race, what usually leaps to mind is somebody whose parents are Black and White. Most people don't consider the dozens of other combinations in between. To me, mixed race also hints at a 'pure' race – an idea that's at best ignorant, at worst dangerous.

TV chef and restaurateur Andi Oliver is mum to TV

presenter Miquita Oliver, whose father is White. Andi, a single parent and a Londoner of Antiguan descent, raised Miquita in west London. 'She grew up in the middle of Carnival,' Andi says, 'so she was always surrounded by a mixed, multicultural panoply of people that helped build her foundations.' However, there were some ugly incidents, including people calling Miquita 'dirty':

The word 'dirty' always comes into it, some sense of purity being sullied. Now more than ever we need to remember we're all human. The idea that people are retreating back into these tribal enclaves, be it about gender, sexuality or race or whatever. We're moving in the wrong direction in an attempt to protect ourselves and it's creating more division.

What advice does Andi have for facing up to racist bullies?

I always tried when I was with the kids never to respond with aggression. I would take them out of the situation and explain that people can be ignorant and unkind. My parenting template was to rise above it. I didn't always succeed though, sometimes the lioness came out and I would just tell people to fuck off.

Unboxing Identity

Of course, you can't always intervene for your kids, but Andi believes if you raise them with a strong sense of self, they will learn to stand their ground. She recalls Miquita having trouble with mean girls at school. 'She got it from both sides – not Black enough, not White enough. But she and her cousin came up with a really great thing: when people would call them 'half-caste' they'd say, "Oh no, we're golden".'

Many people don't get why saying 'half-caste' is offensive, but it stems from the Latin word 'castus' meaning 'pure', and its Portuguese and Spanish derivative 'casta', meaning 'race'. I grew up with this term in Nigeria where it wasn't used as an insult – quite the opposite. Typically, being 'half-caste' meant having coveted fair skin and a higher social ranking. Still, knowing what I know today, it sets my teeth on edge.

Blogger Nomita compares it to an Indian term that sounds innocuous enough to outsiders. When her daughter was born, the health visitor referred to her as 'Anglo-Indian' and Nomita was horrified. 'Anglo-Indian used to be a very derogatory term,' she says. 'It meant the British didn't accept you and neither did the Indians. Usually they were born out of wedlock, like someone having an affair with the help.'

Throughout slavery and colonialism, mixed children were often the result of illicit or abusive encounters – such as between master and slave. As times progressed, more and more inter-racial couples simply fell in love, as humans do. However, many worried about their future children. Would they become social outcasts? Myths were rife about the emotional instability of mixed kids, captured in older literature and Hollywood movies (like *Imitation of Life*) as 'tragic mulatto' figures, destined to a life of misery.

Fortunately, the boom in thriving multiracial families has helped smash some of those stereotypes. However, children of mixed heritage can still grow up with questions around belonging and identity.

Do you have to pick a side to gain acceptance? If you identify as one race, are you rejecting a part of who you really are? And why do others try to box you in, based on superficial things like how you look, sound or wear your hair?

In an article for *Elle* magazine, Meghan Markle wrote poignantly about being asked to check the box for 'Caucasian' by a teacher.[3] She wound up leaving the box 'incomplete', which summed up how she felt at the time.

The pressure to define your race – or even fix racism, somehow – can be a burden for mixed-heritage kids.

What can you do as a parent? Take some pressure off. Give your child space to discover themselves on their own terms.

Entrepreneur and mum of three Shanthi is a happy blend of English, Nigerian, Ghanaian and Indian. Married to Kojo, a Ghanaian-Nigerian, Shanthi describes their kids as 'Black African' on the census box, while checking 'Mixed Other' for herself. However, she's open to things changing as they grow. 'It will be interesting to see how they self-identify.'

Try to support your child through identity shifts. What they choose to call themselves might – and probably will – change over time. Sometimes, even siblings in a mixed-heritage family will identify differently. Children with one Black parent might see themselves as Black, mainly because that's what society sees. The majority of Black mixed-heritage people I know (including my husband's first son, Isaac, whose mother is White) find solidarity with the Black community. Acknowledge that it's ok to explore and that you understand it's not about your child rejecting either parent. It's about becoming comfortable and confident in their own skin.

Nat Illumine, co-editor of the *Afropean* magazine, is a White Jewish Londoner co-parenting with a Ghanaian Brit. She says it's important that their ten-year-old daughter can frame her identity for herself:

It's a dynamic and fluid process; every teenager goes through identity formation as they come of age. Right now, her big thing is 'I'm Brown'. Obviously, she's too young to understand the political ramifications of being Black. But that may change as she gets older; she might decide she's a Black woman, and I'll be cool with that.

Raising Mixed Kids

Nat attributes her daughter's self-confidence to growing up in London. 'Her school is so diverse. I realise that for other people living outside of big metropolitan areas, it's a very different experience. But she's in this diversity bubble. She doesn't question who she is, why she looks like she does. She revels in her skin.'

It can make a huge impact for your children if you can raise them in an environment where their difference is the norm, not the exception. Many mixed families relocate to large, metropolitan areas to find more people who look like them.

Yet for all our ethnic diversity, Londoners aren't free from ignorance. I remember sitting in a north London pub with my husband and his half-sister Mira, who is White. A stranger came to chat her up, and Abiye jokingly intervened. 'You trying to talk to my sister?'

The stranger was confused. 'Which sister? Over the course of what became an excruciating ten minutes, Abiye and Mira explained they were brother and sister, but the stranger wasn't having it. 'You're Black mate, and she's White.'

As we went around in circles, it was obvious this fool wasn't too dumb to understand they had different fathers. But (consciously or not) he wanted to make a point about Whiteness and to deny Abiye access to it. The thing is, my husband and his sister both look just like their mother. Only a blind person could miss the resemblance. Or a bigot.

Sadly, racism isn't solved by having more babies that look like Abiye. Often it just brings it home. Sometimes it's microaggressions from a stranger; sometimes it's animosity from your own family. When you enter an interracial partnership, you might discover your favourite uncle is a closet xenophobe. You might have to confront some of your own hidden prejudices. For

White mums raising Brown and Black kids, it's typically their first personal encounter with racism.

Blogger Ivanka Poku grew up in an all-White community in Slovakia where it was 'rather an exciting experience' to see a Black person. She's married to a Ghanaian living in London and they have twin boys:

Since I had never come across racism before, this is all new for me and it took me a while to accept that racism is real. I'm learning how to teach our children to be confident enough to not let racism impact their life in a negative way. The fact I am White also means I see a lot of things in a different light than my husband does, which nicely balances it out. I see this as a great benefit as we can offer our boys different perspectives.

Business and mindset coach Ruth Kudzi is a White British mum of two girls who's also married to a Ghanaian based in the UK. She says, 'I feel that I am learning the whole time and I now have a different perspective than I did before. The recent press about Meghan Markle has made me glad my daughters can't read.' Although her girls are young, she knows they'll soon have to have deeper talks about race and racism. Once, her eldest was told she had 'dirty skin' by fellow schoolgirls. 'When my youngest daughter was a baby, I took her to baby group and she was told she was exotic and different. I complained to the organiser!'

The word 'exotic' might be said as a compliment. But it can feel dehumanising – like comparing someone to a rare bird or flower. It's code for different, strange, foreign. It also ties in with a troubling, fetishistic narrative around people with multiple heritages being 'more beautiful'. There are many ways to affirm a child's unique qualities without over-emphasising their racial mix or using terms like 'exotic'. For girls in particular, it's better to identify a range of strengths and characteristics that go beyond the physical.

A child who is growing up mixed might worry about not looking like either parent. Talk to your child about how this feels and reassure them that your bond is deeper than skin or facial features. Look through family albums and tell stories about relatives who resemble your child, either visually or in personality. Search for other role models they can relate to – books with mixed-heritage protagonists, strong characters in movies and media, perhaps real-life heroes in your area.

Hair can be a huge issue for children with Black ancestry. If looking after Afro or mixed hair is unfamiliar to you, ask for advice. Visit an Afro hair salon, watch YouTube video tutorials, read natural hair-care sites. Educate yourself on gentle detangling, hydrating and protective styling for your child's hair. Ruth says her in-laws have also helped her greatly with her daughters' hair, which she describes as 'a learning curve'.

No matter your background, having a mixed child makes you part of a multi-ethnic community. Embrace this and your child will embrace it too. If you can spare the time and money, take them to the country where their grandparents are from.

If this isn't possible, look for other ways to bring their traditions into your home – say, through language, food, music and stories.

Ivanka says, 'I think it is amazing that our children have such a rich heritage. We teach each other and discover new facts we would have not discovered otherwise. We learn a lot about other cultures and their traditions. I think our boys can be proud of being half-Slovak and half-Ghanaian.'

Facing up to Racism

Be sure not to shy away from conversations about race and racism. You might feel like you have it covered because it's not an issue at home. However, it's essential to equip your child for the world that exists outside your front door.

For a mixed-heritage child, race is often the first thing people fixate on. On the other hand, if your child looks ethnically ambiguous, they might feel like their racial heritage is overlooked or undermined. Either way, race is something they'll have to learn to navigate for most of their lives.

Engaging in thoughtful, empowering conversations can act as a buffer against the shock of other people's ignorance and vitriol. Remember to keep these discussions age-appropriate. You could start with your own (or your partner's) earliest experience of being made to feel different. Talk about how it felt, how your own parents handled it (or didn't) and what you wish you could change if you could go back in time.

In a personal essay for the *Afropean*, Nat shared her hesitation around bringing up race with her daughter. She was afraid of bursting that 'diversity bubble' and letting the real world in. Now she says their conversations are evolving organically.

As she gets older, it's become easier because she can understand it more. Also, she brings things up herself. We haven't sat down to have one big conversation – we just address stuff as it comes up. I'm a race academic, so I don't want to come across too heavy-handed. I've told her I'm here if she needs to chat.

It can be helpful to reframe conversations with kids from how to cope with mean behaviour to how to treat others kindly and fairly. Shift your child's perspective from potential victim or observer to someone who takes action.

You could talk about how often people discriminate because they are uncomfortable or fearful of what they don't know or understand. Ask your child how they feel when they notice people who are different, whether it's because of skin colour or looks, hair, language, size, gender or ability. Reassure them that it's normal to feel curious or surprised, but staring, pointing or rude comments are never ok. Ask them what they think might be the kindest way to respond to difference and see what answers they come up with. Kids will often surprise you with their natural instinct for kindness, decency and compassion.

If your child seems stuck, you could offer a prompt like 'What if you waved or said hello?' Teach your child to avoid intrusive questions or remarks in the face of strangers. Just as your child doesn't owe anybody an explanation of who they are, neither does anybody else. It's best to save questions for when you can discuss and learn together on your own time.

Ghanaian mum Mercy's two younger boys are 'part-English, part-Welsh' like their dad. She's normalised talking about race as part of family mealtime chats:

As a single parent, I have a strong bond with my kids and have created an environment where they can talk about EVERYTHING. I don't have a specific way of discussing racism, but at dinner time each person talks about their day, highlights and lowlights, and rates the day out of ten. If someone had a particularly bad day, we discuss the issue or incident and offer advice going forward.

If you make it a part of everyday conversation, you'll be more prepared to cope with any questions that come up. Questions about skin tone, hair, identity, nationality, why people look different, what to call themselves, what box to tick where. Many of these questions don't have straightforward answers; some of it you can learn together, much of it they'll have to figure out for themselves.

Your role is to create a sanctuary for your cub to grow. And to remind them, when it matters, that a lioness has their back.

• Talking Points

Q. I'm mixed Southeast Asian and White British. I grew up feeling like I never quite fit in with Asian culture nor did I feel accepted as an English girl. When I go to India, they call me a foreigner and in Birmingham, they tell me to go back to my country. I'm dating a White boy and I'm worried that if we have kids, our children will be even more mixed up.

A. It's tricky always feeling like the 'other' on some level, but it can also be liberating. You have a unique perspective, shaped by the variety of experiences that make up who you are. Every human feels like an outsider at one time or another. You will be in a prime position to help your kids navigate any feelings of not fitting in or never thinking they're enough. I think it's a bonus to have multiple cultures influencing you and, as a modern woman, you can take more of a pick-and-mix approach.

I like the saying, 'Tradition is peer pressure from dead people'. In other words, feel free to hang onto those elements of your inherited culture that you feel connected to, and let go of what doesn't serve you. You will pass on all you love and know to your children and they can sift through what they love and need as they grow. Hopefully, your children will feel at ease with their mixed heritage, but essentially, they will be British just like you and your partner. And regardless of what some believe, the beauty of modern Britain is our diversity.

Q. My daughter hates the term 'mixed race'. What other ways can she describe herself?

A. Mixed. Bicultural. Mixed heritage (what I've used throughout this book). Biracial (a little too close to mixed race?). Or get specific, depending on what her actual ethnic origin is e.g. Japanese Nigerian, Italian Swedish, Lebanese American, Irish Pakistani. Sometimes it feels like we have chopped ourselves into far too many pieces with all our labels. However, for the purposes of categorisation, she can play with different ways of describing herself and choose whatever feels right.

Q. We're adopting a boy from China and we're doing everything we can to educate ourselves about his culture. But we live in a very White area, and we don't have much opportunity to mix with Chinese people. I'm worried that we're going to fail him as parents.

A. You are already way ahead of many parents by even thinking in this direction. Whether we are parenting our own children or adopting kids of the same race, many mums and dads haven't given race matters a second thought (which is why I wrote this book). So you have a jumpstart on all that and there's no reason to think of yourselves as failures. Use what you have at your disposal: books, movies and other cultural resources can help to educate you as a family and provide a sense of connection for your child (see Further Reading, p. 297). Also, there are loads of forums and communities for people in your situation – a simple Google search should lead you to a group either in your area or online.

If you can afford to make a trip to his homeland as a family, it's a worthwhile investment into helping him connect with his ethnic origins. Also do your best to seek out local adoptees and families, ask around for anybody who knows a Chinese family or a neighbourhood where you can hang out. You want to find a happy balance between him feeling part of your community, no matter how White, and also taking pride in his race and heritage. Stay open to his personal experiences, be an active listener, support him where he needs it, keep the conversation going.

CHAPTER 7

History Lessons

Until the lion learns how to write, every story will glorify the hunter.

African proverb

On 5 April 1968, the day after Martin Luther King Jr was assassinated, a schoolteacher in Riceville, Iowa (population 898) played what some called a cruel and divisive prank on her class.

When one asked her, 'Why'd they shoot that King?' Jane Elliott asked these kids, aged eight and nine, what they knew about Black people. They parroted back stuff they'd picked up from parents, their community, the media at large. 'Negroes' were dirty, lazy and fought a lot.

Elliott asked if they wanted to play a game to help them understand what discrimination felt like.

First, she split her class into two groups – Blue Eyes vs Brown Eyes – and told the former they were superior. The blue-eyed children got privileges, like extra time at break period, access to the new jungle gym and second helpings at lunch. Meanwhile, the Brown Eyes were forced to wear blue fabric collars and to sit at the back of the class. They weren't allowed to drink from the same water fountain and Elliott lied to them that their brown eyes made them less intelligent.

It didn't take long for the blue-eyed kids to start acting superior. Interestingly, even their grades and ability to perform simple tasks improved, whereas the brown-eyed kids scored worse on tests, began to isolate themselves and act more subservient.

Elliott was amazed to see her 'marvellous, cooperative, wonderful, thoughtful' third-graders become 'nasty, vicious, discriminating' little children, in the space of fifteen minutes.

The following Monday, Elliott gave the brown-eyed kids preferential status. Although the Brown Eyes enjoyed lording it over the Blue Eyes, it wasn't quite as harsh. When the exercise was over, Elliott got the kids to write down their experiences. Some were published in the local newspaper.

When the story was picked up in the Associated Press, Elliott was invited onto *The Tonight Show* with Johnny Carson and afterwards, she got hundreds of angry calls and letters. One fumed about the 'psychological damage' her social experiments would do to White kids, as opposed to Black kids who 'grow up accustomed to such behaviour'.

Elliott was defiant, wondering why people were so concerned about White children's temporary suffering when Black people experienced injustice for real, every single day.

For decades, she continued running her experiment with schools, prisons, workforces and other institutions. In the 1985

PBS retrospective *A Class Divided*, some of Elliott's former third-grade students were reunited as adults. All agreed it had taught them a lesson for life. One former student said whenever she heard people saying racist stuff like 'go back to Africa', she thought about the fabric collar she'd worn as a child. She wished she could whip the collar out of her pocket and say, 'Wear this and put yourself in their place'.

You can find *A Class Divided* on the PBS website.[1] Watch it with your children and talk about what you learn and how it makes you feel. The lessons are as relevant today as they were in 1968.

How Did We Get Here?

If it sounds nuts to segregate according to eye colour, remind your child that race is made up. It's just as senseless to discriminate based on skin tone or hair. Yet this foolishness has been going on for centuries.

Race took hold as a biological idea in the 17th and 18th centuries, as Europeans spread to the New World and discovered natives who didn't fit their ideas of 'civilised men'. German anatomist Johann Blumenbach invented the term Caucasians (Whites), ranking them above four other 'varieties' of human: Mongolian (non-Caucasian people of Asia), American (indigenous Americans), Malay (South Pacific Islanders) and Ethiopian (Black African).[2] Samuel Morton, known as the father of scientific racism, went on to measure human skulls and claimed that Caucasians were more intelligent, while Blacks were closer to animals.[3] All this pseudoscience came in super handy in justifying the human trafficking of Africans over centuries.

Slavery had been around for ages, but chattel slavery was specific to the transatlantic slave trade. The idea of importing humans as cattle and owning their children and their children's children indefinitely must have been hard for some to stomach. So the lie of White supremacy was spread: God or Mother Nature had designed the White man with superior intellect and breeding to master the Black African and possibly tame the savage out of him.

Now, even though modern DNA kits trace every human to the same African ancestor, that lie haunts us today.

Miseducation

When you have a Western education, you are conditioned to side with the conquerors – the ones who stripped the world while spreading God, Empire and civility. When I was a child in an English classroom, reading about the 'Dark Continent', Africa felt like a wild, dangerous, almost mythical place. Even for someone like me who was born there.

I remember learning the phrase 'from here to Timbuktu', as if that was the most remote place on earth. I had no idea it was a real city in Mali, whose university was home to priceless manuscripts dating back to the 13th century. As far as I knew, ancient Africans didn't read.

Fortunately, my parents and their bookshelves helped me to uncover other stories. To make connections between Igbo creation myths and tales of Israel and Egypt. To understand there was much more to our 'primitive' culture than met the European eye.

At school, the Eurocentric history I learned was simply called History. We crammed on facts and figures and glossed over slavery, unless it was through the eyes of the (mostly British) abolitionists. Until I started reading outside the curriculum as a teen, I didn't fully understand how Britain and its industrial revolution were built on wealth acquired over hundreds of years of slave-trading and colonisation. And I was a mother of two boys before I learned about the Slave Compensation Commission of 1837 that paid 46,000 former slave owners £20 million (the equivalent of £16–17 billion today) for the loss of their human property.[4] That's right – the slave market was so central to the UK economy that ending slavery resulted in the country's biggest financial bailout before 2009. So why has Britain's part in slavery been treated like a footnote in our history books?

Nat Illumine, co-editor of the *Afropean* magazine, says:

I think the British education system needs to be completely overhauled; the way they teach history is disgusting. One of the biggest problems we have is what Paul Gilroy called 'post-colonial melancholia'. An inability to acknowledge the tragedy of the British Empire and how colonialism is linked to capitalism. The way we were taught African history begins with slavery, and how the Empire was amazing and it brought trains to India and all this BS. It prevents us as a society moving forward into the 21st century, into the real world, and addressing a lot of the issues we still have due to colonialism.

Our lack of knowledge about who we are and where we come from continues to destabilise people of colour. Scratch that. It destabilises everyone. How can we learn from past mistakes if we're afraid of looking back with open eyes?

Nat adds:

People ask stuff like, why do you have to bring up race? Slavery was ages ago. And I'm like, no you don't understand the structural ramifications; but to be honest, the system doesn't teach people to think critically whatsoever. Kids go to learn information, but they're not taught how to think.

What Are Our Children Learning?

If racism is an infection passed on to our kids, one way it's transmitted is through our education system. A lot of the time, it's by omission. At many schools, for instance, Black History Month is treated as a cultural exercise – a chance to quote Martin Luther King and eat some rice and peas.

But Black History Month was about something bigger. It sought to reclaim the narrative around people of African descent and how they've helped shape the world. Like Britain's

129

first Black settlers and the African and Caribbean soldiers who fought in both World Wars.

If more Britons knew their history, there would have been more national outrage at the recent detainment and deportation of members of the Windrush generation – Britain's first wave of West Indian immigrants. Men and women who were granted automatic UK settlement rights on arrival, only to have these stripped by a hostile Tory government.

There is so much we haven't been taught. When the show *Watchmen* launched on HBO in 2019, the opening episode blew people away. It told the true story of the Tulsa Race Riots of 1921, when White American militants in Oklahoma dropped bombs on what was known as Black Wall Street. It was a shocking event, particularly for modern Americans who had never heard anything about it. They took to social media to express their horror and disbelief that this was never taught in schools.

For African-American entrepreneur and mother of three Timil Jones, the airbrushing of education comes back to the dirty history of trading humans.

America hasn't taken responsibility for the gruesomeness of slavery and that trickles down into the school system. If adults are uncomfortable with the truths of chattel slavery and its connection to America's wealth and power, then in turn, when they create the curriculum, they can't be honest in their teachings. It's important for all children to learn the truth, but it's especially important for children of colour's history to be taught in a way that doesn't make them feel further traumatised in the classroom.

One way is to balance difficult truths with more life-affirming stories. Just as all children need to see strong, interesting, multi-layered Black and Brown role models in the media, they need positive representation in the classroom and curriculum too.

We need to push for better race education in schools. Because most children will have their first experience with racism in a school setting. TV chef and restaurateur Andi Oliver has painful recollections of experiencing racism as the only Black girl in a Suffolk school. The worst incident involved a teacher.

I had my hair cane rowed for the first time and I was scared to go to school as it was the 1970s and I didn't want to look different. But my mum had put silver beads at the front and I felt pretty. When I walked into my German class, the teacher went: 'Oh my God, what is that? Your hair, your hair!' in German. For the first 15 minutes of the class, he made me stand at the front and had the kids take the piss out of me. There were tears rolling down my face. I was probably about 12. Even now, that story makes me cry.

When I heard Andi's story, it brought tears to my eyes too. I wondered if she told anyone and she said no. 'I was too humiliated. As a child, you take on the shame. One of the worst things about racism is that it makes you ashamed of yourself. You feel ashamed for existing. I had to teach myself that I'm allowed to occupy space.'

Teaching our children to occupy space and to allow others the same is a call to action for all parents, especially parents of colour. However, first they need safe spaces to occupy.

School Ties

A UK schools report commissioned by campaign organisation Show Racism the Red Card revealed stark gaps in race and equality education:[5] lack of diversity in staff and senior leadership positions; teachers who aren't trained or equipped to handle race conversations or racist incidents; unfair or disproportionate punishments for children of colour. Black and Gypsy Roma and Traveller kids were most at risk for racial abuse and exclusion.

For Black boys, exclusion rates are triple the national average. Unconscious bias and institutional racism work together as invisible barriers, edging kids of colour out of the classroom and onto the streets. Young boys are targeted as 'naughty', kicked out of school and children as young as 10 and 11 wind up as 'county-line' drug couriers. In the US, the rate at which disadvantaged Black and Brown kids are failed out and funnelled into a life of crime has become known as the 'preschool to prison pipeline'.

Timil's kids have faced challenges since preschool:

It tends to be in the areas of harsher discipline being given to our children for things we know other children aren't penalised as severely for. It's also shown up in the language used to characterise our boys by teachers. In one instance, we had to get our child placed with a different teacher several weeks after the beginning of the school year when she used criminal-justice language to describe him in a parent–teacher conference.

A UK campaign tagged #ClosingtheGap aims to increase Black Asian and minority ethnic student attainment levels at UK universities. It emphasises stronger leadership, conversations about race and racially diverse environments.

These are positive steps, but clearly we need to intervene much younger.

Raising Critical Thinkers

What would our societies look like if we taught all children that they mattered? That their history was of equal value and that we cared about their futures too. What if all schools were safe spaces where adults and kids alike could have honest, sensitive, open dialogue around race, identity and belonging?

Personally, I think the UK education system is broken and things don't look much better in the States. I'm interested in what's happening in countries like Denmark and Finland. They seem so much more progressive. As Nat says, education should be about teaching children how to think, rather than telling them what to believe.

Sometimes I wish every classroom could sit through Jane Elliott's experiments. But your child shouldn't have to wear a collar around their neck to understand injustice or to develop empathy for their fellow human.

Maybe we shouldn't push our kids to be the brightest in the class, the ones to ace every test, or to win every medal. Maybe what matters more is whether your child is the one to raise their voice and stick up for someone being picked on. If your child notices when another child is lonely or needs a helping hand. What always stuck with me from my boys' school reports was learning how considerate they were with their classmates. In Year 3, Jed's teacher told me: 'If I was eight years old, I would want to be Jed's friend too.' One of my proudest moments as a mum.

What if we made kindness a core part of every curriculum, as central as 123 and ABC?

I know, it sounds a bit woo woo and you might wonder what teaching kindness would look like in a practical sense. I believe it connects with teaching children how to think critically.

In his TEDx Talk on the subject, teacher trainer Brian Oshiro says children, parents and teachers can enhance their creative and critical thinking by asking a series of questions.[6] He recommends following each What question with a series of Whys that help you go deeper and connect the dots. Finally, focus on problem-solving by asking How.

You could try this with a statement like racism is bad. First, ask your child what makes racism bad. Then go deeper by considering various reasons why. Now, how we solve racism is a question too big for global leaders. However, you can break it down for your child. For instance, how can you reach out to that one person in class who doesn't feel included?

Empower kids with critical thinking skills and you are giving them tools to come up with creative solutions for real-life challenges. Plus you are sowing the seeds for a kinder, braver individual by teaching them to resist narrow ideas, to consider other points of view and to embrace the unknown.

Hacking Your Education

I watched a TEDx Talk years back by a super-bright 13-year-old, Logan LaPlante, all about 'hackschooling'.[7] That was his term for homeschooling. He spent his days in libraries or learning to code, but also surfing, skiing and generally being enthused by life. I was almost persuaded to pull my boys out of primary school.

Sadly, I don't have the patience to homeschool. But I can hack my children's education and so can you. Create your own diverse curriculum through cultural events, books, websites, music, movies and travel.

Take time to teach your child life skills they might never learn at school. Learn these skills together. Watch TED Talks or documentaries – anything by Neil deGrasse Tyson or David Attenborough will keep the whole family enthralled.

Personally, I believe stories are our greatest teachers, so don't discount the impact of fiction and drama too. An episode of *Black-ish* Season 5 about colourism (see Chapter 'Different Shades of Beauty', p. 202) sparked questions that led to us watching *13th*, Ava du Vernay's powerful documentary about racism in the US prison system. Jed fell asleep (thankfully, as it's pretty graphic), but Ezra found it highly educational.

Some of the best storytellers are the elders in our community. Encourage your kids to sit with grandparents and senior citizens and listen to their stories.

During one family visit, my father-in-law, Patrick Dele Cole, told us about an incident that happened in the late '60s, when he was a fellow at Cambridge. At a Nigerian wedding in London, a small fight broke out. Although things died down quickly, someone in the area called the police. Within minutes, Patrick and fellow guests were herded into vans. At the station, policemen dragged these Black men in their wedding finery into individual cells and beat them up. Afterwards, they were charged with riotous behaviour, and it was only Patrick's Cambridge connections that helped free him.

Our boys listened intently, no doubt seeing their granddad in a new light. It opened up an interesting conversation about race, privilege, police brutality . . . and partying too loud. An invaluable history lesson.

• Talking Points

Q. My kids aren't being taught about stuff like slavery and colonialism and I want them to know more about this history. However, I wasn't taught any of it at school either. Where's a good place to start?

A. Google is your friend and so is YouTube; although both can turn into wormholes of information seeking, you can also find some really helpful, detailed and free resources on exactly these issues. I've included a list of books and websites (see Further Reading, p. 297). But these are huge topics, so don't try to consume everything at once. Take it day by day, and always check and recheck your sources, as there is also a ton of disinformation out there (often put out by people with their own agenda). Also, don't feel like you have to stick with facts and statistics and true-life stories only. I learned more about the effects of slavery, colonialism and apartheid from reading fiction like Toni Morrison's *Beloved*, Chinua Achebe's *Things Fall Apart* and André Brink's *Looking on Darkness* than I did from any history books.

Q. My son feels like he's being singled out in class and he thinks it's because of his race. I've tried speaking with the teacher, but it didn't get me anywhere. Should I take it up with the head or is there anybody else I can turn to?

A. Absolutely go to the head teacher and ask for support. If they are not supportive, demand further investigation. Trust what your son is saying and also listen to your gut. You know whether your son is more naughty than other boys, and if you feel this is the case, he might have other learning challenges that need following up. However, it's all too easy for a Black boy especially to be labelled as 'difficult' and for that label to stick throughout his school career. Take it up with the school's board of governors, the school counsellor (or equivalent) and, if necessary, go to your local educational authority and make a formal complaint. If you have to contact a local paper, do it. Go the extra mile for your child. This is important. You are his first and his last advocate. It's also important to seek support for yourself and your family while you are going through any trying times. There are usually support groups and forums online, where you can connect with other parents and get advice more specific to your situation. Please see Further Reading, p. 297.

Q. I want my kids to go to the best schools, but I'm worried about them being in a monocultural environment and picking up values that don't suit us as a family.

A. I know from personal experience, having been to school in overwhelmingly White/monocultural institutions, versus the experiences my boys have with more diversity, that a multicultural environment was a very strong value for our family. However, there are many great schools, both state and private, that offer places to children from a range of backgrounds. Every school has its pros and cons regardless, so I would take your time researching and speaking to other families, including any parents in your area who might share your perspective. Also remember that no matter where your child goes to school, the values that you raise them with at home will outlast anything else.

CHAPTER 8

E Is for Equality

Let the water live, and let the fish also live; the water should not dry and the fish should not die.

Igbo proverb

When my youngest was ten, he took part in an educational programme aimed at inspiring more kids from underrepresented backgrounds to apply for highly selective universities. The children visited Cambridge and Reading universities and, over a few weeks, they worked with a Ph.D. candidate who tutored them on concepts like equality, equity and meritocracy. The weekly discussion and writing sessions built towards their final assignment: a 1,000-word essay on Fairness.

'One thousand words!' Jed moaned, as if mentally calculating how many FIFA hours that would cost him.

In the interests of, well, fairness, I insisted he write his papers himself, but if he needed to bounce any of his ideas around, I was happy to help. After writing a couple of paragraphs on equality, Jed stopped two-finger typing and flipped around in his chair.

'I know what equality means in a general sense, but can you give me some more examples?'

So I asked him what he knew about the Civil Rights movement, for instance, and he mentioned Martin Luther King and Rosa Parks. We spoke about the significance of marching on Washington and why they needed to campaign for African Americans to be treated fairly as human beings. We also talked about how global inequality affects people on so many levels, from the climate crisis to basic standards of living.

One thing that seemed to niggle at him was when I explained how some nations were grouped together as the First World. Meanwhile other countries (mostly former European colonies) were described as Third World, or what today are more commonly known as developing nations.

When Jed got down to writing his essay, he stopped again and turned to me.

'Mum, is it ok for me to put First World and Third World in quotation marks?'

I gave him a thumbs up.

'That's Not Fair!'

It's funny how quickly kids catch on to basic concepts that sometimes adults complicate. I could see Jed's eyes narrowing when I spoke about Africa being 'Third World'. Having visited

Nigeria and seen both lavish wealth and extreme poverty, he knows things aren't so black or white.

If there's one thing the smallest child understands very early on, it's the concept of fairness. Kids have a strong sense of justice, even when it's motivated by self-interest. Just try giving a child one lollipop, then giving their sibling two, and watch what happens.

Right up until my boys hit their teens and tweens, there could be no peace on Middle Earth until I'd divided stuff up equally between them. If I took a chip off Ezra's plate, I'd have to take one off Jed's too. If I had a bite of Jed's burger, I'd have to take an identical bite out of Ezra's. The hardest times for Jed came when 'older-brother' privileges kicked in for Ezra, meaning he would get to stay up later, receive more pocket money, have one extra sleepover that month.

There's a concept attributed to American author Rick Riordan that explains how fairness isn't about everybody getting the same, it's about every person getting what they need. For instance, if you have bigger feet than your sister, giving you both the same size shoes simply won't fly. It's the distinction between equality and equity, as Jed learned in his academic programme.

However, just because he understands equity (distribution according to what people need), doesn't mean he applies it to himself. There are times when life feels very unfair indeed and there's not much he can do about it.

Sometimes the gap between the wealthy and the destitute is a measure of hard work, but for the most part it's by pure accident of birth: what part of the planet you live on, whether your parents went to school, how many other mouths they had to feed, what opportunities there are for people of your colour or caste or creed.

'But it's not fair!'

It's tempting to retort, 'Well, tough!' However, what's more useful is hearing your child out when they feel something's unjust. Sometimes, all they want is validation. They want their feelings to be recognised. When you can engage a child on their basic rights, it can be transformative.

A BBC report on a school in Wales revealed that children who were taught about human rights were more likely to open up about feeling unsafe at home.[1] When they learned about the life they deserved and compared it to the misery they endured, it empowered them to ask for help.

Why not share the UN Convention of the Rights of the Child with your offspring? You can find versions online, often in a handy infogram.[2] Adopted in 1989 and now signed by 196 countries, it includes the right to be safe from abuse and neglect, the right to an education and the right to think for yourself.

If your kids are anything like mine, they'll absorb it with interest. Then five minutes later, you'll find them abusing each other's human rights until one of them is crying, bleeding or threatening murder. But take heart. The revolution doesn't happen overnight. You have to rinse and repeat. Just try not to hammer your message too hard or it will bore them into a state of apathy.

I've come to terms with the fact that 90 per cent of what I say to my children is white noise. The more you reinforce it though, eventually something will stick. That's how you find yourself rehashing things your own parents used to say ... all that homespun wisdom you rolled your eyes at when you were younger. Turns out, it was (mostly) good advice.

Tomorrow's People

Anyway, when it comes to equal rights, your kids are probably more clued up than you are. Children growing up in today's ethnically diverse, gender-fluid societies tend to be far more open than their parents' generation. My kids have shared classrooms with people who identify as Black, Brown, mixed heritage, religious, atheist, LGBTQI+, differently abled and neurodiverse. Sometimes all in the same charismatic individual. I'm proud of how well rounded they are as a result. I'm much more likely to raise an eyebrow over stuff they take in their stride.

Still, it doesn't mean you can hit the snooze button on your conscious parenting. Because prejudice will creep in where you least expect. When Ezra was about six, a teacher decided to start a school netball club. Since Ezra was always super sporty, I asked if he fancied signing up. He looked at me, then burst out laughing.

'Netball? What are you talking about, Mum? I'm a boy.'

To my knowledge, he'd never even seen a netball match, let alone considered what kind of balls (or lack thereof) were needed for the sport. We've had many (often amusing) conversations about gender expectations since then and we keep having them. Because just as with racial messaging, gender stereotypes are everywhere. In 2017, Common Sense Media analysed more than 150 articles, books, interviews and other social-scientific research to report that movies and TV shows were still feeding our kids the same old croutons.[3] Between ages two and six, children learn what toys, activities and skills go with which gender and between seven and ten, they attribute different roles and qualities to men and women.

As it turned out, several boys in Ezra's year did join the netball club and Ezra played in a couple of games too. To date, both my sons have female friends, although they still prefer hanging with boys. The other day, while griping about some politician going overboard with her proposals, Ezra started a sentence with: 'I mean, I'm a feminist but . . .' I don't remember what followed; I was just so thrilled he'd called himself a feminist.

Sexism, racism and other isms are the white noise of our lives. It can be exhausting as a parent, keeping up with the times, while constantly disrupting the nonsense your kids pick up from all around. At the same time, you're attempting to model the kind of culturally sensitive, socially aware, decent human being you want them to become.

Intersectionality for Kids

Our first trips to Nigeria opened my kids' eyes to the stark differences between the haves and have nots. It's literally in your face as you drive in from the airport and beggars squash their palms against your car window. I would watch the boys' expressions as they saw street kids hawking their wares, amputees pushing themselves along on makeshift skateboards, so much poverty and desperation. They were full of questions. 'Where are their mummies and daddies?' 'Don't they have anywhere to live?' 'Do they have to sell this stuff all day long?' 'Should we give them more money?'

I told them what I tell them when we're walking the streets of London, in the dead of winter, and we pass homeless people sleeping rough. Life can be very unfair. You can never judge a person by their circumstances. And unfortunately, you can't take on all the world's problems at once. However, you can work on changing one thing at a time: try to brighten one person's day; offer one person a helping hand; put some time or money towards a cause you care about.

Visiting Nigeria also taught my boys that privilege is multi-layered. That in London, sometimes we scrimp and save, whereas in my birth country, we live in relative luxury.

Blogger Nomita says taking her daughter back home to India since she was a year old has acclimatised her to vast income and class inequality:

India is trying to evolve as a society. We're breaking down the caste system, but class is still very much an issue. In England, your child can go to school and the child next to her might be a plumber's kid or the son of a banker. But in India, you don't mix like that.

She says things are changing gradually, as more schools and top universities hold places for people from underprivileged backgrounds. 'My parents' driver has been with us for ages. Now his kids are going to university and they won't be drivers or domestic help. There's still a long way to go, but the society is changing, even if it takes a few generations.'

Nomita was surprised at first that her daughter never asked her about the poverty in India. She thinks it's because she has tuned in to the class and wealth structures in Britain:

I don't think she looks at servants in India any differently than she would waiters in a restaurant in the UK. Also, in England, maybe on the surface it's not as blatant but there's definitely a snobbery about background. You can tell that people look down on others who do certain jobs, come from certain places. It's just not spoken about.

From travelling to their mother countries, our kids have learned first-hand how class, power and culture intersect. The theory of intersectionality was first defined by sociologist Kimberly Crenshaw in 1989, to explain how White feminism and Black male chauvinism worked as twin forces to exclude Black women from making progress. It's become one of those words loosely tossed about by activists and derided by cynics.

Intersectionality is a bit of a mouthful for kids. I prefer to think of a layer cake (cake is always the answer): how each layer that makes up who we are can also serve as a barrier in society. If you are Black, gay and from a working-class background, you face a different set of challenges from somebody who is Asian, middle class and living with a disability. When a child can think about their own layer cake, how each layer is essential to their identity, they are more open to appreciating other children's multi-layered experiences. When we are free to embrace our multiple identities as individuals, we create a fairer world for all.

Works in Progress

We have to model what we want to see in our children. We also have to keep reshaping the dominant narratives. Like most British mums, I carry the majority of household obligations, such as grocery shopping, family laundry, cooking and cleaning up, the never-ending mental load (birthdays, school trips, doctors' appointments, etc.). When we visit my in-laws, I serve my husband like a good Nigerian wife. However, the boys also see their dad at home, frying up breakfast, cooking a roast, sorting his own laundry. He does the handiwork and the gardening, drives us everywhere. Most importantly, we get the boys to chip in with errands and chores. Often there's grumbling and arguments but it gets done. Our version of equality is not about man vs woman or splitting equally down the line. It's about everybody contributing in whatever way they can. Not quite perfect, but a work in progress.

As parents, we have an awesome opportunity to help remake the world. Culturally, many of us are conditioned to fall into various patterns because it suits us. Because that's how it's always been. But we can create tiny revolutions every day, starting at home with our children.

After Donald Trump was elected, I took the boys to the Women's March in London. They were happy to go because they'd seen Trump hating on Black people as well as women, Latinos, Muslims, Africans, homosexuals, people with special needs. He was an equal-opportunity hater. This was intersectionality in living colour.

They loved being out, marching in solidarity with the crowds. The sound systems and stages. The placards and pussy hats. We were small, but we felt powerful that day. And although we couldn't shift him from the White House, we knew we had made a dent in his ego.

Harness your child's natural instinct for social justice. If they think something isn't fair, ask them what they would do to make things fairer. Challenge them to take action or learn to live with it. Put those critical thinking skills to work. Give your child tough choices and watch them grapple with the right thing to do. Talk about the ways they've observed and experienced inequality and what gives them an advantage – whether it's skin colour, gender, social background, education, physical ability. If this advantage (or privilege) was an actual superpower, what world problem would they solve first?

Remind your child that true change starts with every one of us. Fairness isn't only about how you cut the slice. It's about showing up in all your layers and flavours, and inspiring others to do so too. Be the cake you want to see in the world. Everything else is icing.

• Talking Points

Q. I want to bring my kids up to support equal rights for all humans. At the same time, I want them to understand that the world isn't really fair, and that competition is part of being human too. How can I reconcile the two?

A. Gandhi said: 'The earth has enough for everyone's need, but not enough for everyone's greed.' It's important to raise our kids with an abundance, rather than a scarcity mindset. There is more than enough for everybody, we just have to learn to be content with what we have and be generous with what we can give. Sure, we aren't born equal – some of us are taller, some of us are faster, some have quicker brains and stronger hearts. Everybody has something that they can do better than most other people. Some might call that a competitive advantage; you could also see it as your part to play in the grand orchestra of life. There is nothing wrong with being competitive, especially as competition helps us to grow, achieve greater things and inspire generations after us.

However, where competition and humanity clash is in the scramble for resources and the mad dash to be on top. Maybe you were born super tall not so you could tower over others, but so you can lift someone much smaller onto your shoulders and help them see further. Competition is the drive that has helped our species to survive, but cooperation and fairness are what make us thrive. Everybody deserves free will and we can exercise our right to choose to be kinder and fairer to each other,

especially in the face of so many other things that seem unfair
and totally out of our control. Teach your child that competition isn't only about coming first. It's about becoming the best
version of themselves they can be. And that is exactly what
equal rights is about too – being the best version of ourselves we
can be as humans. There really is no conflict between the two.

**Q. I'm a White father of a mixed-race daughter with
special needs (mild cerebral palsy) and I only really
started opening my eyes to feminism and racism and
ableism since becoming her father. Now I consider all
the challenges she'll face growing up and it fills me
with anger and despair. How can I encourage her
without getting her hopes up too much?**
A. Your daughter will face many, many challenges throughout
her life. That is without question. However, it isn't your job as
a father to put a cap on what she might expect or how she
dares to dream. Quite the opposite. Encourage her to go
further, to look deeper, to reach higher than either of you
could possibly imagine. Empower her until she's bursting with
affirmation. Fill her with hope until it overflows. You can
never have too much.

**Q. I support Black Lives Matter, but my child asked if
it's a racist statement and shouldn't we say All Lives
Matter? How should I respond?**
A. Tell your child that when you support a cause, it doesn't
mean you don't care about anything else. You are simply

trying to draw attention to a specific problem that needs solving. So saying Black Lives Matter doesn't mean you don't care about other lives; it's just that you want to highlight how some people treat Black lives as if they are worth nothing. If you walked around with a sign stating 'Dolphins Need Love', it wouldn't mean that you don't support other living creatures. And wouldn't it be weird for someone to challenge you with a sign reading 'All Animals and Humans and Plants Need Love'? You support Black Lives Matter because you believe all lives should matter, but too many Black people are getting a raw deal.

CHAPTER 9

Bananas in Public

▬▬▬▬▬▬▬▬

Why did they throw a banana peel at him? What does that even mean?

Jed, age nine

My boys had reached the ripe old ages of 9 and 12 before they learned an ugly fact about the humble banana.

Jed was to bananas what Cookie Monster was to cookies. Sometimes I'd find him in the kitchen, a banana in each hand. He'd clamber up for story time, cuddling against me with his banana breath. Over the years, he's fallen in and out of love with most of the fruit basket, but bananas are still *bae*.

So it was with a heavy heart that I had to break it to the boys that bananas had become a weapon against Black people.

I had shared a powerful photo of Arsenal's top striker Pierre Aubameyang, standing tall and proud after he'd scored a goal. By his feet lay a banana skin, tossed at him by a hater in the crowd.

'Why did they throw it?'

I inhaled.

'They're trying to say we're monkeys.'

I explained how the lie that Black people were apes had been spread since slavery, as a way of dehumanising and humiliating us. That even in 2018, idiots tried to bring us down by comparing us to chimps. Professional Black footballers had been dodging bananas and skins throughout their entire careers.

'But look how Aubameyang is standing like a king.' I showed my boys the picture again. 'It doesn't bother him one bit. I bet whoever threw that banana skin is feeling very stupid right now.'

In fact, the offender was caught and convicted. Hopefully, he had plenty of time behind bars to contemplate his stupidity. Ezra and Jed listened, expressed their annoyance, then got distracted by whatever they were watching on YouTube. But I couldn't stop thinking about Aubameyang's mother. I imagined her anger, her feeling of helplessness.

Bananas in Football

My sons have been footballers since they were in nappies. Like most young boys their age, they fantasise about playing for our local club.

For the most part, I encourage it. Seeing Jed power a shot into the top corner. Watching Ezra dribble through multiple players to slide in the winning goal. When your child is playing like nothing else matters, it can take your breath away.

For so many kids in deprived communities, football is a way out. A chance to use their natural talents to pursue a better life. However, their hopes of Premier League success are slim. And even if they make it into a football academy, the path to professional football is a chequered one.

The first Black footballers to walk onto the pitch in the '70s had bananas and harder weapons thrown at them. Some got beaten up after matches. Cyrille Regis was getting ready to make his debut for England in 1983 when a letter came through his door. It contained a bullet and a warning shot: 'If you put your foot on our Wembley turf, you'll get one of these through your knees.[1]

To this day, there is so much extra pressure on Black players. Pressure to be that dazzling baller on the pitch. Pressure to hold yourself to a higher standard than your White teammates, because you will be judged more harshly. Pressure to make it, to be the winner, to lift up the community, to provide for your entire clan and crew. Pressure to carry the team, followed by the flash of anger from fans when you don't deliver.

Star players like Mario Balotelli, Marcus Rashford and Paul Pogba have had racial abuse from their own fans for missing penalties. Chelsea player Tammy Abraham missed a penalty and someone posted Tweets calling him a 'fucking nigger' alongside a video of a Ku Klux Klan lynching. In press interviews, he admitted it had reduced his mother to tears.

And it's not only skins and chanting, it's the culture that surrounds it. In a viral Instagram post, footballer Raheem Sterling challenged the media on how their biased football coverage can stoke racism. It caused the pundits to sit up for a minute. But the bananas kept piling up.

According to Home Office stats, football-related hate crimes rose 47 per cent in England and Wales during the 2018–19 season.[2] It continued spreading across Europe, part of a rise in fascist politics. England's Euro 2020 qualifier against Bulgaria was interrupted by a group in the stands singing racist chants and giving Nazi salutes.

Asian players meanwhile are sidelined, since scouts don't tend to visit football grounds outside of the mainstream. South Asian footballers rise up through their community groups but face an impossible barrier when it comes to turning pro. Imagine being a football fan and never seeing any players who look like you or your family. To date, only three South Asian players have featured in the history of the Premier League.

As a Black mum, I have a love/hate relationship with this game. I'm happy to do soccer-mom duty. But I dread either of my sons being attacked with racist abuse. Because it's increased not only in men's clubs, but in women's and youth football too.

Ahmed Maravia, vice chair of the Black, Asian and Minority Ethnic Football Forum (BFF), collects reports of discrimination across youth community football clubs.[3] He runs a club in Leicester and records hearing monkey chants and Islamaphobic remarks at games with kids as young as seven. Some of his under-14s have left the pitch in tears. One boy got offered a banana by a parent, who said 'they should be used to it'.

When Jed's school football team got an invite to Wembley to

watch England vs Montenegro, I fretted. Would there be monkey chants or bananas flying through the air? What would teachers do to make sure my boy felt safe?

After sharing my concerns with Jed's teacher, she reassured me they would leave at the first sign of trouble. When I spoke with Jed about it, he said: 'How about I wear earmuffs, so I can't really hear any racist chants?'

I hugged him. Luckily, the match passed without incident. Jed came back buzzing as England won 7–0. All his schoolmates had been calling him Jadon Sancho, because of his new haircut. Jed couldn't hide his pleasure at this, especially since Sancho had scored one of England's winning goals.

Every year, the boys have new favourite players. They wear their names and numbers on their backs with pride. When someone lobs a banana at Aubameyang, I look at my boy in his Aubameyang shirt and my chest tightens.

Monkeying Around

I am eight or nine years old, standing in front of our colour TV, clapping and dancing to 'Bare Necessities'. It's after bath time and I'm wearing my long, itchy nightdress, talcum powder sprinkled everywhere and my beloved brown bear, Honey, is dancing with me. I sit to catch my breath and, before I know it, those cartoon monkeys are singing and strumming and Mowgli is bopping along to another irresistible tune. I'm up and grooving again.

Of all the films I couldn't wait to watch again with my own children, *The Jungle Book* was near the top of my list. The babes were pretty young when we saw it playing at a family festival. They were singing and dancing too. However, I watched it with new eyes.

King Louie the orangutan and his band of be-bopping monkeys. 'I Wanna Be Like You' is one of Disney's catchiest songs. I can't help but click my fingers and hum along. But what am I humming? The underlying theme played over and over in music halls and movies of the day: those negroes aren't much better than monkeys, but they sure can swing.

Apparently old Satchmo, legendary jazz trumpeter Louis Armstrong, was considered to voice King Louie but the Disney team worried people would accuse them of racism. Instead, they cast Louis Prima, a White jazz musician. A White guy known for playing traditional Black music in cartoon Blackface, pretending to be an ape. You couldn't make this shit up.

Maybe it's no surprise that *The Jungle Book* is based on the stories of Rudyard Kipling, someone George Orwell described as a 'Prophet of Imperialism'. Kipling's writing is not so much seasoned with colonialist sentiment as fully marinated in it. When Jon Favreau made his version of *The Jungle Book* in 2016, he changed King Louie from minstrel-show orangutan to a gigantopithecus voiced as a mob figure by Christopher Walken.[4]

Flip through Disney's back catalogue, and you'll find racist elements in *Dumbo*, *The Lion King*, *Aladdin*, *Lady and the Tramp*, *Peter Pan* . . . And it's no secret that Disney films are also riddled with sexist stereotypes. In the latest Disney movies, they've introduced more kick-ass heroines instead of impossibly tiny-waisted princesses awaiting salvation from brick-jawed heroes. It's taken a while longer to include more Black and Brown faces.

In 2019, Disney announced a Black actress – Halle Bailey – would play Ariel in a live action version of *The Little Mermaid*. Thousands of fans flipped their tiny minds. Their argument? Ariel was a redhead, Hans Christian Andersen was Danish and mermaids were 'European'. Let's get past the fact that the mermaid pops up in many cultures, including West Africa where we call her Mami Water. Or that Hans Christian Andersen didn't invent the Little Mermaid legend; he merely rewrote it in his own image (some say it was a coded story about his forbidden homosexual feelings for a Danish prince). The really crazy thing is that Disney's original Ariel was a cartoon based on a mythical creature. So why all the fuss about the character's authenticity?

When I saw pictures of Halle Bailey, it struck me that with her big almond eyes and button nose she looks more like a Disney heroine than about 99 per cent of people you meet on the street. Still, the outrage continued with protest groups on Facebook and a trending hashtag #NotMyAriel. However, others spoke out in favour of the casting. In a tweet with more than half a million shares, White author Hillary Monahan pointed out: 'White people complaining they cast a black girl as Ariel: Disney created 49 films from 1937 to 2009 before delivering their first black princess with Tiana. Black girls watched an entire catalog NEVER seeing themselves. For 70 years. You spoiled, racist brats.'[5]

I especially liked Hannah Palframan's Tweet in response to complaints by redheads that their icon was being erased. 'When I was younger, I loved *The Little Mermaid* because Ariel had hair like mine. That was important to me, people were mean. And now, a different group of kids are getting a Little Mermaid that looks like them. Representation is really important to kids.'[6]

More Public Bananas

Representation matters. Before the film *Black Panther* came out, Jed had already declared it his 'favourite movie ever'. The film was released on his birthday and we took him and two of his friends, both White, to watch it on the big screen. Like millions of Black families around the globe, we fell hard for Marvel's African Utopia starring a mostly Black cast. They were cool, they were sexy, they were badass. They had never been enslaved or colonised. After the film, Jed's blond mate Atti kept pulling out his lip to show off his 'Wakanda tattoo'. Another sign of how great storytelling puts you in someone else's skin.

Like other kids his age, Jed was born into a world where the most important man on the planet was a Black man. So many children walked taller and reached higher because of US president 44.

When Barack Obama was running for office, a bar owner printed T-shirts featuring Barack as the monkey Curious George. There was some national debate around these T-shirts, over whether it was racism or a harmless joke. After all, George

Bush had been compared to Curious George too. Wasn't this just liberals getting their panties in a bunch? While the Obamas were in office, Michelle Obama was called 'monkey face' by a prominent Colorado doctor. An 'ape in heels' by a West Virginia county employee. A 'poor gorilla' by a teacher's aide. A caricature of Michelle as a monkey topped Google images, despite efforts to remove it.

In 2016, a Belgian newspaper published a 'satirical' image of the Obamas morphed with monkey faces.[7] Nigerian-born author Chika Unigwe tweeted an image of the spread, noting it was symptomatic of a race problem in Belgium where Black people were unseen and unheard. The editor of *De Morgen* apologised for the slip-up, claiming: 'We wrongly assumed that racism is no longer accepted, and that in this way it could be the subject of a joke.'

Isn't it hilarious?

See No Evil, Hear No Evil, Speak No Evil

When H&M put a Black boy in a shirt proclaiming him to be 'The Coolest Monkey in the Jungle', the public outcry was instant. H&M said they never intended to cause offence. The boy's mother thought it was an innocent mistake. But I have questions: what message were H&M trying to send and to whom? Were they really so 'colour blind' to believe nobody would make that link? More importantly, who was in the room when it happened?

When a story like this hits, talk about it with your children, your peers, your community. This is important for Black or Brown families who might feel directly affected. It's equally important if you're White. You need to engage with as much passion as if that was your kid in a national campaign, the object of ridicule and ignorance.

We can't keep covering our eyes, ears and mouths to racism. Because even our babies aren't safe.

More than 10,500 racial hate crimes in the UK recorded by police between 2017 and 2018 included attacks against babies and toddlers.[8] In May 2019, *Guardian* columnist Lola Okolosie wrote of her sister's experience in Bradford when a stranger shouted 'fucking dirty wog' not at her, but at her nine-month-old baby.[9]

Days after royal baby Archie was born in 2019, funny man Danny Baker tweeted an image of a royal couple emerging from hospital with a chimpanzee. It hit me like a punch to the gut. I'd anticipated something like this after I saw that gorgeous photo of the Queen posing with her grandson, Harry, Meghan and her Black mother, Doria. The picture of a modern multi-cultural family. I knew it was only a matter of time. Somebody would have to ruin the moment.

I argued with a close friend over the Danny Baker incident. She was adamant it was a faux pas, not a racist statement. She said he was known for telling monkey jokes. What I tried to get across was that even if it wasn't deliberate, it was a show of implicit racism. After all, he hadn't compared any other royal offspring to chimpanzees. The fact he would put out that image without thinking twice, without considering the impact, was racist in itself. The fact he could tell monkey jokes on the regular was a sign of systemic racism. Can you picture a Black comic making a career out of monkey jokes?

You are so vulnerable after you give birth and all you care about is protecting your newborn. I felt deeply hurt for Meghan and her little boy, so quickly served up for racist appetites.

Maybe I bruise too easily. I should take a leaf out of Josephine Baker's book.[10] The African-American icon was born in 1906 in the slums of St Louis, Missouri. At just eight years old, she worked as a maid for a White mistress. Reportedly, one employer burned her hands for putting too much soap in the laundry. By age 11, she had witnessed a race riot. By 15, she was already on her second marriage. Yet she turned her life around, playing on her wit, her sexuality, and a big bunch of bananas.

Josephine moved to Paris and reinvented herself as a stage icon with the infamous 'jungle banana' skirt dance. It sold thousands of Josephine dolls across Europe and she became one of the highest paid artists of her time.

But she wasn't just shaking it up at the Folies Bergère. During World War 2, Josephine also worked for the French Resistance as a spy, hiding Jewish refugees and weapons in her castle. She was a sub-lieutenant in the Women's Auxiliary of the French Air Force and a lifelong campaigner against racism. During the March on Washington in 1963, she spoke alongside Martin Luther King. She adopted a 'rainbow tribe' of 12 children from around the world to reflect her beliefs that the human race is one big family.

And she wasn't wrong. Every living thing is connected by our billion-year-old relationship to a single-celled ancestor. Scientists say we share 96 per cent of DNA with the chimpanzee. We share more than 60 per cent of our genes with bananas too. Like it or not, we are all related. We are part-monkey and we are a bit bananas. It's all relative and yes, a bit ridiculous.

So maybe we should all be a little more Baker (Josephine, not Danny). Encourage our kids to be more Baker too. Be daring and creative and funny as heck. Keep going, no matter what life throws at you. The late yogi Ram Dass once said: 'You can do it like it's a great weight on you or you can do it like it's part of the dance'.

Life can be ugly and heavy but if we wear it lightly sometimes, we inspire our children to wear it lightly too. Tbe future belongs to the one who knows it's all a dance. The kid who understands the banana in your hand is pointing at you.

• Talking Points

Q. My daughter is mixed heritage and she was so happy when Meghan Markle married her prince. But all the negative attention in the press and social media since then has really affected her own self-confidence. What can I say or do to give her a boost?
A. The press has been beastly to Meghan and (by association) Harry and I think they sent a powerful message that they refused to take it lying down. This is a great lesson to pass on

to your daughter: that no matter how strong or influential you might become, there are often those who look to tear you down. However, you can also stand your ground and fight your corner with grace. You can hold your head high and know that, despite the haters, there are so many more people who have your back. Show her the amount of support Meghan and Harry also receive and that it's never just one story. Also, it's a useful lesson that marrying a prince doesn't guarantee a fairytale ending. There are many other role models she can look to for a confidence boost. Help her find other strong women of mixed heritage that might inspire her, whether family members or public figures (not necessarily entertainers). Another idea, depending on her age, is to do what you can to limit her access to news and even social media, since both can be a minefield of negativity and bigotry.

Q. My son plays in a local squad and at one game, the other team's coach made a racist comment in front of him (I didn't hear it). I complained immediately and the coach has been sanctioned, but I'm worried about letting my boy play other matches, especially when I'm not there. Football is his passion, but I hate what the game has become.

A. Football can get ugly, especially as feelings run high and people lose all sense of perspective. However, racist language is unacceptable under any circumstances. If you are worried about the atmosphere at the club where your son plays, you can make further complaints and try to get support from fellow parents to ensure nothing like that happens again. You can think about switching him to a different club if things get out of hand. However, I wouldn't restrict him from playing altogether as that feels like punishing your son for somebody else's problems. Unfortunately, most footballers will grow up to experience a certain amount of verbal and even physical violence. The important thing is to try to be present for your son when you can, and teach him to avoid trouble or getting involved in any kind of altercations. Remind him the majority of his time on the pitch will be focused on doing what he loves rather than responding to haters. Ultimately, he wins by being the best player he can be and continuing to show up even when bigots try to keep him away.

Q. I took my daughter and her friend, who is Black, to a match where there was racist chanting. I took them both out immediately, but felt powerless otherwise. How can we talk to our kids about racism without making them feel powerless too?

A. You did the right thing by taking the kids away once the atmosphere turned nasty. And when you talk about racism with kids, it can feel overwhelming. However, you can empower them to see themselves as part of the fight against racism, whether that's through educating themselves or advocating for themselves, their friends or family. Unfortunately, we cannot protect our children from evil, but we can help them to identify it and give them the tools to choose a different path.

Remember, your words and behaviour set an example to your child. So when faced with a difficult choice (e.g. watching your favourite team play or walking out), make sure you choose the path you want them to follow.

CHAPTER 10

Please, Don't Touch My Hair

I think judges should wear Afro wigs. They'd look funky.

Ezra, age eight

'Your daughter is so pretty.'

I held back a smile, as four-year-old Ezra glared up at the lady peering down at him.

'I'm a boy!'

'Oh, really? But you're such a beautiful boy. And just look at that hair.'

Without warning, the woman plunged her hands into his thick tangle of curls. Ezra snapped backwards, practically growling. A frown cut his forehead like a middle parting.

'He doesn't like people touching his hair.'

'I'm sorry,' the woman said, not looking remotely apologetic. 'I couldn't resist. What amazing hair.'

I've come across children of all complexions with adorable hair: golden dreadlocks, strawberry-blond ringlets, big, soft

Afros, bouncy auburn curls, purple mohawks, sculpted 'frohawks, jet-black glossy hair that was almost bum-length. Never would I reach out and snatch some child's hair in passing. A child I don't even know? Why would anyone think this is ok?

Recently, an Instagram clip showing a White lady fondling a woman's Afro in a salon and talking about how 'strange' it was sent some of my Black friends into a frenzy.

'No, she did NOT!'

'Aww, HELL no. Nope.'

'You will definitely not be touching my hair.'

My niece Mayowa had a more pragmatic response. 'You just have to do it back until they get uncomfortable.'

Both my boys were born with jet-black straight hair that added to queries about their heritage. Japanese? Chinese? Maori? Ezra lost his fine baby hair, turning shiny bald and then growing soft little curls that became thicker and twistier as he got older. Washing his hair became a daily fight. He's tender-headed and the mere sight of a wide-toothed comb would send him into a tailspin. Some evenings I would dedicate more than an hour to applying sulfate-free shampoo, deep conditioner, oiling and detangling. While Ezra screamed blue murder.

Owing to their Scottish New Zealander ancestry (from their nana, Helen), my children's Afros have a slightly looser curl pattern. Jed's is a little wavier. Ezra's folds into itself naturally, strong and stubborn, like his personality. Strangers used to ask me how I got his hair to twist and lock like that.

'I just let it do its thing,' I'd admit, with a shrug. Outside of our washing battles, I pretty much left it alone. I wanted my

169

kids to embrace the hair they were born with. But it was a source of consternation for my mum, who couldn't work out why I let her grandsons go around like 'dada' (a Nigerian term for the madman walking half-naked in the street, muttering to himself and scratching his matted hair). On rare occasions, when Ezra let me comb his twists out into a springy, Brothers-Johnson-style Afro, my mum would nod with relief.

'Eh-hen. See how handsome he looks now. Very respectable.'

A Black Hair Story

Black hair and respectability have a long and knotty history. For centuries, we have been judged by our hair and judged ourselves more harshly. In certain circles, you can't step out with a strand out of place. Your 'edges' (hairline) and your 'kitchen' (back of your head) have to be on point. Unkempt Afro hair can provoke feelings of deep shame and self-loathing going back to the days of slavery.

Africans held as slaves were often left dishevelled, as part of the propaganda to depict them as subhuman. Images were distributed of enslaved people either naked or with torn, grubby clothing and hair like scraps of burned wool. Slave owners kept their dogs and horses better groomed. Sometimes slave mistresses would shave their female slaves bald to ensure their husbands didn't find them attractive. Not that it stopped Master sneaking into the slave quarters at night or assaulting slave girls by the cold light of day.

No matter your complexion, one feature that screams 'I have African heritage' is your hair. Therefore, it was one of the easiest ways to debase Black people. Anybody with tight, curly hair growing up in a Eurocentric society has been taught to despise this particular feature. Curly or (gasp) frizzy hair is seen as unruly, untamed, unmanageable. We've been sold on the model of long, silky, preferably blond hair. The Farrah Fawcett. The Jennifer Aniston. Remember that *Friends* episode when Monica gets cornrows on holiday? Then she removes them and her hair takes on a life of its own. It's hilarious watching Monica's hair expand in the humidity. But the racial undertones aren't quite so funny for any of us who have been ridiculed for having 'puffy' hair.

Author, podcaster and relationships expert Natalie Lue is of Jamaican Chinese heritage and grew up in Dublin. She's married to a Sierra Leonean and has two daughters. She remembers feeling like the odd one out as a young girl at her all-White private convent school. Until she got braids in her hair that helped her fit in more. With her own kids, she's done her best to give them more confidence:

From the outset, we encouraged them to know and love their hair, to play with, read and watch things where they could see themselves. That doesn't mean that they haven't both wanted at times to have 'princess hair' or 'to have hair like the other girls so that people stop touching it or telling me that it feels weird'.

At one point, the comments and 'othering' turned into outright bullying:

This girl and another sat behind my daughter and they dissected her hair loudly, as my daughter smarted with humiliation. 'Why do they have hair like that? It's gross . . . Do you think it's dirty? . . . Look at it. It's so weird . . .' and on and on. She was distraught, wouldn't eat, didn't want to go to school. Terrified that if I spoke to the teacher, the girl would beat her up. Of course, I had to speak to the teacher, and they dealt with the bullying swiftly. But my daughter insisted on having her hair braided a few days later and wouldn't wear it out at school for the remainder of Year Seven.

Former journalist Rachel remembers her own struggles for hair acceptance when she moved from Nigeria to the UK at age 12. She was determined her daughters would grow up feeling positive about their hair and praises it daily:

I'm really proud of them. They can wash, plait and style their own hair from an early age. I tell them our hair was born to stand up, our hair was born to shrink. Embrace the shrink, it's beautiful, it's lovely. There's nothing wrong with how you look, what your hair does. You're gorgeous.

Tangled

It can take years to untangle hair-esteem issues. How does a child grow up feeling comfortable in her skin when the hair that grows out of her head is seen as unworthy?

Lekia Lee is founder of Project Embrace's #Afrovisibility, an award-winning billboard campaign promoting positive images of Afro hair and beauty. She says:

For Black girls, #Afrovisibility means validation. It means self-worth. For the rest of humanity, it means they can enjoy the full potential of Black and Brown girls. They will be able to see them for who they are and not through limiting stereotypical lenses. When anyone is given a chance to be who they can be, everyone benefits. Also, it is good for White girls and boys to see others as equal. Seeing yourself as superior brings with it a kind of pressure that can be quite damaging to one's mental health.

For decades, we have soaked up negative messages through social conditioning, media and music videos, and Black people can be our own worst critics. Comedian Chris Rock made the powerful documentary *Good Hair* in response to his daughter asking him, 'Daddy, why don't I have good hair?' 'Good hair' is a common term used mainly by Black people across the African diaspora. 'Good' meaning anything but Afro.

I had a friend at secondary school called Anahita who told me how, when she was little, she would cry about not having a 'fro. She wanted Afro hair that she could wear in two bunches on her head. I would stare at Anahita's long, tousled locks – the stuff of dreams – and think she was batshit crazy.

Even before I came to the West, I fantasised about hair that I could flick over my shoulders. I would wear tights on my head and swing it to effect, making myself dizzy. My sister and cousins and I would put on our 'hair' and strut out to the tunes of Diana Ross, Donna Summer and Chaka Khan. We were Hot Stuff. We were Every Woman.

Back in the day, the only way a Black woman could become 'beautiful' was to deny her Afro. According to Victoria Sherrow's *Encyclopedia of Hair: A Cultural History*, enslaved women found ingenious ways to fix their hair, such as curling it with butter knives or using a mixture of potatoes, lye and egg that often caused severe scalp burns.[1] It was worth it though to look more acceptable and earn more privileges in society. Lighter skin? Check. Longer, straighter hair? Check check.

After emancipation from slavery, certain elite Black churches would hang a comb outside their door. If your hair snagged in the comb, you weren't allowed inside to worship. This might sound like an urban legend, but a similar method of segregation happened during the apartheid era in South Africa: the pencil test involved sliding a pencil through your hair, especially if your racial origin was uncertain. If the pencil fell to the floor, you could pass as White. If the pencil stuck, tough luck. You were classified 'Coloured' or (if the pencil didn't move at all, no matter how you shook your head) 'Black'. The bottom rung of society.

It's telling that America's first self-made millionairess was Madam C. J. Walker, who made her fortune from hair-straightening creams. Her hair relaxers were so in demand that she helped spawn a billion-dollar global industry. Relaxers have been linked with a number of severe health problems, from fibroids to endometriosis, recurring miscarriages and cancer. Yet huge companies are still dealing in them.

As a child, I used to wonder at the term 'relaxer' as I never found processing hair in any way relaxing. Perched in a hard-backed salon chair, bracing myself for the assault of chemical smells, the cold relaxer cream, and the sensation of ears and scalp on fire. The risk of scalp burns didn't bother me.

The first time I had my hair relaxed, I was one of the happiest little girls alive. The joy of swishing my hair, feeling it blowing in the wind. It was the closest I could get to the visions of beauty on magazines and TV screens. No wonder I chased that high again and again, for another 25 years. If my hair wasn't relaxed, it was in braids, again giving me the illusion of hair that drops rather than springs up.

Braiding your hair as a child was almost as stressful as relaxing it. I have memories of sitting clamped between the burly knees of a market woman in my dad's hometown, Onitsha, as her fingers wove someone else's hair into my own. Flies buzzing, the smell of her lunch hovering, my scalp stinging as she sectioned my hair with a fine-toothed comb. Any time I would move or squint or whimper, she would clamp me tighter and instruct me to be still. Be silent. Don't interrupt the work or we would be there all day.

Beauty is pain, they say, and your hair is your crown. As a young Black girl, keeping your crown beautiful could feel like a form of torture. Taking your braids out was another laborious task. I would carry my braided look to boarding school and leave it in well past its due date. The embarrassment of sitting in class and spotting one of your tiny braids come loose. Schoolmates running after me holding the evidence.

'Your hair fell out!' they'd shout, half-amused, half-horrified.

If my hair was relaxed, I'd do anything to avoid being out in the rain. Water was like kryptonite to straightening creams, turning a sleek mane back to a headful of frizz. Swimming was a no-no. We were imprisoned by our hair, but we felt free. At least a little more acceptable in mainstream society.

I have a photo of my late mother in 1961, on the deck of a ship from France to New York. She was one of only four Nigerian women to win an Aspau academic scholarship to pursue her first degree. My mother attended Mills College, a women-only college in San Francisco, where she continued to excel academically. This journey would change her life, as it would eventually lead her to UCLA where she met my dad, a young doctoral student. It would eventually lead to me.

I love seeing her in this picture, standing proud among the Africans and European men, a far-off look in her eyes. She is wearing what looks like a short, straight wig. As one of the few Africans in her college, my mum told us, one of the banes of her daily life was keeping her hair 'did'. How the Black women would hide out in their dorm rooms, searing their scalps and ears and foreheads as they worked out kinks with burning hot combs. Every single night. Otherwise, they'd invest in wigs that showed off the latest styles like bobs, bangs and beehives. Even when the Afro came into power in the mid-'60s, most of them had traumatised their natural hair so much, they had to resort to Afro wigs.

Nowadays, the natural Afro hair movement is in full bloom. I love the creativity and versatility of Afro styles. The fact that more young Black kids can grow up fully embracing their God-given curls.

Throughout history, the only other 'tribe' of people that have faced wide-scale hair prejudice are people with red hair. Strangely, this is mainly in the UK; typically, redheads are revered in the US, Latin America and Scandinavian countries. National Redhead Day (also known as Love Your Red Hair Day) is a worldwide festival for people who've been described as having 'fiery' locks.

In a similar vein, World Afro Day is a global celebration of Black hair. Founder Michelle De Leon launched it on the day the State of Alabama passed a law allowing companies to deny jobs to people with dreadlocks. She writes: 'I was incensed, the rage boiled up inside of me. How could a law be passed against Afro hair in the 21st century? The race was on, I wanted to put World Afro Day on 15 September 2017 to mark this dreadful law.'

World Afro Day hold the Big Hair Assembly every year to promote positive messages around Afro hair, and the event in 2019 was livestreamed to 7,000 schoolkids around the globe. They also provide school and media training, an awards show and a Hair Equality Report.[2] The report addresses the hair discrimination, particularly against Black children, that has been going on unrecognised for decades.

In BBC coverage of World Afro Day 2019, there's a lovely interview between pop star Jamelia and her daughter.[3] The singer talks about why she chose to let go of her long, straight weaves and show off her natural 'fro. She wanted to be a better example for her little girl. For her daughter, it was a revelation because she'd assumed her mother's hair was straight, and suddenly she realised 'oh my gosh, we have the same hair! And I felt like, that means my hair is nice as well.'

The look of pride on her sweet little face is everything.

Who Owns Our Hair?

Black women still spend thousands every month buying hair from Asia and the Middle East to use in wigs and attachments. Afro hair is a trillion-dollar industry, mostly controlled by men, very few of them of African descent.

And while many Black customers carry on buying into a Eurocentric hair ideal, there's a wave of Westerners and Asians adopting traditionally Afro looks. We all remember the Bo Derek cornrows (à la Monica in Barbados – see p. 171). Recently, I've seen videos of Asian men transforming their straight hair into Afro twists and fades. The response from Black people ranges from amusement to encouragement to feeling personally affronted. 'Cultural appropriation' is a phrase often lobbed at anybody who dares to step outside ethnic or cultural lines. Personally, I'm not bothered by a Chinese dude who wants to try out a fade or a 'fro. I think it's pretty cool. What does grate is seeing celebrities praised as 'edgy' for wearing box braids or cornrows. With no authentic context or accountability, they are merely coasting off another culture. A culture that's otherwise deemed inferior.

While Kendall Jenner sashays down a catwalk, swinging her braids freely, a Black woman wearing the same protective style to work is being told to remove it and adopt something more 'corporate' instead. Black boys with dreadlocks have had them snipped off at school, at work, at sports events, by people who decry them as unacceptable. Many schools in the UK discriminate against African hairstyles, whether it's overt or coded in school uniform policies. According to the Good Hair Study by the Perception Institute in 2017, 'a majority of people, regardless of race and gender, hold some bias towards women of colour based on their hair'.[4]

I'm not against borrowing from or paying homage to foreign traditions. We all do it in one way or another. But it can be a slippery line between appreciation and appropriation. If in doubt, leave it out. You might not fully understand how deep something goes until you bother to learn the history.

When I first heard about Native American resistance to having a baseball team named the Washington Redskins, I assumed it was because the word 'redskin' is belittling to Indian heritage. Digging a little further, I discovered that 'redskin' was a term used by White aggressors during the genocide against indigenous Americans. They would take scalps as symbols to show off the 'redskins' they had managed to slaughter.[5]

Native American kids were packed off into boarding schools and had their hair routinely cut, as part of their forced assimilation into White American society. Hair is a prized feature, with spiritual as well as cultural significance for their communities, and it was like losing a part of their essence.

So think twice before you or your children put on somebody else's culture as a joke, a costume or a fashion statement. Do your best to learn where it comes from and what it means. For instance, African braided or woven hairstyles today date back to ancient civilisations. Your hairstyle would signify your clan, your social status, even your occupation. Hairstyles were as distinguishing as tribal marks. Even today in some African societies, how you wear your hair tells what village you come from.

Your hair can even be your way home. During slavery, some people fleeing capture devised an ingenious way of sharing escape routes. They wove them into each other's hair. An underground railroad transcribed via cornrows and flat braids. Passing on messages, sharing identity, telling stories through our hair is something that connects us historically, from Africa throughout the diaspora. So the idea of a Kardashian supposedly making these looks 'hip' leaves my scalp tingly with irritation.

Let Kids Be Kids

Sometimes though, we take hair far too seriously. It's just dead weight, after all. For me, one of the most empowering moments came ten years ago when I shaved the damn thing off.

A 2019 H&M advert featured young girls who looked like they'd just left school and slipped into their everyday clothes. All the girls had hair that was slightly messy, not properly tied back or combed, in keeping with the campaign styling. One of them was Black with natural hair and she was singled out, with critics going into convulsions on social media over the way she looked. She was a 'hot mess', they said, and 'somebody should have taken a comb to that poor child'. Yet all the other girls were allowed to be their playful selves, so why couldn't she?

Sadly, the majority of people wigging out were Black women. The same women who've been held captive for years to a silent war against our bodies and our hair. Supposedly the criticism was dished out in the spirit of love. The same way you'd tell a sister if her lipstick was bleeding or her skirt was tucked into her underpants. However, it was directed at a little girl.

When I heard about this latest 'controversy', my first response was to roll my eyes emoji style. Then I felt a wave of sadness for the child. She must have been so proud to get that gig. To see herself starring in a national campaign. Only to have her image debated to shreds by cultural gatekeepers.

I felt sad for little Zahara Jolie too, when the same thing happened to her. All the Black women who slammed Angelina Jolie for not taking proper care of her daughter's Afro hair might have had a point. But in their need to look out for the sisterhood, they forgot to look out for Zahara. A young girl still discovering herself in a multicultural family, in a mixed-up world.

Please don't touch our children's hair. Just let it be. Celebrate every tone and texture, every crimp and curl and wave. If your child is happy to sit still for combs and brushes and braids and bunches and slides, more power to you. But if they prefer to keep locks free and less defined, let them wear it with pride. Let's not keep dumping all our hang-ups on their little heads. Do look after their hair, teach them how to treat it with tender loving care. But look after the child first.

As parents, we should encourage our children to show respect and appreciation for the way different cultures wear their hair. If your child is curious about hair that seems 'strange', you can flip it so they imagine themselves in another country, where they are the odd one out. How would they want people to treat them? What comments about their own hair would make them happy, and what might make them feel bad? Ask your child if they can come up with three kind, positive and empowering words to describe their own hair and someone else's. See if they can switch out terms like 'greasy' or 'bushy' for happier words like 'smooth' or 'free'. Remind them that every day they have the choice to dim somebody's light or to help somebody shine. Sometimes all it takes is a kind word . . . or three.

Rites of Passage

When Ezra turned 13, his father took him to the barbershop as a rite of passage. I'd been trimming the boys' hair since their second year of primary school, but this was Ezra's first official haircut. He opted for a clean, super sleek, low-top fade.

I sat at home with butterflies in my belly, wondering what version of my child would walk back into the house. As Ezra strolled in, grinning from ear to ear, my eyes welled up. He looked so grown, a young man now, undeniably. He was absolutely beautiful, his features sharper than I'd ever seen them. I went to hug him and my hands reached for his head, but he ducked away.

'Don't touch the fade, Mum,' he warned, laughing.

Nowadays, whenever I feel his hair, it's by invitation only. Even as his mother, I can't overstep his boundaries. His journey from boy to man is also a journey of self-ownership.

Jed's hair is still frisky and free. However, I've noticed as he's gotten older that strangers are less likely to grab it, more willing to appreciate from afar. His hair is his power, his self-expression, his crazy, his fun, his spirit animal. His hair is Black boy joy. Please don't touch it.

• Talking Points

Q. I've seen my child put their hands in their Black friend's hair before and reading about it here, I feel embarrassed. What should I tell my child?
A. You could talk to your child about boundaries and consent (two very essential discussions for parents) and how it's not ok to put your hands on anybody without their invitation or their permission. Tell them that even if they are only touching their friend's hair because they like it, it's better to share their appreciation verbally. Otherwise, it's by invitation

only, or else they are invading someone's personal space. Remind them that it's ok to be curious about how other people look, but it's more important to act with kindness and consideration first.

Q. A little Asian girl I know asked me why African women use Asian hair to make their own hair longer. It was pretty awkward. How do I handle such a discussion?

A. Well, it's a very good question and one that doesn't necessarily require a long answer. I would say that many people from all different cultures have sold or donated their hair for a variety of purposes throughout history. Sometimes it's to make wigs or extensions for people who have lost their hair due to illness, other times it's for cosmetic reasons. You could say that for a long time, African women were told that their own hair wasn't beautiful, so they borrowed hair that was straight rather than curly. However, nowadays many African women prefer to wear natural hair (you can give examples like actress Danai Gurira and singer Solange Knowles), while some still like to change their hair a lot and use other types of hair to get different looks. Many Black women wear their hair in styles like braids, extensions and wigs, to protect against the harsh European climate that doesn't suit our natural curls.

Aim to keep the conversation positive and empowering; you can state that it's a great thing for women to be free to wear their hair (or cover it up) however they please.

Q. I'm a White mum and I struggle with how to look after my child's hair properly (she's mixed). What advice can you give me?

A.If in doubt, head to YouTube where you will find hundreds of hair video tutorials for every texture of Black and mixed hair. Also do reach out to any Black mums you know. Are there women in your daughter's extended family who can help out or offer tips? It's worth visiting a Black hair salon not just for the professional touch, but also for the experience and insight into your daughter's Black heritage. If you feel hesitant, do remember that on a regular basis most people of colour, including your daughter, have to navigate spaces that weren't built for them. You have to be bold enough to take extra steps towards your daughter's and your Black family's culture too.

CHAPTER 11

What's in a Name?

A name pronounced is the recognition of the individual to whom it
belongs. He who can pronounce my name aright, he can call me, and is
entitled to my love and service.

Henry David Thoreau, American
essayist, poet and philosopher

Obianuju, O-bee-an-oo-joo. It's a melodic name, if I do say
so myself. A name with a powerful, some might say mystical
meaning.

I was born in 1974, four years after the civil war that nearly tore
Nigeria apart. During the struggle to create a separate state of
Biafra, more than a million men, women and children died, mostly
from starvation. For some time after the war, the Igbo people struggled to pick up the pieces and pull their lives back together. My
father, a young lecturer in political science at the University of
Ibadan, had been called to office when the war started. At just 31,
he was appointed Administrator of Eastern Region, the area that
had remained under federal control when Biafra broke away.

My dad accepted what was described as an 'insane' challenge. He firmly believed in one Nigeria, a stance that came

close to splitting up his marriage, driving family away, making him an outlier among his own people. He was seen as a traitor, a saboteur, a puppet of the Nigerian government. It would take decades to turn this image around in certain circles. After the war, he introduced a number of groundbreaking policies to rebuild, restore and revalue Igbo lives and livelihoods.

Through it all, he remained an idealist, and a believer in our national identity. My dad referred to the Nigeria–Biafra conflict as 'our family war'. He named his first child Obodoechina, meaning 'my country will not die'. He named my sister Nkiruka, meaning 'the future is better than the past'. Four years later, he named me. Obianuju. It means 'born in a time of abundance'. Our names are more than markers, they are stories of survival, hope and regeneration.

Uju Think You Are, Then?

I go by the name Uju, a popular shortening of Obianuju. You, jay, you. Three letters, two syllables. Yet somehow, for the average Westerner, it's a mouthful.

'You ji? Ooh-jee? You jay?'

It doesn't matter how you try to butter it up. Whether you serve your name with honey on the side. If it's 'weird' enough, somebody's tongue will smack the taste out of it. The worst is in emails, when the sender finds multiple ways of misspelling my name, despite seeing it clearly written in my signature. I've found myself in passive-agressive sparring matches where

I deliberately misspell the sender's name until they get the point.

But sometimes I have to shout it out in all caps.

'By the way, my actual name is UJU.' Not Uji. Not Uzi. Not Uzu, or whatever you feel like calling me today.

'Ah, so sorry about that. Uju? What a beautiful name.'

My siblings and I still chuckle over a story my dad told us about having to repeat his surname over the phone so many times he lost his patience. So he spelled it out.

'A for Asinine, S for Stupid, I for Idiot, K for Kangaroo, A for Asshole'.

There was a long pause on the other end.

'Oh. ASIKA? Gotcha.'

After I wrote about the impressive meaning of Uju on my blog, a friend of mine said she would only call me 'Abundance' from now on. I joked that Abundance actually sounds like the kind of name Nigerians drop on their hapless kids. Then they'll be yelling it through the house like: 'Abundance! Come and pick up your socks *ojare!*'

I wasn't always so fond of my deep, powerful name. There were times I flirted with shortening Uju to something snappier like . . . I don't know . . . Henrietta. When I was little, I wanted a name that sounded normal. A name you might find on a keyring or mug. But most don't even bother with the letter U.

I envied Nigerians with names that already sounded English. Ada. Lola. Even my sister Nkiru got to be called 'Nicky' by some of her besties. Uju marked me out as 'different' from the start. Names are like accents, in that when yours sounds 'strange', then strangers make assumptions about you. At best, they find you exotic. 'Ooh-jooo, where's that from? So pretty. I wish my name wasn't so boring.' More often, they stamp you as FOREIGNER. And with that come other, less visible labels: invader. Inferior. Ignorant.

Roll Call

Raise a hand if you've ever sat sticky-palmed in a classroom as the register was read out? I see you. You're steeling yourself for that pause. The inevitable swivel of heads as the teacher clears her throat and hacks your identity to pieces.

The name shaming of kids that happens in education, often by adults who should know better, deserves its own book. Author, podcaster and relationships expert Natalie Lue shared her daughter's experience at primary school. 'My eldest was called another Black girl's name by her teacher for an entire term. Also, her surname was misspelled as "Sambo" and it took a week and three separate complaints for it to be corrected.'

When your name is too much like hard work, some teachers will go as far as christening you something else for convenience. Like the French teacher who decided to call me Bijou. I didn't mind so much when I found out it meant 'jewel'. I hadn't yet learned the term 'microaggression' in primary school.

Your name is something to treasure. But you can't be too precious about what people call you when you're a schoolkid. Especially as a dark-skinned kid in a pale-skinned school.

'Uju, are you a Jew?' 'Uju think you are, then?' 'Uju Nicko-Bollockoff!'

The jokes flew thick and snappy. I got off lightly, as it happens. My brother Obi has had a lifetime of 'Obi Wan Kenobi?' comebacks. Innocuous enough. But his middle name Ogbogwu (Oh-bwor-goo) got him the less appealing nickname 'Obi Wog'. Luckily, he was a legend on the sports fields. As a person of colour with a name nobody can pronounce, it helps if you can leap tall buildings in a single bound.

Even sports stardom won't stop people from bastardising your heritage. It grates listening to English football commentators butcher African, Latin American and even some European names. It wasn't until I saw the name 'Aya Nacho' spelled out that I realised he was actually an Igbo footballer named Iheanacho (Ee-heh-nah-chor) and not a corn snack. I insisted the boys learned to say his name correctly. And I insisted they taught the correct pronunciation to their friends. It's a mark of respect.

If you listen right, a name can be a thing of beauty, bursting with lyricism and potential. Names have power. They are the symbols of who we are, where we come from, and in many cases, our destiny. Your name is not just your calling card; it's your calling.

I've lost count of the number of Nigerians I've met who've chopped their names into something easier for Western contexts. I understand the impulse, but when I meet you, please tell me your original name and give me the chance to say it right. It's the least we can do if we want to meet each other fully as human beings.

One of my favourite celebrity interviews featured award-winning actress Uzo Aduba of *Orange is the New Black* explaining why she never changed her name.[1] She said her mum always told her: 'If they can learn to say Tchaikovsky and Michaelangelo and Dostoyevsky, then they can learn to say Uzoamaka.' Damn right. I also loved watching actor David Oyelowo on *The Tonight Show*, pronouncing his name with all its Yoruba intonation.[2]

I often think about how much happier I would have felt about my name while growing up, if I'd had more people who looked and sounded like me on film and telly screens.

Lost and Found

Between the 1500s and 1800s, during the transatlantic slave trade, more than 12 million Africans were captured and sold as slaves to America and the Caribbean. More than 2 million died during the journey, known as the Middle Passage. Some of those who survived were renamed after their slave masters as another way to strip them of their origins. If you had no name, other than the name that owned you, soon enough you would forget where you came from. Your languages and tribes and customs would be erased. You would lose yourself completely.

During the birth of the Civil Rights movement in the '60s, many African Americans began to reject their 'slave names'. Some adopted African or African-sounding names. Some took on names embracing a new faith or philosophy. Possibly the most famous was the boxer who, having risen to fame as Cassius Clay, converted to Islam and called himself Muhammad Ali.

Renaming and Reclaiming

Of course, changing your name to rebrand yourself was a celebrity rite of passage. Speccy youth Maurice Micklewhite became screen icon Michael Caine. Shy brunette Norma Jean Baker became Marilyn Monroe. Krishna Pandit Bhanji, born to a White mum and Kenyan dad of Indian Muslim descent, became Oscar winner Ben Kingsley.

The less 'ethnic' you sounded, the easier it was to pass for the White Anglo-Saxon Protestant ideal. I wonder how far any of this lot would have made it with their birth names: Natasha Nikolaevna Zakharenko (Natalie Wood), Issur Danielovitch Demsky (Kirk Douglas), Frederick Austerlitz (Fred Astaire), Ilyena Lydia Vasilievna Mironov (Helen Mirren), Ramón Gerardo Antonio and Carlos Estévez (Martin Sheen and his son Charlie).

In a 2019 interview, Martin Sheen's son Emilio Estevez revealed casting agents had told his dad: 'If you want to work in this business, you've gotta have a more Anglo-sounding name.'[3]

According to Emilio, the first time his grandfather came to watch his son Ramón in a Broadway show, he looked up at the marquee and saw the name 'Martin Sheen' instead of his family name. And he shook his head in disappointment.

'My father saw that,' Emilio said. 'So when I began to get into this business, we had that conversation. And he said, "Don't make the same mistake I did".'

Emilio pushed back at this because he thought he didn't look especially Latin American. But his dad said the face of Latin America was changing:

And I realise this now on a much deeper level, but it was honouring the Hispanic heritage. And I own that and the Hispanic community has embraced me because of that. And I can't tell you how many people on the street have stopped me and said, you know, just seeing your name on a poster, just seeing your name on screen, meant so much to me you have no idea.

Sometimes changing your name was about survival, as it was for many Jews fleeing persecution after World War 2. For many, it was a passport to freedom. The first wave of immigrants to America at the turn of the 20th century were quick to assimilate. According to a study, 77 per cent of immigrants between 1900 and 1930 dropped their original names for something that sounded more 'American'.[4] Even if your last name sounded foreign, just changing your first name could give you a leg up. It helped with fitting in and, crucially, with finding jobs.

According to a research paper published in the *American Sociological Review* in 2016: 'Native-born sons of Irish, Italian, German, and Polish immigrant fathers who were given very ethnic names ended up in occupations that earned, on average, $50 to $100 less per year than sons who were given very "American" names.'[5]

Your Name as a Barrier

Flash forward decades, and we haven't made much progress in the job market. Study after study from US, UK and European sectors shows job seekers face a massive hurdle if their names sound too 'ethnic' on their CVs. A joint study by Stanford University, Harvard Business School and the University of Toronto revealed only 11.5 per cent of Asian applicants got callbacks when their CVs showed foreign-looking names or references to their heritage.[6] For African Americans with names that sounded 'Black' or allusions to their background (belonging to a 'Black' association, for example), callbacks went down to 10 per cent.

A Swedish report from 2018 cited an example of three applicants with the same level of education who applied for 'similar and comparable' jobs.[7] A man with a Swedish-sounding name ('Anders') received a higher salary than both a Swedish woman ('Eva') and a man with a foreign-sounding name ('Ahmed'). In a French study based on fake CVs sent by researchers at the Paris School of Economics and Stanford University, two typically French-sounding names got 70 per cent more callbacks than four other names that sounded North African or foreign.[8]

This discrimination cuts across countries and affects everything from where you can work to where you can live. In Switzerland, researchers sent out 10,000 rental applications using Swiss and non-Swiss names.[9] The non-Swiss names were 10 per cent less likely to be offered a viewing.

When Barack Hussein Obama ran for president, it didn't take long before people (Donald Trump, mostly) started picking on his Kenyan ancestry and his 'funny-sounding' name. Some went as far as calling him Osama. It meant everything that number 44 not only clung to his identity, he rocked it. In a long line of Georges and Thomases and Teddys, Barack Hussein Obama stuck out like a black diamond.

After the names of the 9/11 terrorists were broadcast worldwide, we told my brother's friend Hamza that his days of international travel were numbered, since his name was on the World's Most Wanted List. We were joking, but the world had changed for all of us. Just getting past border control became harder for anyone with a passport suggesting Muslim, Arab or African roots. My friend Joyce had named her daughter after an Egyptian goddess. However, following a wave of terror attacks on London and other major cities, she decided to call her something else. It's a shame, as Isis is a beautiful first name.

How We Name Our Babies

Choosing a name for your child is one of the biggest decisions you make as a parent. What you name your child can, and probably will, affect them for the rest of their life. It's a ton of pressure, but lots of fun too with oodles of possibilities.

Google 'baby names' and more than 740 billion results come up. You can search up what names are popular today; what was popular the year you were born; what type of parent you are, according to how you choose to name your child. Many of us want to instil a sense of ancestry and cultural pride in our kids. But are we saddling them with years of playground abuse, social interrogation and boardroom discrimination?

Vicki Broadbent (née Psarias) has made her name as a film-maker, blogger, author and entrepreneur. She's had to deal with people othering her and mispronouncing her last name for what feels like for ever. But it was her first name that gave her parents pause, after their negative experiences as Greek Cypriot immigrants to the UK in the late '70s and '80s: 'I was called Vicki and not Vikentia after my grandmother because my parents feared I would be targeted. Two years later they defiantly called my brother Solos, somewhat regretful they had felt pressured to hide my ethnicity as their first child. I was named after their first cat!'

I'd be lying if I said we didn't try to give our sons the best of both worlds. When picking their first names, we thought about what would be easy to pronounce for Westerners as well as Nigerians. We considered possible nicknames and tested them against their father's surname (luckily, everything goes with Cole).

My stepson is called Isaac, so we wanted another strong biblical name for his brother. I'd been coming up with all sorts – Zachariah (too much like Isaac), Zebedee (too *Magic Roundabout*), Nehemiah (no flipping way, said Abiye). A few nights before our wedding, Abiye called me up. He had the perfect name for our firstborn, already curled up in my belly making his presence felt.

'Ezra,' he said.

'Ezra,' I repeated, smiling.

Our little Ezra. He would be a prophet, as well as a poet, unique among his classmates. Fourteen years on, we've met only a handful of Ezras. And none quite like ours.

For our lastborn, it was my turn to choose. Again, we went Old Testament. I liked the sound of Reuben and Ezekiel, then I came across Jedidiah. It's one of the names for King Solomon and it means 'beloved of God'. We would call him Jed for short and he would be a king among men. He would also be a Jedi, which pretty much swung it for his dad.

As tradition dictates, my mum and Abiye's dad also gave names to our kids: long, strong, Nigerian names from their respective languages. I made sure each name was listed on their birth certificates and that their passports contain at least one of their Nigerian middle names. Since their surname sounds passably English, it was important to me that their official documents revealed some Naija heritage.

Your Name as a Blessing

In Igbo culture, your name is so significant there's a special ceremony held typically seven days after your birth to mark this moment. We are not alone in this. In Yoruba culture, Jewish culture and some Asian societies, the naming ceremony pre-dates baby-name encyclopaedias and Google naming charts. At this ceremony, the members of your family offer you names as blessings. It is a baptism of sorts.

Sometimes, though, a name feels more of a curse than a blessing. If you have a family name that rhymes or aligns with something silly, or rude (in whatever language), you might get teased mercilessly.

What do you do when your child comes home from school crying because somebody made fun of his name? Or when your child asks if they can change their name to something less 'weird'? What if it's your family name that offends? How can you get a child to embrace this core part of their identity?

Start with a story. Tell them about the roots of their name, where it comes from, what it truly means. Let them know which cool people in their lives or in history or literature had that name before them. If the name is brand new, emphasise how they are a total original. Tell them about people (famous and familiar) who walked tall with names others found tricky.

Names have energy. When you hear a name, it can stay with you for ever. When you lose a name, it can haunt you for life. I miss the way my mother used to call my name, especially when she was angry with me, saying the full name with extra heavy intonation on the final U. Back when I was young, it was always an interruption, one that would make me roll my eyes or, at times, strike terror into me – what had I done this time? Nowadays, I would do anything to hear my mother calling me. Or to hear my father whistling out the syllables of Obianuju.

When Abiye and I visited the 9/11 memorial in 2015, I read as many names as I could out loud. Every name tells a story. Every name holds an entire life within it.

I remember teaching my boys the right way to say their grandfather's name, Ukpabi (Ooh-kpa-bi; the kp sound is what my dad called an 'imploded implosive'). That night, I heard Ezra and Jed calling his name all the way up to their bedroom. Ukpabi, Ukpabi, Ukpabi. Somewhere in the afterlife, I'm sure my father was smiling.

There is no such thing as an easy name. There is no such thing as a difficult name. There are only names you have taken the time to enunciate. What matters is not that you remember a name instantly or that you pronounce it perfectly. What matters is that you try. Even if your tongue trips over itself, give it another go. It's worth the effort. A name can be your first expression in another language. An invitation to communicate across cultures.

When you take the time, you can say any name correctly. So take your time. Teach your child to take their time with other people's names. Teach your child to say their own name as it's meant to be pronounced. Tell them: your name is your birthright, your destiny, your legacy. Own it. Claim yourself.

• Talking Points

Q. We're Yoruba and my son hates his name. He's always shortening it and says he's going to change it when he's older. But it's the name my late parents

gave him and that would make me really sad. How can I get him to appreciate the power and meaning of his name?

A. If your son is quite young, then I wouldn't sweat it too much. It's probably just a phase. If he's older, have a discussion about why he hates his name so much. Really listen to his experience before you wade in with your own personal feelings. Does he know that his grandparents gave him that name? You could tell him stories connected to his name – stories are often more powerful than your personal opinion. Talk to him about people he admires, famous figures who had difficult names and stuck with them. Remind him there is power in a name, especially one that sounds original or one that is rich with meaning and tradition. However, remember that what he chooses to call himself will be his right as an adult. Maybe you can persuade him to keep his Yoruba one as a middle name, but he gets the final decision.

Q. The other mums at school are still calling me and my child the wrong name, even though I've corrected them multiple times. Can our names really be so hard to say or are they doing this on purpose?

A. Whether it's intentional or a faux pas, calling somebody you know by the wrong name over and over again is a micro-aggression. You are entitled to point this out and tell them (once again) the correct spelling and try to help them with pronunciation. Make it clear that by naming you wrongly repeatedly, they are insulting your names and your heritage. If all else fails, you could go the passive-aggressive route and call each of them by the wrong name too, until they figure out what's happening!

Q. Our family is Welsh and people get our names wrong all the time. But surely it's not racist?
A. People of all backgrounds can have their names misspelled or mispronounced. However, there's a specific type of othering when you are of a different race. There's nothing wrong with someone getting the pronunciation or spelling wrong if they're unfamiliar with your name. However, if they refuse to try to say it correctly or they call you by something else entirely, that is a bigoted choice. We must teach all our kids the importance of learning and saying names they might find difficult at first. Being respectful is always worth the effort.

CHAPTER 12

Different Shades of Beauty

Mirror mirror, on the wall, who is the fairest one of all?

The Evil Queen, in *Snow White*

My brother had a mate, a fellow Nigerian growing up in Britain. His middle name was 'Black as night'. Not by birth, of course, but everybody called him that. Looking back, I sometimes ask myself if we were being cruel? He didn't seem to mind. His brother had the same skin tone and became a movie star. I do wonder though, did he ever question his looks in the quiet hours? We meant no harm by what we named him. But it wasn't exactly a compliment.

Beyond race, there's caste. Beyond caste, there's colourism. People hating on each other (and themselves) for the lightness or depth of their complexions. I've heard sometimes White people are surprised by the shades of shadeism that can exist among Blacks, Asians, Hispanics and West Indians. As far as they're concerned, we're all 'people of colour'. But for the most part, we didn't make up these rules. Colourism is one of the uglier legacies of colonialism and the slave trade.

In the US, throughout and beyond slavery, there was a distinct hierarchy between lighter-skinned African Americans and their darker brothers and sisters. Often the product of sexual assaults (or illicit liaisons) by slave masters, mixed-heritage children would get special privileges. Enslaved Africans were divided into 'house negroes' (domestic workers) and 'field negroes' (those toiling outdoors) by dint of their skin tone and hair texture. The more 'high yella' (fair-skinned) you were, the higher your rank.

When freed slaves were setting up communities, many would segregate along colour lines. Just like the hair test (see p. 174), upscale churches and clubs devised a test to check whether your skin was too Black for admission. Raise a brown paper bag to your face and if your skin was any darker than the bag, you couldn't come in. It sounds wicked, but in those days, it could be a matter of survival. At the time, very light-skinned Blacks were able to pass as White and move up through society. Otherwise, thanks to the 'one-drop' rule (one drop of African blood meant you were classified as 'Negro') you might get stuck at the bottom like other African Americans.

Oprah Winfrey told a story about going to Milwaukee as a young girl to live with her mother. Back then, her mum was rooming with a lady, Ms Miller, who was passing for White and who didn't want too many Black people in her home or it might blow her cover. Oprah revealed her mum had a younger daughter who was very light-skinned and she was allowed to sleep inside. But Oprah, being darker-skinned, had to sleep outside in the hallway. 'My mother went along with it because other-wise we would have no place to sleep.'

Oprah says her favourite book is Toni Morrison's classic *The Bluest Eye*. It tells the story of a little Black girl who prays for blue eyes. It's a book about colourism and the quest for self-worth. After Toni Morrison appeared on the Oprah show in 2000, hundreds of women wrote in describing their pain of never feeling loved, never feeling accepted. Dark-skinned girls from South America to South Asia said it was the first time they felt seen.

Colour Coding

If you've ever wondered how deep skin prejudice goes, hop on YouTube and search for a BuzzFeed video (July 2016) titled *What Dark Skinned People Will Never Tell You*. It makes for painful but revelatory viewing. The video shows men and women from different backgrounds, all of whom are the 'darkies' among their clan. It doesn't matter whether you're a Southeast Asian, Brazilian, Korean, Haitian, Nigerian, Trinidadian . . . if your skin is perceived as darker than average, you are likely to grow up feeling like the proverbial 'black sheep'. This is a side effect of racism, but it's also its own animal. After all, it can happen within families where the gene pool simply throws a curve ball. And in some cases, it pre-dates our modern concepts of race.

While researching this book, I learned more about how the pale face ideal pervades the world. I learned that in Japan and

Korea and some parts of China, people are so obsessed with whiteness that they stay out of the sun at all times. Some carry parasols everywhere or sit on the beach fully clothed, wearing face masks to block the sun. There are beauty creams claiming to get your skin to the ultimate whiteness. Of course, thanks to the global White supremacy effect, some Asian men and women will go to extra lengths to get that 'Anglo' look, from blond hair transplants to having surgery on their eyes. However, ancient Japanese and Chinese scrolls also seem to show a preference for whiter skin. This goes back to the Han dynasty, from around 202 BC, way before any European invasions.

Even in Africa, you can find ancient Egyptian papyri revealing the darker-skinned masses either working or worshipping below their fairer rulers, gods and goddesses. The theory in all these cases is that skin tone was an obvious way to separate the high-born from the labouring classes. It was easy to spot because lighter-skinned folk stayed out of the sun, presumably being fanned, fed and hydrated by their servants. Meanwhile, the workers and slaves toiled all day outside and burned to a crisp.

Until the early 20th century, staying out of the sun and powdering yourself to oblivion was all the rage for European aristocracy too. Men and women tried out sickly remedies like mercury and leeches to achieve that ghost-like glow. You only see the trend shifting as we enter the 1920s, when rich folk wanted to show off their jet-set lifestyles with perma-tans.

In India, colourism goes hand in hand with class and caste prejudice.[1] There, the preference for fairer skin is embedded in a tradition that's difficult to understand as an outsider. The caste system is a source of pride for some, while most say it's an outdated form of oppression. While America sells its dream and Britain purports to let its citizens educate and work themselves out of the lower classes, in India if you are born into a caste, you stay there until you croak. Then you're reborn and you die and you're reborn in the same caste again ad infinitum. No get-out-of-jail card for you. The castes include numerous subcastes and your status can affect anything from where you work to who you marry. Skin colour is a big part of that package.

The caste called Dalits (formally known as the untouchables) are on the lowest rung. People in this caste do all the jobs nobody else wants to do and typically, they can be identified on sight because of their darker skin – again, supposedly from working outdoors in the sun.

Fair and Lovely

Blogger Nomita tells me in India, when your baby is born, one of the first questions you'll hear after 'boy or girl?' is 'fair or dark?' 'Especially for a girl child,' she says. 'And if she's dark, the whole tone changes. Nobody says anything as such but the fact that they ask that question . . . it's like if you failed an exam or something. "Oh, what a shame, never mind." If she's fair, everyone's really happy. It's so ridiculous.'

Ridiculous, yes, except that skin tone is actual currency in India. Lighter-skinned girls are considered marriage material and matrimonial ads openly ask for 'fair skin'. If you're fair, you're more likely to get a job or a promotion or feature in a movie or magazine. Indian movie stars tend to be on the paler end of the spectrum and many of them help advertise skin lighteners to the browner public. Fair and Lovely, India's leading whitening product, is also the country's number-one selling beauty cream.

In India, as in Nigeria and other post-colonial nations, it's quite common for middle- to upper-class families to employ house help, such as maids, cooks and gardeners. Nomita says:

One of the perks for every maid we've hired was that you had to promise them some Fair and Lovely cream. Because everybody wanted to be fairer-skinned. I never cared about being pale. I'd happily go and get a tan. But of course, my aunties would be warning me to stay out of the sun.

Nomita describes herself as 'unusually pale' for an Indian and her mum was the same, to the point that most people thought she was Parsi, a descendant of Persians. 'I used to get so many comments, not just about my complexion, but people asking, "Is your mum Parsi?" It didn't really affect me growing up. I didn't question it. Now I have a different perspective.'

She says she's not sure why Indians are so colour obsessed, although she assumes there's a link with British colonialists arriving in India and claiming superiority for White people. 'I mean, up until the late '60s or '70s, thanks to the British we had a famous country club in Bombay that had a sign stating "No dogs and Indians allowed".'

A 2012 study by a health charity in India revealed childless couples paid more for a surrogate who was fair, even though it had no genetic impact on the baby.[2] Another study in 2014 showed nearly 90 per cent of girls in India described skin lightening as a 'high need'.[3]

According to a report from Global Industry Analysts, the skin-lightening industry will be worth $23 billion in 2020 (with projections of $31.2 billion by 2024).[4] More than $430 million of the market share is consumed in India. Apparently, skin lighteners make up close to 90 per cent of ads on prime-time TV in India and Pakistan.

Most of these skin-bleaching creams include toxic substances like mercury and hydroquinone and aren't exactly kind to your body. Side effects range from scarring to skin cancer and nerve, liver, kidney or brain damage. And people don't stop at lotions, they're using pills and injections and chemical 'baths' to achieve that pearly-white illusion.

I saw a video doing the rounds on social media – it's a whitening process that shows what appears to be a woman bathing in some kind of skin stripper.[5] You can watch as her 'beautician' literally peels the Black off her skin. It's nauseating. I thought about the victims of acid attacks in Nigeria, Pakistan, Lebanon, London. The people – often young girls – who are walking around with third-degree burns for which they've undergone multiple surgeries to repair.

Your skin is not for decoration. It is a living, breathing organ whose key function is to protect your insides. If you strip it away, ruin it for ever, what's left to protect your flesh, your bones, your heart?

My heart hurts for the sweet little Black girls being raised on a Snow White diet. I was one of them. Growing up, even in Nigeria, our vision of what was attractive was reinforced by TV, movies and music videos from overseas. American media dominated the airwaves. Throughout my childhood, teens and twenties, it felt like every hot chick you dreamed of being (or men dreamed of bedding) had a caramel or honey complexion: Halle Berry, Vivica A. Fox, Lisa Bonet . . . all the way to Beyoncé and RiRi.

Entrepreneur Shanthi is of mixed African, Indian and European heritage and says colourism didn't really factor for her until her teens:

It was only when I got to around 15 or 16 when most women are self-conscious about their looks that the idea that more European hair or lighter complexions were more desirable started to surface. But often this is a narrative pushed more loudly from within the Black community. So maybe I was actually less affected by this because I went to school in a mixed environment. It's Black people who would remark that I had 'good hair', not White people.

Author, podcaster and relationships expert Natalie, who is of Jamaican Chinese descent, said being fair-skinned didn't always work in her favour – in fact, quite the reverse:

I hear conversations about how 'lighter-skinned' people have always had it good – that is not my experience. As my parents broke up just before I was three, and I was 'yellow skin' like my dad, I grew up with a lot of negative comments about my appearance without having to step out of the house. In my early years in England, there was far too much talk about skin colour. I wanted to be darker, although obviously, I would have still experienced colourism and racism.

Yellow Fever

In Nigeria, the 'yellow babe' (light-skinned hottie) is like the 'blond bombshell' is to the European: arm candy, a status symbol, that woman who turns every head in the room. Our nation's colour complex was also a colonial hangover, one of the lingering effects of Eurocentric values imposed on the continent, until the Year of Independence in 1960 when 17 African countries broke free. You can raise your own flags, take back your lands, but liberating your mentality is a lot harder.

Former journalist Rachel is a Nigerian who spent her forma-tive years in eastern Nigeria, living with her family, including her grandmother who hailed from Wales. 'Colourism was definitely a factor,' she says, 'although I never grew up thinking I had this advantage, because I had a White grandma. Probably people around me treated me differently sometimes. I guess it was the unfortunate colonial legacy of being regarded as coming from a privileged background.'

In Nigeria, 77 per cent of women use skin-lightening agents, in Senegal 57 per cent, in Togo 59 per cent.[6] Togolese superstar Dencia has turned her blond hair and skin into a commercial opportunity. She's launched a product so any girl with a song in her heart and a craving for creamy skin can get her look. She calls it Whitenicious. While more African governments are banning these toxic products, celebrities proudly show off their sheen. Despite critical feedback, South African singer Kelly Khumalo posts defiantly on Instagram: 'Ima bleach until Jesus comes'.

In Africa, we aren't plagued by eating disorders. On a continent where hunger and starvation could be just around the corner, the final stand of powerless girls is not to reject food. It is to starve your skin of melanin.

Who taught us so much self-loathing? Colourism feels superficial, but its impact is profound. It turns out that not only in India but all around the world, dark-skinned women are less likely to find a marriage partner. Dark-skinned women are given longer prison sentences. Dark-skinned people in general are more likely to be unemployed. In fact, one study shows job interviewers actually remember educated Black people as having lighter skin.[7] It's part of what is called the 'halo effect' (when you unconsciously attribute positive characteristics to people you remember favourably). The gap in pay rates for dark-skinned and light-skinned men is similar to the gap in pay rates for Black and White men.

This stuff is hurting our kids too. Young Black girls are more likely to be excluded from school if they are darker-skinned.

Black boys face quicker judgments and sterner punishments than their lighter peers. In 2019, the NSPCC reported that schoolgirls as young as ten are using whitening make-up to avoid racial bullying.[8]

Writer and social critic Ahmed Olayinka Sule says anti-Blackness should get its own category as a form of extreme racism that affects billions worldwide. Anti-Blackness dates back to those phoney scientists who first created racial categories and put Africans at below zero. This fear of a Black planet pops up everywhere from attacks on African immigrants in India, to the lesser status given to darker-skinned Brazilians, to the Dominican Republic's shameful treatment of their darker, Haitian neighbours. In her book *White Fragility*, Robin DiAngelo calls Black people the 'ultimate racial other'. But as we can see, it's not just an anti-Black thing. It's a global colourism complex.

Colour Me Beautiful

When I was little, a White boy I liked ran up to me and grabbed my hand. My heart lurched. He turned it over and stared in wonder at the rose gold of my palm. I stared at him. Should I say something? Did I need to explain? I wanted to tell him my skin is not one thing and neither am I. But he had already let go and run away.

Flashback to when I'm about four years old, browsing a supermarket in Enugu. There's a row of dolls, including Black ones with curly hair. But I'm transfixed by the Barbie: blond, skinny, pointy breasts, zero waist. That's the only one I want, not the Black one. Not even Sindy with her chubby face. I want Barbie.

I grew up wanting to look like my mother who was dark-skinned and, in my eyes, the epitome of glamour. But part of me also wanted to look like Barbie, with her blue eyes, swishy golden hair and unattainable figure. So many of us were sold on that fantasy.

Even girls who grew up visibly 'White', like British Greek Cypriot Vicki Broadbent, felt the pressure to conform to an even Whiter beauty standard:

There were very few if any visible role models who looked like me during those formative years. Most children in books or on TV were blond and blue-eyed. Later, at university when women like J-Lo rose to fame and then much later, the Kardashians, as well as directors like Gurinder Chadha, I started to feel not only were women who looked more like me accepted and celebrated, I had role models.

In the landmark 1954 case Brown vs Board that resulted in the desegregation of American public schools, something called 'the Doll Test' played a key role. Based on a 1940s study by psychologists Kenneth Bancroft Clark and his wife, Mamie Phipps Clark, it showed Black children between ages three and seven favouring White dolls over Black dolls when they were given a choice.[9] Each kid was asked which doll was 'nice' and 'pretty' versus 'bad' and 'ugly' and overwhelmingly, the White doll came out on top. The researchers concluded that anti-Black bias, even among African-American kids, was harming a generation. Citing the Doll Test in his decision to end school segregation, Chief Justice Earl Warren wrote: 'To separate from others of similar age and qualifications solely because of their race generates a feeling of inferiority as to their status in the community that may affect their hearts and minds in a way unlikely to ever be undone.'

The experiment has been recreated time and again, including for a Birmingham, UK study featured in the documentary *The Doll Test: The Birth of Self Hate*.[10] You can find clips of these tests on YouTube but, be warned – it can be hard to watch.

The good news is that we have the power to disrupt these attitudes, starting when our kids are very young. Studies show if you raise a child in a household where Black and Brown beauty, excellence, joy and creativity are highly valued, they will have higher self-esteem, no matter what the outside world tells them.[11] Seeing Blackness in a positive light benefits White kids too. When everyone is celebrated, every child thrives.

Take little Sophia Benner, a two-year-old who became famous for her own 'doll test'. When Sophia, a White American, picked out a Black doll for herself in a supermarket, the cashier tried to change her mind. 'Are you sure this is the doll you want, honey?' the cashier asked. 'She doesn't look like you. We have lots of other dolls that look more like you.'

Sophia was insistent. 'Yes, she does. She's a doctor, like I'm a doctor. And I'm a pretty girl and she's a pretty girl. See her pretty hair? And see her stethoscope?'

Even at her tender age, Sophia knew the truth: beauty comes in every shade and real beauty is more than what you see. Your skin is not one thing, and neither are you.

Mirror, Mirror

Walking down the Cally Road in north London, I see a White mum dragging her rosy-cheeked daughter. The mother's complexion can only be described as Oompa Loompa with a coating of Trump. She's heading to the tanning salon. I've heard you can fall sick under those machines. I've heard also they can become addictive. Just like skin bleaching becomes addictive. Because you can't let it slip, you have to maintain the lie. If you don't keep tanning, you might pale into insignificance. If you don't keep bleaching, you might fade to black. I worry for the little girl, where her head is at and what her body will look like in ten years. Will she succumb to her mama's habit? I hope someone in her life tells her that her skin is beautiful, no need for additives.

At secondary school, the girls would compare tan lines. 'You tan so easily. I wish I could get brown like you.' 'But you're much darker too.' 'Yeah, but not like you. You're nigger black.'

I let those memories wash away because my Blackness is a source of joy. I love the sun and the sun loves me. My sister used to describe me to friends as 'cute, short, dances, kinda yellow'. I'll take it all apart from 'yellow'. If you really want to go there, I'd say I'm dark milk chocolate. At least 45 per cent cacao, baby.

Second emoji from the right. I might get slightly paler in the winter months, but catch me in summer and I'm darker than you remember.

What we see as beautiful is shifting, as people power starts to push back, particularly on social media. If your child worries about looking weird, you can bet there's an Instagram account dedicated to their peculiar brand of gorgeousness. Dark skin or albino, ginger hair, tattooed, people with vitiligo, transgender, differently abled, elderly, you name it. Occasionally, there's a hint of fetishism, but on the whole it's a powerful and positive move forward. I love the sight of Lizzo in a bathing suit, lounging in her dark-skinned glory, like so many full-figured, confident, beautiful African women I know.

Dark-skinned activists share campaigns like #unfairandlovely #Blackgirlmagic #melaninpoppin #ilovemybrownskin. In 2019, for the first time in history, the winners of five major beauty contests were all Black. Not just Black, but different hues and expressions of what Black looks like.

Beyoncé sings 'Brown Skin Girl' and dedicates a verse to Lupita Nyong'o. When she shares it on social media, Lupita is radiant with joy.[12] She can't disguise how much this means to her. It's easy to imagine her as that little Kenyan girl who was told for so long that she wasn't enough. The Black girl who felt she could never be as precious as her light-skinned sister. *Sulwe* is a picture book Lupita wrote about her own journey to self-acceptance. For all the little girls who dream of being loved just as they are.

What we find ugly or unbecoming can become magical in the right light. All we need to do is change the way we see and the words we use. When you talk to your child about appearance, teach them to celebrate every skin tone, gender and ability. Tell your child true beauty comes in looking for and expressing the beauty in others. Kindness looks good on you.

On holiday in Antigua, after a week of non-stop sun and sea, my husband and two boys are as brown as I am ordinarily. I am darker than I've ever seen myself. Getting dressed after swimming, we spot the pale moons of our bum cheeks in the mirror and can't stop laughing.

Shortly after my return to the UK, I bump into one of my aunties. After the initial pleasantries, she greets me with the usual insults that Nigerians mistake for small talk.

'Uju, you've added weight.' She takes me in from head to toe. 'Ah ahh, but you're looking so black.'

'Thank you,' I reply, with a smile.

• Talking Points

Q. My little girl tried to bleach herself with a pigmentation cream and I'm devastated. How can I get her to love the skin she's in?
A. Be clear about the dangers of bleaching creams. Tell her they'll ruin her skin and can make her very sick. You'll find plenty of reports and images via Google to support your statements (although try not to scare her). Talk to her about why she wants to make herself lighter and how much you love her just as she is. You can listen to artists and songs like Wizkid and

Beyoncé's 'Brown Skin Girl' or read books like Lupita Nyong'o's *Sulwe* (see Further Reading, p. 297) that are all about claiming your natural beauty. You could also make a vision board together filled with dark-skinned people you admire. The journey to loving herself for your daughter might be a lifelong one, but it starts young and often it starts with you, her parent.

Q. My son feels he's out of place in our family because I'm White, his father is dark-skinned and he's very pale Brown. What can I say to make him feel like he belongs?
A. Your son is a wonderful blend of you and his father, so show him that. If he's little, it might be fun to mix paint colours together or even milk and cocoa powder to show how your individual colours have created such a beautiful combination. Tell him that you realise he will have his own experiences as a brown-skinned boy of mixed heritage but that there are many people like him all over the world. He never has to feel alone. You can look out for role models within and beyond your families. As always, books and movies are a helpful conversation starter (see Further Reading, p. 297).

Q. My daughter's best friend is Korean and has the prettiest eyes, but she's been talking about having surgery on them when she's older. Should I bring it up with her mother or is it not my place?
A. I would certainly mention it to her mother. It's not your

218

place to cast judgment, so make sure to frame it more as a question (curiosity) than a criticism. You could say something like: 'I heard from my daughter that your little girl wants to have surgery on her eyes. Do you mind if I ask why? Have you discussed this with her? I think her eyes are gorgeous and it would be a shame to change such a pretty face.' It's also most important for you to talk about it with your daughter, to see what *she* understands about her friend's wishes and to steer her in a direction of self-acceptance, cultural appreciation and the beauty in all faces.

CHAPTER 13

Books Will Save the World

I'm almost in the 11th chapter of my life. I like saying chapter instead of year. Because it's my story.

Ezra, age 10

The first time I saw a golliwog was in the Noddy picture books. Reading those stories as a young girl in Nigeria, it never occurred to me there was anything racist about this character. I didn't know what racism was. I had never seen a minstrel show. I liked his big head, natty suit and bowtie. That colourful smile.

On one of my first nights at boarding school in England, I spotted a golliwog on a girl's bed. As I lit up in recognition, another child took it from my hands.

'Look, it's a wog like you.'

I had never heard of a wog, but I soon found out what it meant. I looked at Golly, a teddy wearing Blackface, with new eyes. Most of all, I saw somebody different in the mirror. Noddy would never be the same. And neither would I.

Wog. Darkie. Foreigner. Go back to where you belong.

Paper Houses

Where I belonged was in a house of open doors and mosquito-screened windows, ceiling fans whirring and walls lined with bookshelves. Legs propped up on a pouffe, nose buried in a book. In the distance, my mother's voice calling my whole name 'Obianuju', beckoning me to the dinner table or to whatever task I'd abandoned.

Every school holiday, our home in Enugu, Eastern Nigeria, turned into summer camp. Cousins would pile in from every direction and settle in for weeks. My parents welcomed all and sundry in for food, conversation, family sleepovers.

The adults gathered in air-conditioned living rooms and studies cloudy with pipe smoke. The kids ran around barefoot, chasing dogs, climbing trees, plucking unripe guava and bruised mangoes overhanging from our neighbour's garden. The older children would send us younger ones, aka the 'small rats', to the corner kiosk to buy sweeties. Spicy Tom Tom and Trebor Butter Mints.

I remember us cramming chunks of Bazooka Joe bubblegum in our mouths as quickly as possible, so we could read the comic strips inside the wrappers. Reading was my superpower, something I had mastered by age four. I lived in two worlds: one made for family and one made out of stories. A book was a passport. A magic-carpet ride. A paper house strong enough to hide inside. Through these portals, I discovered all kinds of characters, places and flavours I couldn't wait to see, touch, taste.

I read authors whose names tripped off my tongue with ease. Chinua Achebe, Buchi Emecheta, Wole Soyinka, my auntie Flora Nwapa. I also read tales of people who were nothing like me on the outside, but whom I absolutely knew deep down. I saw myself in girls named Jane, Anne, Jo, Matilda, Sophie, Emma . . . women who kicked against some unseen system.

When I came to England, I got several sharp knocks to my fictional identities. I was no longer the protagonist, the author of my destiny, the girl at the heart of the story. Far from being Jane, I was the woman in the attic. Unseen, untold, unspeakable. If I had imagined myself as Huck Finn, riding my boat into adventures new, the world saw me as Jim, the runaway slave. During English lessons, I would cringe as the teacher asked me to read as Othello. I could feel all eyes on me as I lowered my voice. But I was not the Moor; I was Desdemona, the beauty of Venice. I wasn't Mammy or the maid, I was Scarlett O'Hara. Why couldn't anybody see me?

We move like black ink on a white page. We do the work you cannot see. We carry the weight of the words, but you never truly look at us, any more than you notice the whiteness surrounding everything. Yet without us, you couldn't begin to tell your stories.

Mirrors, Windows and Sliding Doors

Every child should have the chance to lose themselves inside a story. However, they need to find themselves there too.

In a famous essay about the lack of Black and minority ethnic representation in children's books, education scholar Rudine Sims Bishop described books as 'mirrors, windows and sliding glass doors'.

Writer Sunny Singh, co-founder of the Jhalak Prize for Book of the Year by a Writer of Colour, elucidates:

All of us but especially kids as they are growing up need mirrors, windows and sliding doors – so books that can reflect them, give them access to different worlds, and teach them to recognise commonalities even when there may be some differences. Giving children access to the widest range of books is the only way possible.

A comprehensive report by the Centre for Literacy in Primary Education (CLPE) on the state of UK children's book publishing revealed an alarming stat: out of 9,115 children's books published in 2017, only 1 per cent featured a Black, Asian or minority ethnic (BAME) main character.[1] That's despite 32 per cent of primary-school kids in England coming from minority ethnic origins. And this population is growing.

In a quarter of the books surveyed, BAME characters showed up, but only in the background. It's the same story we see on our screens repeatedly. The sassy Black sidekick. The geek chic

Asian roommate. They are dependable, expendable, only there to prop up the White hero or heroine.

According to the Cooperative Children's Book Center, in American publishing things aren't much better. In 2018, only 10 per cent of kids' books featured a Black character.[2] By contrast, more than double that number (27 per cent) had an animal hero or a character that wasn't even human.

I never read any studies on publishing as a child, but I got the message loud and clear. The very first story I wrote was about a family of fruits and vegetables. My first attempt at a novel, 'published' in an exercise book by my friend Tamsin, was about a family of White protagonists. It took several tries before I found my voice. Before I felt free to put myself and people like me into my own stories.

As a teenager, I began seeking out books by authors whose words made me feel seen. Simi Bedford. Audre Lorde. Ntozake Shange. I used to feel quite possessive of Toni Morrison. To me, she looked like Mama, my paternal grandmother. When she died in 2019, I mourned her like a relative. Toni was unapologetic about writing Black stories for Black people, and for Black girls in particular. She belonged to us. Yet I've heard from so many White friends and readers whose lives were turned around by books like *The Bluest Eye* and *Song of Solomon*. We need other people's stories as much as our own.

Changing the Narrative

There is nothing quite like curling up with your child and sharing a bedtime story. To become a co-pilot on their adventures. But for kids who are constantly written out of the story, or added as a footnote, it can be hard to sustain any interest in reading. Research shows Black boys are the least likely to pick up a book and it's no wonder when so many of their stories remain untold.[3] However, this isn't just about representation. Boys of a certain age tend to be more distractible and can wind up losing interest in books, in favour of more visceral thrills like gaming or sports.

Now my boys are in their teens and tweens, we still read books together. Sometimes their dad reads aloud to all of us or we listen to an audiobook. When they were little, they loved the tales I would spin for them after lights out.

I'm a huge fan of classics like *Where the Wild Things Are*, *Winnie the Pooh* and *Goodnight Moon*. Coming back to my favourites was like comfort food. But I was disappointed by the overall Whiteness of what was available. I had to go searching for books that featured characters who looked like my children.

As a White mother raising her half-Nigerian boy in Cambridge, England, Helen (my 'mother-out-law') had an even bigger challenge. In the late '60s and early '70s searching for people of colour in children's stories, or indeed any stories, was a tall order. Helen scoured second-hand bookshops and academic friends' houses and came up with a few treasures.

Abiye has kept some of his childhood books in pristine condition, and when Ezra was very small, I was delighted to come across an old picture book featuring a Black boy with thick Afro hair on the cover.

'He's got my name too,' Ezra squealed, pointing at the author's name: Ezra Jack Keats.

What I loved about this book, aside from its warm storytelling and poignant illustrations, was that the boy being Black isn't the focus of the story. Peter is the central character in seven of Keats' books and in each one he's simply a boy doing his thing. I think it's great there are more books now for children about embracing their skin colour, hair and heritage. But it's just as important – more so, I would argue – for Black and minority ethnic kids to see themselves in books *as* themselves. Ordinary, everyday kids getting on with the sweet, sticky mess of life itself.

Ezra Jack Keats, an American of Polish Jewish descent, began his career as an artist and illustrator before turning his hand to children's books. What changed everything was deciding to make a Black boy his hero. Keats wrote: 'None of the manuscripts I'd been illustrating featured any Black kids – except for token Blacks in the background. My book would have him there simply because he should have been there all along.'

Climb Into My Skin

As a parent, you have to be intentional about the books you read with your children. Representation is important and it's not always a race thing. I remember stumbling across *The Incredible Book Eating Boy* in the library years ago and laughing out loud. You see, Jed used to eat books as a toddler, happily munching away on paper and cardboard. I'd often find whole chunks of picture books missing with Jed's telltale bite marks. I also recall Jed's utter delight at finding himself, an actual Jed, in a book gifted to him by his nursery as a leaving present, *Zed's Bread*. Jed could barely read but he devoured that book (metaphorically speaking).

Children need mirrors. But remember they also need books as windows and sliding glass doors (see p. 223). It's a powerful thing for a child in a council estate or a leafy suburb or a small town in Finland or a village in Sri Lanka to discover how children live elsewhere. You can watch all the TV and films and music videos but there's nothing like the written word to put you right inside someone else's head. Reading stories by and about people of colour, LGBTQI+ and differently abled children teaches your child to care about stuff outside their own experience. It can help your little one grow into a sensitive, thoughtful, more compassionate individual.

My boys are drawn to stories about other boys. Jamie Johnson juggling footballs and family troubles, Tom Gates and Wimpy Kid doodling their way through school. But especially as they get older, I am deliberate about steering them towards more books with female protagonists. I believe learning to see the world through the eyes of a girl is essential to their development as whole human beings.

To paraphrase Atticus Finch in *To Kill a Mockingbird*, reading helps us climb inside another person's skin and walk around in it for a while. And we are forever changed.

What If the Author Is Racist?

What happens when you love a book so hard you can quote it from back to front, its pages are dog-eared, you've recommended it to everyone you know . . . and then . . . you discover something upsetting. What if one of your beloved authors turns out to be racist?

Let's take another look at old Atticus Finch, social-justice warrior and liberal icon. I had always wanted my kids to read *To Kill a Mockingbird*, Harper Lee's seminal tale of crime and prejudice in the American south. It was way ahead of its time on race relations and it's filled with some of my favourite lines. However, some contemporary readings take issue with how the Black victim is portrayed (practically mute) and its repeated use of the N-word.

Harper Lee is far from the only author to come under scrutiny by modern readers. Enid Blyton, one of my childhood staples, managed to push her bigoted ideas on an unsuspecting youth. In her book, *The Three Golliwogs*, she writes about three characters called Golly, Woggie and Nigger. Their favourite song is – wait for it – 'Ten Little Nigger Boys'.

'Ten Little Niggers' was a popular children's rhyme about

ten Black kids dying off one by one. It's the original title of one of Agatha Christie's most famous murder mystery novels. Later, the title was changed to *Ten Little Indians* and eventually it became *And Then There Were None*. I read so many Agatha Christie tales under the covers way past lights out. Twisting my brain to work out whodunnit. *And Then There Were None* was Christie's masterpiece with that killer ending. It's one of the best-selling books of all time.

Up until May 2020, when a successful petition on Change. org forced its removal, you could still find a copy of Christie's *Ten Little Niggers* on Amazon. The cover features a golliwog hanging from a noose. One happy reviewer gave it five stars, adding: 'What a title?!! We should all hold hands around the Palace of Westminster and lament this shameful act of social injustice! Or we could get a life. Anyway . . . Great book!'

In 2020, no publisher in their right mind would put out a book with such an inflammatory title, cover and content. But if you're taking your kids on a nostalgia trip through literature, stay vigilant. Look out for racist caricatures. Buck-toothed Asians, big-lipped Black pirates, stomping mammy figures. They pop up everywhere, even Asterix, Tintin, Tom and Jerry cartoons, all over Disney's back catalogue. These are images little kids can internalise, whether or not you point them out. But especially if you say nothing at all.

Some say you shouldn't read too much into historic racism. They'll excuse someone they love – whether it's a family member or a celebrity – by saying it was all so long ago when people were all shades of ignorant.

Frankly, that's a piece of crap. The past isn't a free pass. Sure, people were more racist and less educated about different cultures. However, unlike many of our ancestors, these people also had choices. They could make a choice, as artists and story-tellers, to take a broader view on humanity. To use their voices to change the narrative rather than spreading more little white lies. These authors chose wrong and they don't deserve our apologies or excuses.

That doesn't mean I'm into cancel culture or burning books. I prefer recentring to outright censorship. If Enid Blyton was not writing for me, perhaps it's poetic justice that her books not only gave me pleasure, but certainly boosted my literacy and eventual writing career.

I teach my kids to look at who is telling the story, who they are trying to reach, who is left out? What would the story look like if someone else was the hero or the villain?

As a mum, I think it's my right to curate my children's book-shelves. But as they grow older, I want them to be able to make their own informed choices. Jed is a fan of *Green Eggs and Ham* (the picture book, not the dish). He loves listening to the audio-book. When I became aware of Dr Seuss' racist leanings, I wanted to switch off. Instead, I told him about Dr Seuss and some of his faulty thinking and how that colours what he writes and how it's received. Jed listened, thoughtfully.

'But I can still sing "Green Eggs and Ham", right?'

I hate that I live in a world where telling my kids any of this is necessary. Being Black means always having to watch your back, even with something as innocuous as a picture book.

The good thing is there is a universe of books out there, more books than we can ever hope to read. More writers are born every day, more stories springing to life. More of us are finding versions of ourselves in picture books and biographies and literature and poetry. If an author no longer speaks to you or your children, there are a hundred other books you can pick up instead.

Also, be careful not to write off an author based on hearsay. Do your research and make your own judgment calls. I'd heard a negative rumour about the Peanuts Gang and how the Black character Franklin came about. However, when I read the backstory, I discovered a true tale of courage, kindness and resistance.

It started with a White American schoolteacher and mother of three, Harriet Glickman, writing to Charles Schulz to ask if he'd consider introducing a Black child into the Peanuts Gang. This was after the assassination of Martin Luther King and Glickman believed this simple act could be a powerful force for change. My favourite part of Harriet Glickman's letter to Schulz comes at the end when she asks Schulz to include more Black characters if possible and 'please, allow them a Lucy!'

At first, Schulz resisted, thinking it would be condescending to African Americans. So Glickman enlisted two of her Black friends to write to Schulz as well, urging him to integrate Peanuts. Their gentle persistence won him over. One day on a beach, a Black boy returns a ball to Charlie Brown and they start chatting. Franklin was born on 31 July 1968 – now celebrated as #FranklinDay.

Franklin had to do some heavy lifting for the culture. He is every Black kid sitting alone in a classroom of White peers. When I dressed Jed up as Franklin for World Book Day once (easy peasy costume, if you need it), not one of his friends knew the character by name. But at least Franklin is still here, representing his little socks off.

The Stories We Tell Ourselves

Not long ago, numerous articles foretold the death of the book. They couldn't have been more wrong. The book is the greatest technological invention of our age and nothing – not e-readers, not mobile phones, not VR – will change that.

Books are conversation starters, badges of honour. Seeing a book in someone's hand can be like a secret handshake as you recognise you're part of the same club. I love catching my kids reading furtively under the dinner table, or squinting by torchlight in bed or even flipping pages as they walk down the pavement. I'll tell them off, but secretly it thrills me, as I remember doing the same.

They say if everybody put down a gun and picked up a book instead, we'd be living in a very different world. I'm not someone who never lets their kids play with toy guns. However, I will make sure they always have more books than toy bullets at their disposal.

Research shows reading fiction does everything from developing your language skills to slowing down memory decline and Alzheimer's symptoms; reading rewires your brain to be more empathetic.[4] You become a kinder, more compassionate person by sitting inside someone else's story for a while. Books are one of the fastest ways to 'show and tell' kids about what makes us all unique and what binds us together. If you want to grow a better human, grab a book off the shelf. If you want to start a conversation on race, identity or any big life issue, turn to page one.

Stories are transformative. And there is nothing more powerful than the story we tell ourselves about who we are. It can shape our whole world. We need more voices in this story, more faces, more imagination. Make space for more Franklins and allow us our Lucys too. Any one of us can be a hero or a villain or an everyday kid getting on with the sweet, sticky mess of life. Write each of us into the narrative. We should have been there all along.

• Talking Points

Q. I was shocked to hear about racist views from Dr Seuss, Enid Blyton and other children's authors we love. Should I ban those books in our house? My daughter's favourite book is *The Cat in the Hat*. Am I teaching her racism by reading it to her?
A. This is something I've struggled with as both a parent and a reader. It always throws me for a loop when I discover some of my favourite books and movies were created by people with

racist sympathies . . . or even outright fascists. As I've shared in this chapter, I am careful about curating what books we bring into the house. I also stay open with my kids, tell them what I know, have conversations about why authors might have certain attitudes, invite them to ask questions and give them the chance to choose how they engage with particular stories and their creators.

Remember that much of English literature is racist and sexist by omission, with its heavy focus on White/male narratives and very little space for women and writers of colour. Yet that doesn't mean you have to scrub your entire library and start again. It does mean being intentional about what you consume, what you read with your child and also where you draw the line according to your own personal values. Does reading *Mein Kampf* count as an educational exercise, or are you helping to support the ideology of one of the most evil minds in human history? That's for you to decide.

Q. I have bought a range of books with diverse characters for me and my child to read together. I'm not sure how well the message is getting across though. Should I be doing more?
A. It's wonderful to share stories by and about diverse people with your child. However, don't just read these stories in 'colour-blind' mode. Talk to her openly about the differences you notice, such as skin, hair, language. Use them as opportunities to start conversations around race and racism. Help her to think more deeply about these stories, who is

telling them, the message behind them. You will be raising a critical thinker as well as a child who is comfortable talking about race. And of course, don't limit her interaction to books and media alone. Get out there and engage with people from different backgrounds in real life.

Q. Where can I find a list of inclusive and diverse reading resources for kids?
A. I have just such a list at the back of the book (see p. 297).

CHAPTER 14

Babes in the City

In London, everyone is different and that means anyone can fit in.
Paddington Bear, from the movie *Paddington* (2014), screenplay
by Paul King, story adapted from the books by Michael Bond.

There's no place like London. I have lived and worked in some
of the world's most exciting, cosmopolitan cities. New York.
Paris. Lagos. Yet London takes the biscuit. Its blend of old-
world charm and new-school cool. Its patchwork of cultures
and personalities. Unlike Paris or even New York, where various ethnic groups tend to flock together, Londoners are like one
big, sometimes fractious, but mostly-we-get-along family.
Standing on the overground platform waiting for a train, I smile
as Mayor Sadiq Khan's message comes through the speakers.
'London is open and everyone is welcome.'

We live in Islington, one of London's most diverse boroughs.
From boutiques and buzzy restaurants to corner shops and
council estates, there's never a dull moment. Every day hums

with possibility. My boys go to school with children from all different backgrounds, speaking many different languages. There's no chance of either one of them being singled out as the only Black or Brown child in the classroom.

There's no place like London. Every other day, we wake up to news of another stabbing. Knife crime slashes through newspaper headlines. Kids carry weapons to school and drug gangs recruit tweens to smuggle their stash between boroughs or to neighbouring towns. One mum from Haggerston tells me that in her area, teens are shooting fireworks at each other, the latest tool of casual youth violence. When I pop to the shops, I give a wide berth to the boys lurking on their bikes and mobile phones. The pavement is littered with broken glass and laughing-gas canisters. On the corner of our street, another teenager gets knifed. A former student at my boys' primary and secondary schools. They knew him by name.

We get letters from school, warning us about an increase in muggings, telling us what parks the kids should avoid, what streets are safer to walk after dark. They hold a special assembly about the boy who died. Police say he was stabbed by rival gangs from another postcode. He was only 17. His whole life ahead of him – but what kind of life? It's starting to feel like *Boyz n the Hood*. Politicians blame grime and drill music and turn a blind eye to the poverty cycles their policies help to perpetuate. Leaders ignore how cuts in police, fire and other services are devastating communities. I listen to the children's names read out on the nightly news like a liturgy. So many are Nigerian or Ghanaian. African immigrants whose parents dreamed of a better life now seeing their futures cut short, their hopes dashed and bleeding on the streets.

Big City of Dreams

I blog about this city of dreamers, a city I'm so proud to call my home. London is alive with culture. The hub of Europe. I don't want to leave. It's the only place in the Western world where my Blackness doesn't define me or isn't called into question frequently. My boys are born Londoners. During the 2012 Olympics, we bounced along on the buoyancy and hope that infused this city. I get a bounce in my step any time I walk along Waterloo Bridge, taking in the sights. The London Eye blinking at me, Big Ben glowing like a smiley face.

I walk London and remember I am treading on the dreams of those who came before me. A city that built itself on the backs of slaves. A city that grew rich off gold and other minerals stolen from my ancestral home. We take the boys to the British Museum to see galleries stuffed with looted goods. Benin bronze heads from Nigeria, Egyptian statues with broken noses. Parliament, even by moonlight, is the seat of power that helped prop up an apartheid government. As we tour the city, sometimes we catch dirty glances from others who don't think we belong. Yet we are here, we have been here and we aren't going anywhere.

We are Londoners and we are outsiders. Sometimes I have a love-hate relationship with London because this city is also a danger to my kids. Raising Black boys in an environment where they are dying every week is not for the faint-hearted. It's a dilemma faced by many modern parents. We can't afford the lifestyles we want in the big city, yet the cost of moving out is far too high. Then again, the price of life in London seems to be on a downward trend. The price of a Black child's life is losing value by the day.

Knife crime hit a record high in 2019, with 44,076 offences barely six months into the year. The majority of the attackers and the victims were from Black or ethnic minority back-grounds.[1] Far too many of them were under 20; the youngest, Jaden Moodie, was only 14.

Sometimes I stand by the window in the evening, peering out, waiting for my 14-year-old to come home from football training. Like his secondary-school mates, Ezra likes to drop roadman slang. I worry one day someone will mistake him for the real deal. Many victims of knife crime and gun violence are gang related, but some are innocent bystanders. Just kids walking through who got caught up in some beef they never saw coming.

Tashaun Aird, 15, died from a stab wound to the lung in May 2019, one of the youngest victims to date. A family state-ment described him as: 'passionate about his music and he loved drawing. He was a loving, caring boy with an infectious laugh. There are no words to avoid this empty void we now have.' At the scene of the crime, a woman could be heard screaming: 'It's my son, it's my son'.

Making Moves

There comes a time when almost every city parent considers moving out of town. Sometimes it happens before the nippers arrive. You look around at the high-rises and traffic, dangerous levels of pollution and reports of childhood asthma at an all-time high. A little voice inside you whispers that this is no place to raise a child. Sure, you want your kid to be independent and streetwise, but you also want to preserve their innocence and sense of freedom. You want them to be able to ride a bike into the centre of town with their friends. Or to play out in the streets until sundown, like you did as a child.

Whether you're in Paris or Johannesburg or Mumbai, big-city life can feel like a pressure cooker. So many beings crowded into the same space. The abnormally hectic pace of life. You worry your kids will grow up way too fast. In the city, you are more likely to be victims of violent street crime or a terrorist attack. A bomb on a bus, a train, a shopping centre, a concert stadium. A lorry going off road and ramming into pedestrians. If you are Black, your child is more likely to be assaulted in a turf war or roughed up by police searching for someone who 'fits the description'. Whenever you escape to the countryside or seaside, you breathe a sigh of relief and think about quitting city life for good.

However, the world outside the city can feel too small, too insular to make that leap. Some days, I fantasise about waking up and looking out across fields of rolling green. Farm air mingling with morning coffee. Starry nights unfiltered by the

London smog. Then I remember how isolated I felt way out in the middle of absolutely bloody nowhere as a little girl. I don't want to raise my children in a monoculture, where they feel hyper-alert to their difference whenever they walk out the front door. London comes with its troubles, but at least my kids can stroll down the street without feeling all eyes on them.

Safe, Free, Happy

'White flight' is an American term from the '70s, referring to White families who, as their boroughs became more multicultural, packed up and fled to the suburbs.

Blogger and political activist Laura grew up in Detroit, USA, which she describes as racially segregated, even today. As a Civil Rights activist in the 1960s, her mother worked on the South Side of Chicago, helping transition mostly African-American families into newly built public housing. Her mum told her about real-estate agents ringing up to advise her that a Black family had recently moved into the neighbourhood and they might like to consider selling their home. A tactic known as 'block-busting'.

Despite their political leanings, her parents made a choice to leave Detroit after the city riots in 1967, because they were expecting their first child. 'My mother and father were guilty participants in "White flight",' says Laura. 'At that time, the city had become crime-ridden. My uncle's best friend had been shot dead on his way into his home one evening.'

Laura says the unintended consequence of a childhood learning about the African-American community in the Midwest is that she was really learning about White supremacy:

My parents left Detroit and did not have to worry about the cops pulling them over in their new suburb. The banks gave an affordable mortgage to a White couple buying a home in a white neighbourhood. We went to schools that were mostly White, and guess what? They got lots of kids into universities.

Now living in south London, Laura welcomes the fact that her children's upbringing is so different to hers. 'My son is often the only White boy in his year.'

Not all Londoners are so keen. White flight was the subject of a documentary in 2016, *Last Whites of the East End*.[2] It focused on Newham, in east London where the Cockney locals were described as an 'endangered species'. One resident comments, 'You come out of the Tube station and it's like Baghdad.'

Reasons often cited for White flight include seeking bigger, more affordable housing, better schools and quality of life. But research also shows race is a factor. For instance, one study of Glasgow residents revealed White families are more likely to leave the neighbourhood if people with Pakistani or Muslim names move in.[3]

However, many White parents lean the other way. Joan (name changed) told me she was in a dilemma with her husband about moving out of town. Their family was expanding, but like many Londoners being squeezed out of the property market by inflated prices, they couldn't afford a bigger flat. They had their hearts set on a house in the country suburbs. But she was torn because of what it would mean for their environment and her child's upbringing. What impact would pulling her out of a diverse school and placing her in an all-White space have?

Business and mindset coach Ruth Kudzi spent her childhood in semi-rural Buckinghamshire. She says, 'I certainly heard racist comments on a semi-regular basis and it made me feel uncomfortable.' Now married to a Ghanaian Brit with two mixed-heritage daughters, being around a wider variety of cultures and backgrounds was a number-one priority. 'We live in Sydenham, south-east London, which is relatively diverse. This is something that is important to us, as we enjoy the diversity and think it is important for our daughters to grow up with others who look like them.'

London Mums magazine founder, Monica Costa, lives in cosmopolitan south-west London, a totally different scene from her own upbringing:

I was brought up in Italy in the '70s and '80s at a time when there was little people movement and I don't remember having a single foreigner in our classes. Looking at my school photos I can see only White Italian children. The London reality where I am bringing up my son is very different and I love it. I wanted him to grow up bilingual and in a multicultural society.

243

Living in an ethnically diverse community has been shown to increase cultural sensitivity, reduce prejudice and broaden social networks. But there's more. According to research reported in the *Journal of Personality and Social Psychology* in 2018, living in racially diverse neighbourhoods actually makes you a kinder human being.[4] The study showed people in diverse neighbourhoods were more likely to have offered help to a stranger in the previous month. They were also more likely to 'identify with all of humanity'.

On the flip side, some major urban areas in the UK with large minority populations like Bradford and Birmingham are self-segregating, creating more racial and ethnic intolerance. And thanks to gentrification, middle-class families taking up space where ethnic populations once thrived can totally change the look and vibe of a community. These clusters of wealth can leave poorer families feeling edged out. However, reports on gentrification show it has less impact on diversity than it does on social mobility. Children from working-class and minority backgrounds growing up in such areas are more likely to wind up wealthier and more educated than their parents.

As a mama, I want my babies to be free, but I also want them to be safe. More than anything, I want them to be happy. And for the most part, the home we've chosen makes them happy. London is their playground and their classroom. They get an immersive cultural education, not only from the theatres and arts spaces and bookshops on our doorstep, but from the wide variety of people they meet. One of the ways we come together is through our food. As Londoners, we can break bread with people from all over the globe. My kids and their mates are fluent in dishes like ramen and pho, mezze and shawarma, jollof rice and plantain.

Of course, they see and hear things you wish they hadn't. The drunken brawlers stumbling out of bars. The hobo squatting to take a dump outside a neighbour's door. Walking back from school one day, we passed a woman in the park lighting an illegal fire, crack pipe at her feet.

'What is she doing? Isn't that dangerous?'

Indeed. But it sparked a conversation. I've also had good walkabout chats with the boys about bigotry, inequality, homelessness, elderly care, alcohol abuse, gambling, mental health. Every strange encounter creates a learning opportunity (or a story to tell the grandkids one day).

Our boys do enjoy getting out of the city. They feel the lure of country lanes, seaside piers, cleaner air and endless space to kick a ball around. But they're always itching to get back home.

'It's nice on the beach,' Ezra says on a weekend break. 'But I don't think I'd want to live here. I mean, look around. Do you see any other Black people?'

I've spoken with parents about growing up in rural areas as a person of colour and how they wouldn't wish it on their kids. Yet some mums, like blogger Tinuke Bernade, are happy to move out of London, taking advantage of cheaper accommodation and a relatively quick commute. Above all, she has more peace of mind: 'I moved out of London because as a

245

working-class family with Black skin, I didn't think it would be a safe place to bring up my kids as they got older.'

The downside of living in a small Hertfordshire village is that her daughter became the only Black girl in her primary school. 'I spend a lot of time reinforcing positivity with regards to my daughter's hair and ethnic identity. Simple things like creating Pinterest boards and using loads of positive words to describe her amazing, versatile hair.' Once when schoolboys teased her daughter's Afro, Tinuke spent an evening with her watching videos of strong Black women with natural hair, like Jill Scott, Solange and India Arie. 'She rocked her Afro to school the day after and the day after that.'

Coming Home

Wherever you settle as a family, you and your child might have to navigate unfamiliar neighbourhoods, difficult people, tricky situations. In London, I teach my boys to walk tall but stay alert. Never flash your wares or stroll down the street staring into your mobile phone. If it's after dark, choose a well-lit street and if possible, walk with a group. Choose the route you know best and follow the quickest path home. At any sign of trouble, turn around and never get into an altercation if you have an option to get away. In case of an attack or mugging, hand over your possessions without challenge. Your life is worth more.

Just typing this passage makes my shoulders clench with anxiety, but these are conversations we have with our city kids. But like any hard talks, we also keep it light and don't fill their heads with gloom and drama every day. We share personal anecdotes, open up about our fears sometimes, and focus on the things we love about where we live. Love has a wonderful way of driving out fear, so focus on what you love.

There is no place like paradise. Bad things happen everywhere. We can't swaddle our babies in cotton wool. And being a parent means always having something to worry about. It comes with the territory. We can't control what our children will face through life. What we can do is bring them up with kindness and respect as core values. Everybody wants a better neighbourhood. Let's do our part by raising better neighbours.

No matter who we are, or where we come from, we all come back to the same question: where is home? There's no simple answer, but it lies somewhere between who you were and the life you wish for your children. What I wish for my kids – what I wish for all our children – is that they grow up in a world where they can find a home anywhere. That place where they feel less pressure, more room to breathe. Somewhere they belong without question.

• Talking Points

Q. We are moving out of the city as it's too expensive and getting more violent. However, my eldest is

worried about going from a really diverse school to being surrounded by White kids only.
A. Talk to your child about their worries and be open about any of your own too. Discuss the extra steps you will take to ensure they still have access to diverse cultures and relationships. There are so many ways they can stay in touch with current friends, and of course they will make new ones. Ultimately, children are adaptable, and the most important thing is that they feel happy and secure in who they are (not just where they're going) – and that starts at home.

Q. My son is about to start secondary school and I'm having sleepless nights at the thought of him moving around London independently as a Black boy, when knife crime and drug violence are so high. Do you have any advice?
A. The transition from primary to secondary school can be hard. The best solution is to work on what you can control – your relationship with your son. Make sure you check in with him regularly to know how he's doing and let him know he can always come to you with any concerns. Do your best to familiarise yourself with his friends or the type of people he's hanging out with. Stick him in any after-school clubs or activities on offer, so his schedule is too packed to get in any extra trouble!

Do give him freedom to explore, to express himself and gain some independence. Keeping him cooped up could backfire if he decides to rebel. If you hear of any local incidents,

inform him right away and make sure he knows what to do
and who to turn to if something goes wrong. Remind him to
be sensible and respectful out and about, also to be vigilant
and not to stroll around advertising his phone. Ultimately,
there is only so much you can control, but remember that
parents across the world are all coping with their own set of
worries. We also know that so much worry is in our heads and
we have to keep practising the art of letting go.

**Q. It depresses me that my area has become so gentri-
fied. How can I raise my children to share some of the
community values and colourful experiences I
enjoyed growing up, when so much of that has been
lost?**
A. Gentrification can be a painful reality for people who grew
up in some of the city's most ethnically diverse areas.
Sometimes it feels like the soul of a neighbourhood is being
sucked dry. The thing to remember is that part of what made
certain areas more vibrant was the arrival of new immigrants.
And that immigration is as painful for some as gentrification is
for others.

Change is inevitable and it's important to teach our kids
how to welcome change while having an appreciation for what
once was. You can talk to them about your own childhood and
how things have changed (include the positive changes as well
as the stuff you miss). Introduce them to gallery and museum
owners, shopkeepers, elderly locals and others who keep a
record of what things were like back in the day. Think of ways

you can recapture some of the essence of what you held dear – say, through photographs, music, fashion, food. Discover new places in your neighbourhood and beyond, where you can take your kids to start brand-new traditions. Share your ideas of what makes a community and how your children can begin to build their own networks.

CHAPTER 15

Raising Global Citizens

You know, I don't think of myself as anything like a 'global citizen' or anything of the sort. I am just a Nigerian who's comfortable in other places.
Chimamanda Ngozi Adichie, author

The journey to your true self can take a lifetime. For those of us who grow up between cultures, it feels longer because we live multiple lives. You are always a foreigner, even in your birthplace. In England, I was the one with the strange name and funny-looking food. When I went back to Nigeria, they would call me 'away girl' and laugh at my attempts to answer the elders in Igbo. In England, I wore Blackness like a second skin. In Nigeria, I wore my heritage like a wrapper two sizes small.

They call us third-culture kids. We carry at least two passports and multiple stamps. We have lived in more homes than we can count and enrolled at more schools than we can remember. We are bilingual or multilingual or we speak with motherless tongues. Our accents either thinned to suit our surroundings, or thick with longing for distant lands. Home is a language we can never fully master.

Code Switch

I had a schoolfriend called Sonia, a bubbly girl from India. I remember once her mum and auntie came to visit at school. To my surprise, Sonia's Queen's English accent disappeared and took on the cadences I recognised from watching too many Bollywood movies in Nigeria (Bollywood was bigger than Hollywood there). I couldn't hide my curiosity . . . so Indians also spoke their own version of English with family and friends? Over the years, I've discovered this isn't just a Black thing or even an immigrant thing. People I've met from Dublin or Edinburgh, Somerset or Leeds, all report their accents morphing back into how they speak at home.

Code-switching – flipping between languages, dialects or modes of behaviour – is something that connects so many of us. Yet growing up, at times it felt like a guilty secret. I worked so hard to be 'normal' that any sign of my foreignness would fill me with shame. I remember wanting to run and hide some-times when my mum and dad came to pick me up from school. They were the opposite of the English parents in their stiff shirts, Barbour jackets and tweeds. My dad would emerge from a car in a cloud of pipe smoke, flared suit, belly protruding, Malcolm X goatee. My mum was even more flamboyant, some-times with bright red or purple Afro cropped short, dramatic make-up, a cigarette dangling from elegantly manicured fingers. My parents were born to stand out. All I wanted to do was blend in. 'Is that your mum and dad?' My schoolmates were amused and awed in equal measure. It took years for my shrinking African violet to blossom into pride.

There's a point in your teens or early twenties when you start to revel in your uniqueness. Before that, all you care about is fitting in. Looking back, I realise my friends were hungry for more of me. They wanted to taste my food, hear my Nigeria stories, learn pidgin English expressions, pore over love letters from boys crushing on me back in Enugu. They welcomed the British me, but they wanted to connect with the other Uju too.

If you're raising a child in another culture, do whatever you can to keep them in touch with their roots, even if they fight against it. You might embarrass them with your loud clothes and exotic food, but one day your child will thank you for it.

Mumboss author Vicki recalls growing up in Ilkley, Yorkshire in the '80s. Bilingual from birth, Vicki says:

My mother told me that when I started school age four, on my first day, once home, I announced I would never speak a word of Greek again. I clearly felt a pressure to assimilate with my schoolfriends. I'm sad to admit remembering feeling a great sense of shame at a young age that my parents were 'unusual' . . . that loud Greek music would play in the car and discussions were often more 'surround sound' than gentle conversations. My mother is a quiet character, but my father was and is a huge personality and I often wished he would dial down his Greekness. Something I now love, of course!

Former journalist Rachel is deliberately bringing up her children with a bicultural outlook:

I wanted to raise kids who embraced being British born, but also Nigerians, listening to the music, eating the food. They love okra soup with all the 'obstacles' – the tripe, the cow foot, the oxtail. I love that they'll also eat smoked salmon and scrambled eggs for breakfast. When friends come round, jollof rice is on the menu. For school lunches, I pack rice and stew in the flask. Sometimes I think maybe I'll slide in some okra soup but they're like, no Mummy, I want to eat in peace! It's about being comfortable being yourself, not being ashamed of where you come from and who you are.

Being a third-culture kid can come with multiple challenges, not least mental-health ones. Children who grow up between cultures often report higher levels of anxiety, particularly separation anxiety, insecurity and a feeling of rootlessness. As adults, they can struggle with depression and grief, because when you are a family that relocates again and again, you are always saying goodbye. When you are based far away from your nearest and dearest, you live with a constant sense of loss. On the flip side, you have friends and can make friends anywhere. You gain an adventurous spirit and an open mind. You become adaptable, resilient, a true child of the globe.

London Mums magazine editor Monica says:

As an Italian mother bringing up a child in a foreign country, it is as challenging as you allow it to be. For me, it is extremely rewarding to raise a child with two cultures. I am proud and I only see advantages, benefits and rewards. Both our families are in Italy, so the biggest challenge is having to rely on ourselves and our own strengths alone to overcome any issue we might have to face. This makes us stronger and more resilient. My son is developing his own mixed identity, which is also lovely.

An Immersive Education

One of the most immersive ways to raise anti-racist kids is to bring them up as citizens of the world. And you don't even need a passport. In spite of leaders building walls and breaking unions, the world is more fluid than ever. I'm surprised when I hear English kids using Naija slang like '*no wahala*' (it means no worries), then I remember how we picked up Yiddish and Italian slang terms growing up. All across the globe, people of different backgrounds dance to azonto or salsa or ceilidh, swap the same YouTube memes, use chopsticks like it's second nature. The more we spread, the more we become each other.

I'm at a crowded breakfast spot, bashing away at my laptop and cursing the poor wi-fi. Then I see a young deaf boy with an iPad, talking to his dad in sign language over FaceTime. Sure, technology has its dark side. But it also connects us in ways our forefathers could never have imagined.

From when your children are young, be intentional about showing them a wider world. The Internet will take you anywhere, but a book or a film can take you further. As soon as they're old enough to read subtitles, watch a foreign film together. One that made a huge impression on me as a child was the 1983 movie *La Rue Cases-Nègres* (*Sugar Cane Alley*). It's an affecting coming-of-age flick featuring a young Black boy and his grandmother trying to break free from poverty on a plantation in Martinique. I'll never forget the colours, the characters, seeing a Black child in the central role. I had no idea where Martinique was on the map, but I wanted to know more. I loved the sound of the French Creole, the call and response '*Ye krik, Ye krak*', how familiar it was and how foreign at the same time.

The first subtitled film I watched with the boys was memorable for a different reason. *Zarafa* is a sweet animation about an African boy and his famous giraffe. Jed was still a toddler, barely able to sit through a movie. Ezra was gripped. There's a particularly sad moment when (spoiler alert) the giraffe's mum dies. Ezra was inconsolable. As he sobbed on my shoulder and told me how much he 'hated this film and why did you bring me, Mummy?' I did have second thoughts (and a very wet shirt). However, it was important to show the boys that rare glimpse of a hero who looked like them. Also, to show them how deeply you can become part of the story, even in a language you don't understand.

There's a lot of grumbling in some circles about foreigners who come to our country and refuse to learn our language. I invite you to free yourself from this colonial mindset, *osiso* (Igbo: quickly) and think global. In many London classrooms, kids might pick up Turkish, Urdu, Greek, Bengali, Somali, Yoruba, Cantonese or Slovak from their friends. Imagine how much more inclusive our communities would feel if we all learned to speak each other's native tongues.

I'm often embarrassed by how well people speak English in other countries, while I'm stumbling along with Google Translate. I have rusty French and Spanish from A-levels and an Igbo language app to practise with the boys. Our parents never spoke Igbo at home, so my siblings and I grew up without it. I regret missing out on conversations with my paternal grandmother because she spoke mostly Onitsha Igbo and I spoke mostly 'smile and nod'. Teach your child the language their grandparents speak, but also encourage them to keep trying, keep learning other tongues. Even a word or two in their language with a local shopkeeper, or with someone asking for directions, can brighten that person's day.

Imagine this: learn a sentence in another language every day and in 365 days, you'll be conversational. Did you know languages are like superpowers? Speaking two or more can boost anything from cognitive skills to future job opportunities. It can even keep Alzheimer's at bay. A child who speaks another language learns the simple truth that some things don't translate. In a world where so many of us feel misunderstood, we need more little humans who can appreciate nuance.

Blogger Michelle Chai says she plans to raise her future kids the way she was raised:

Being educated in the UK schooling system helped me to adopt more British habits, but at home I spoke Cantonese – it's my first language – and we ate Chinese food with chopsticks, we celebrated Chinese holidays. I want to raise them bilingual right from the offset, so they'll be able to speak to my side of the family and feel a real connection to one half of their unique identity.

Leave Your Comfort Zone

If you want to raise a child with a global mindset, you need to welcome new faces, places and cultures into your life. Pop into a Korean or Turkish supermarket for groceries, shop at a Ghanaian or Senegalese stall. Visit a Nigerian church service on Sunday (make sure you're dressed to the nines). Celebrate street festivals and cultural holidays. But don't treat it as a spectator sport. Immerse yourself, connect with real people, eat all the food. In London, you can eat your way around the globe in seven days. Or do a search online and try a variety of global recipes.

Take your kids to discover new neighbourhoods, find out how communities are constantly shifting and redefining themselves. Travelling is a lifetime education and you can start locally, with a trip to the library, museum, or theatre. A short day trip can help a child see life from a new angle. If you can afford it, take them overseas. Psychologists say that rather than throwing money at toys, we should invest in experiences like travelling. The benefits are countless – from becoming more confident and tuned in to other cultures, to enhancing empathy, humility and intelligence. When you go somewhere you don't speak the language, for instance, you learn to talk less and listen more. Your senses are heightened, your instincts are sharpened. You grow.

Travelling With Young Kids

People often say that going on holiday with children is never an actual break. Most of us need a holiday when we come back. For the average parent, going abroad with kids means doing all the same cooking, washing, shopping, feeding and bedtime routines, except in a foreign country. However, with a little research and planning, you can enjoy the trip of a lifetime.

I've been travelling with Ezra since he was nine months old and with Jed since he was just six months. We've been on long-haul trips where fellow passengers went out of their way to compliment us on our outstanding babies. We've also had hellish journeys on budget airlines, arriving to broken strollers and missing luggage. On one memorable flight, both kids came down with an infection. As the plane took off, one vomited and the bawling began. It didn't stop until touchdown. As we were about to land, the wailing hit siren level and one passenger shouted, 'Oh for FUCK'S sake!' At which point the other boy promptly turned and vomited all over me. To be fair, the man was mortified and apologised. He just couldn't help himself, any more than my babies could hold their screams.

I'm telling you this story to illustrate that, yes, travelling with children can be the stuff of therapy bills – yet I'm still encouraging you with all my heart to do it. Grab those kids and go. (Also, pack spare clothes for yourself, not just the little ones.)

Head to the shore and see the wonder in your baby's eyes when they catch sight of the ocean. The pain of sleep deprivation fades when you're awake for the most beautiful sunrise. Watching your kids blossom on holiday is magical. Sometimes the fussiest toddler will surprise you when they're away and try something like frog's legs or pickled cabbage or goat meat. You see them overcome some of their hang-ups, maybe dip their toes in the sea for the first time. I'll never forget the sight of my three-year-old, too afraid to get in our local pool, boldly riding a kayak out to sea with his dad in Corsica.

I have a sweet photo of the boys with three French kids in Nice whom they'd hung out with all day. Despite the language barrier, they had spent the whole afternoon laughing, chasing and playing in the park. Leave them to it and kids from any country can find common ground, anywhere in the world. My boys have made friends with children from a variety of nationalities, both overseas and on home turf. Sometimes all kids need is a football, the global circle of trust.

Travelling While Black

'But is it safe to go there?' some friends ask when we're planning a trip. 'What are they like about Black people?' These are things we must consider before we launch ourselves into new territory. Can I get there without issues? Will there be anybody like me? Is it safe for my family?

As a Black mother, the thought of dropping everything and roaming the globe with a knapsack and a map is laughable. This isn't to suggest Black people don't travel – far from it. My Igbo brethren go all over: you'll find Igbo communities everywhere from Atlanta, USA to Guangzhou, China. Companies like Blacks Abroad and Travel Noire help smooth the way for Black travellers to reach far-flung corners of the globe. It's just travelling can be more challenging when your skin tan is permanent.

I was heading to the US at 18, before I was naturalised as a Brit. I made the mistake of carrying my Nigerian passport in my hand as I moved through security, immigration and passport control. I was stopped at least five times by officials who took me aside to inspect my handbag, question what I was doing, where I was going and why. Apparently, I was a quadruple threat: Nigerian (criminal), single female (drug mule), African (economic migrant), Black (suspicious). The idea that I was simply a young girl on her gap year didn't seem to fly.

My sister was once visiting relatives in Atlanta when she was stopped at immigration. They ushered her into a separate room and strip-searched her. She was only 15. She said it was harrowing because they kept her for hours and she wasn't able to reach my uncle by phone. They insisted the face in her passport wasn't hers. (Side note: many Black women change hairstyles so frequently it's common not to look like their passport photos.) She was also accused of lying about her age as they thought she looked more mature. Funnily enough, when you compare her passport photo now and 20 years ago, she still looks the same age.

Once I came off a flight from Nigeria and all the passengers were sent into a closed room. Police arrived and set sniffer dogs on us. I sat there in a silent panic, praying nobody had put something in one of my bags.

Another friend says he's routinely interrogated every time he travels to and from the Caribbean. They've body-searched him, inspected his dreadlocks, threatened to deport him for no apparent reason. Most times, they pull him aside and 'chat' with him while they go through every single item on him. 'They say it's a random inspection,' he scoffs, 'but ain't nothing random about it.'

Nowadays, with my British passport, I pass through most airports without a hitch. However, the last time we visited Barcelona, we couldn't help noticing we were the only family picked to have our luggage opened and searched while everyone else was waved through.

It's hard when it happens in front of or to your kids. In July 2019, author Nikesh Shukla tweeted about being selected for extra checks at the airport and his daughter being forced to have a body search. 'Having to explain to a two-year-old what is happening and why a stranger is frisking her and what they are looking for and why it's us and no one else was really hard.'

We understand the need to keep everybody safe. But incidents like this are a horrible reminder for people of colour that our bodies – and even our children's bodies – will always be subject to scrutiny. If your child has questions about why you are stopped and searched, give a factual response according to their age. Even if you're raging mad, you don't want to frighten them. You can explain the rules for international travel and why everybody needs to show they can board a flight without hurting anybody else. When you have a cooler head, or if your child is older, you can talk about why people of certain ethnicities or religions get targeted for inspection. Be ready to answer questions and be open about how it makes you feel. No matter your child's age, it's a good time to talk about how not to judge a book by its cover. And also about touch and boundaries and when it's not ok for someone to invade your personal space.

Once you make it through the airport, you might have to contend with being in a country where Black people are an oddity. You are the object of stares, kids pointing fingers, strangers touching your hair or asking intrusive questions. On a recent holiday to Venice, Abiye said he could feel a certain edge in the air. He blamed it on a combination of Brexit, the rise of fascism and anti-immigrant sentiment. He made a point of stopping to talk with destitute Africans on the street and giving them spare cash.

My niece Vanessa travelled to southern Italy with some friends after graduation. They had several encounters with racism, the worst of which involved a bus driver refusing to let them get on the bus. He began hurling racist slurs at them

('Your skin looks like poo', etc.) and none of the other passengers intervened. Vanessa captured the whole thing on her Instagram stories.

Of the attitude back home, Monica says:

I feel Italians can be quite racist at times, because until recently they haven't seen many people from other races. Now that lots of people from Asia and Africa have arrived in Italy, the situation has changed and Italians are not at ease. This deeply saddens me, because I believe that growing up in a multicultural and multi-ethnic society broadens our minds.

I want my boys to be able to go wherever they please. But they need to be careful. They're keen to visit the States when Trump is no longer in charge. I have open conversations with them about the hazards of travelling as a Black male in a country where some say they are being hunted.

To my sons, I hope our travels inspire you to show up in your fullness, in as many destinations as possible. Avoid war zones and terrorist hotspots if you can, go off the beaten track if you must, but keep showing up. You might change somebody's world just by your presence. Visit Portugal and Bali and Hawaii and Iceland. But also visit Mali and Angola and Barbados and Saint Lucia. Places where you might find more familiar faces and feel a spiritual connection.

If you get the chance, take your children to your ancestral home. Some of my happiest memories with my kids were made in my birth country. The boys love it out there. All the colours, noises and flavours. Seeing so much prosperity, and income inequality, filled them with questions and an urge to make things better. The last Christmas we spent in Nigeria, before my mother died, is one of their best Christmases ever. A house crammed with family members, sleeping in a jumble on mattresses on my mother's bedroom floor, running everywhere barefoot. As we drove back to the airport, Ezra wept in my arms saying he didn't want to leave. Several months later, his grandmother passed away.

Whenever you can, take your children back to where their roots began. Take them home to see their elders before it's too late. Let them see a world where everybody knows them, everybody loves them.

Reframing Your World

As your child grows, take advantage of school trips or study-abroad programmes. When they're older, they might consider volunteering overseas. It can be a powerful and humbling experience to see how nearly half the world gets by on less than $5.50 a day. However, be mindful of the 'White saviour' approach. Case in point: TV reporter Stacey Dooley snapping photos with random African babies to promote her work with Comic Relief. This inevitably backfired as critics accused her of using human beings as props for her social media.

Raising a child with a global mindset means you have a responsibility to teach them they are not anybody's saviour and no country is their charity case. Some nations are wealthier than others, very often by virtue of the wealth they took from others. Even the richest nations have wealth distribution issues that need addressing. I talk to my kids about letters we get from school telling us to 'help the children of Africa'. I remind them we are children of Africa and we don't need help. We talk about ways to help children in need all over the world. How we should open our eyes and wallets to the homelessness and poverty in the UK. Don't let your child buy into that single story of Africa or Asia or South America as an entire continent in need of handouts. And for the most part, it's not charity, it's centuries of debt.

For children, being citizens of the world can be liberating but it can also feel overwhelming. As you learn more about the planet, your emotional investment and sense of responsibility grows, but so does your sense of helplessness. The refugee crisis, climate change, a virus turning into a pandemic . . . there are not enough lifetimes to fix this mess. Your kids might lie awake at night fretting over global warming, just as we used to worry about nuclear war. Just as we still worry.

I encourage my sons to focus on small things we can do to make a difference. Try to be a good neighbour, a good friend, a helpful member of your community. Do one kind thing for someone every day. Despite what the news tells us, I want my kids to believe that most people are decent at the core and want the best for each other.

Any time the boys got in a state when they were little, afterwards I would take them to a window. I'd ask them to look outside and tell me what they saw. A bird in a tree. Traffic below.

How people look smaller from up above. They would calm down fully as they became absorbed in what they were seeing. My goal was to take them outside of themselves for a while, so they could get a sense of perspective and realise nothing is as big or as bad as it seems. I didn't know it then, but I was practising the art of reframing. According to research, the happiest people on earth (the Danes, voted 40 years in a row) are masters of reframing.[1] Looking at experiences in a new way and seeking out a positive angle.

Adopting a global mindset helps you reframe your entire life. Encourage your kids to look out and remember how big the world is beyond their four walls, beyond whatever they're fretting about in that instant. It's not about you, tell them. There is so much more.

Here's another exercise. Take a map or a globe and look at it with your child. See how fine the lines are between countries, how small the lakes and oceans look against the palm of your hand. Imagine someone looking down on our planet from way out there in the galaxy, where we are a dot in existence. A mere blip in time. Imagine the distance between any of us is nothing at all.

• Talking Points

Q. We're thinking about a European tour this summer but as a Black family, we're concerned about what racism we might experience. Should we forget Europe and stick to Africa or the Caribbean instead?

A. The stress of 'travelling while Black' (and with kids) can be off-putting. However, don't let the racists win! We've had our share of unpleasant vibes and experiences in Europe; but we've also enjoyed some of our best trips there too. Before visiting Croatia, I had concerns about Eastern European anti-Blackness I'd perceived in press reports. While in Pula on holiday, I definitely stuck out like a sore thumb at several places; however, I never felt unwelcome or unsafe.

You should adopt a mindful-traveller approach as a Black family in Europe. Also, don't assume you won't have issues in Africa or the Caribbean. Bigotry comes in many packages. Take the opportunity to talk with your kids about what they might experience abroad and how you will handle anything negative. Be sure to have a good chat with your other half too, so you are both on the same page about how to respond to a racist incident.

Q. My eldest daughter leaves school this summer and is planning to volunteer for a charity in India. I'm so proud of her but I don't want her to come across as a 'White saviour' figure. What advice can we give her to avoid this?

A. Tell her to follow the White Saviour Barbie account on Instagram. It's a light-hearted and satirical take that will give her a fresh insight and a sense of perspective around this issue. I think it's a wonderful thing for anybody, especially a teenager, to volunteer their time and experience for the less fortunate. The important thing is that her attitude is not patronising or self-congratulatory. She should remember that every person she meets, no matter how poor or needy, is an individual with hopes, dreams, talents and desires. If she keeps her focus on serving rather than saving people, and on learning as much as she can from the experience, then she should be ok. Just remind her to always check her privilege and leave her ego at home.

Q. We don't have much money to travel overseas and we prefer to support local businesses and have stay-cations. But we still want to raise our children as citizens of the world. What other tips can you suggest?

A. There are plenty of ways to raise a global citizen without travelling. With so much access to other worlds via books, music, media, restaurants, movies and the big old Internet, you should never feel stuck in one spot. Why not create your own around the world virtual tour where you stop off at a different location every week or month. You can eat that country's food, read up on local history, visit an exhibition or museum, explore their traditional dress, watch a movie with subtitles, read a native author, learn some phrases in their language, keep up with what's happening politically . . . or brainstorm a list of other activities to try with your kids. Happy travels!

CHAPTER 16

Don't Feed the Monsters

We make our own monsters, then fear them for what they show us about ourselves.

Mike Carey, British author

I learned a lot about anger from my family. My husband and eldest both suffer from 'hanger' – that volatile mix of hunger and anger. In the early days, it shocked me how a skipped meal could flip one or the other from Jekyll into Hyde. I get grumpy when I'm hungry, but Abiye and Ezra turn into ravenous beasts. Nowadays, I can read the signs. It's always a relief when we realise the sky isn't falling; they just need a bite to eat. I have vivid memories of Ezra's rages as a toddler, when I'd send him to his bedroom only to hear him turning it upside down. 'I hate this family. I hate this room. I hate these books. I hate this bed. I hate this world. I hate everything!'

I couldn't help but chuckle as he ran out of things to rage about. Afterwards, we'd read *Angry Arthur*. It's a beautifully illustrated picture book about a boy named Arthur who becomes so angry it destroys the world and everything in it. What's left at the end of the book is Arthur, floating through space, wondering what made him so angry in the first place.

As parents, when our children get angry, we dismiss it as tantrums. We punish them with naughty steps and early bedtimes or we take away privileges and playthings. However, anger needs recognition. It's a voice crying out to be heard. Look for safe, physical outlets for your child's anger. A cushion to punch, a pillow to scream into, a bat against a balloon. Think of anger as energy that needs release, otherwise it can fester, shape-shift or erupt when you least expect it.

Hot Blooded

In my birth family, my mother was the hot one. She came from a household of 17 fiery sisters (her five brothers were generally more chill). I have memories of aunties breaking glasses over each other's heads and throwing each other down the stairs. These are fond memories, believe it or not, because they always made up afterwards. In fact, half of them are Bible warriors now. To this day, they can argue tooth and nail, but if anyone crosses them, they band together like the Dora Milaje (*Black Panther*'s Amazonian warriors). My mum and her sisters once beat up a man who had been punishing his wife with bruises behind closed doors. They were not to be trifled with.

When I was little, it felt like my mum could blow her top at any little thing. Nigerians call it 'sparking'. My mum could spark if you answered her the wrong way; sometimes all it took was a look. Over the years, she mellowed to match my dad's temperament. He never lost his cool in front of us. He was also more inclined to bottle stuff in. I am Daddy's girl; I too internalise my emotions. This does more harm than good. I have read that anxiety is anger turned inwards. A couple of years back, I sought therapy for anxiety. I had been angry at so many things for so long and it didn't gel with my shiny, happy persona. Instead, my nerves began to tangle and knot. Therapy sessions helped me unravel the sources and to understand the importance of giving my anger a voice.

My mother-in-law, Helen, is a psychotherapist specialising in anger management. She says anger is not something that needs to be quashed or set aside. It's a valid emotion that deserves as much attention as any other. What fascinated me was when Helen explained how sometimes in a relationship, the person who seems like the quiet one is masking their own anger. This can ignite the more heated personality, causing a raging fire neither can control.

Some days, it feels like the whole world is at boiling point. If you get sucked into the echo chambers of social media, it can be hard to emerge without feeling beaten down or bunched up. You walk around clenched, just daring somebody to say the wrong word, or look at you the wrong way. And as a person of colour, there are so many hostile spaces to navigate.

Why is everyone so angry? We are angry because people are hurting. We are angry because we feel helpless or guilty or scared. We are angry because no matter how loud we shout, nobody's listening. Because everybody's shouting and so few are making sense. We are angry because we don't want to acknowledge how vulnerable we are or how ignorant or how alone. We are angry because a handful of billionaires have taught us how to turn on each other. Because we are stuck in a cycle, caught in a web, we have forgotten how to switch off. We are angry because of words like privilege and supremacy. We are angry because we don't feel privileged, we don't feel supreme. We are angry because the right to opt out of being labelled is a privilege in itself. We are angry because tomorrow something will make us angrier than today. Because our children are dying in the street. Because our kids are asking questions and we are running out of things to say.

For Facebook executive Ebele, some conversations are just too difficult. 'My unarmed brother was murdered by police for walking down the street. It has devastated our family. But I have not been able to bring myself to tell the children how he died. They think it was a car accident.'

No Justice for Chinedu

On the day I celebrated my own brother's birthday, Ebele's brother Chinedu Okobi was tasered to death by US police in an unprovoked incident. They said he had been walking erratically through traffic and, when they tried to apprehend him, he lashed out. But he was unarmed and there's no evidence of him behaving violently or needing to be subdued by brute force. In movies, tasers are used for comic effect. In real life, they have caused thousands of deaths and injuries. Chinedu was tasered twice, sending him into cardiac arrest. His last words: 'Somebody please help me.'

Chinedu had a history of mental illness and his family had been concerned about him for some time. It was devastating for him to be killed in the streets by the very force sworn to protect its citizens. Yet for Black people in America, death by police has become an everyday hazard. There have been too many burials, not enough answers.

On the day Chinedu died, his father put out a message on Facebook asking if anybody had seen or heard from his son. I'm still haunted by that message because I imagine somewhere, deep inside, you never stop looking for your missing child.

Ebele and her husband, Richard, had left the States because of police brutality. They didn't want to raise their children in Trump's America, an environment where many believe Black people are being hunted. Then Ebele woke up on 3 October 2018 and her worst nightmare had come true. Chinedu was her younger brother, a poet, a devoted father, a beloved son. He called his mother 'sunshine'. He was the baby of the family.

The Okobis campaigned tirelessly for justice for Chinedu, while the San Mateo County police denied responsibility. His death was ruled as a 'homicide' and yet an inquest cleared the officers involved.

Every time I think of Chinedu, anger rises like a fist in my throat. Every time I celebrate my brother, I remember Chinedu and all the brothers and sisters who never made it.

Outrage Is a Monster

Some days, I'm so angry it feels like my head will explode. I can't take another gut-wrenching tragedy, another historical atrocity. I can't read one more news piece about a child being shut out or picked on or shot down. Another mother burying her baby. My head might blow up. My heart can't take it. Somebody stop the planet, pull the plug, let the oceans empty for ever.

Anger can feel overwhelming – but it isn't the enemy. Anger is a motivating force, an energy to harness for change. Anger raises its voice, writes letters that demand action, pickets against oppression. We need to separate anger from its cousins: rage and the weaker, more insidious outrage. Anger can be channelled, but rage is a wildfire and outrage is what fans it out of control.

We are living in the age of outrage. The Internet has always depended on the outrage of strangers. The armchair activist, fingers numb from Twitter spats. Outrage leaves us sluggish, stupefied, a monster soaking in its own fat. It is everybody in their feelings and nobody in their facts. Outrage leaves little space for compassion, for humour, for growth. Social media is rearing a generation of Angry Arthurs tearing shit up, losing sight of what made them so outraged in the first place.

One question parents ask me is how you tell your children about racism without filling them with too much anger, fear and dread? How do we teach about hate without breeding hate inside them too?

You have to tip the scales in favour of positive stories. Take a step back from all the rage and the outrage and look at things objectively. There's a popular theory that what you think about expands. What you feed, grows. If you're thinking about the colour purple, you start to notice it everywhere.

When I started writing this book, all of a sudden it felt like everybody was at odds with each other all the time. Like, oh my goodness, we're living in a race war – how do I arm my kids? And do we need to choose sides? My head began to throb. My heart was ready to combust.

I learned to practise self-care. To consume news in bite-sized pieces, or not at all. After a whole year of Brexit drama and a Christmas election, my husband and I decided to stop watching the news. One day, after the footie, the news was about to come on and Abiye switched it off just as the newsreader began with, 'The worst . . .'

'That's all you need to know about the news,' Abiye said. 'It's literally the worst. How can that be helpful to anybody?'

You can switch off the news cycle and still be switched on to the real world around you. Tip the scales in favour of hope. Follow inspirational stories, read blogs like 'The Happy Newspaper' that focus on good things happening. Spend time with people who do not live in thought prisons or huts thatched together with hate.

If your child is (rightly) angry about racial injustice, teach them how to use that anger wisely. Show them the benefits of positive activism, joining a protest march, signing up for humanitarian organisations. The power of sticking up for a friend. But don't let them rage, because that only stokes more rage. And try not to feed outrage either. Show your child how to step back from volatile encounters. Role-play situations, so they learn when to raise their voice, when to stand their ground, when to walk away.

Silence Is a Monster Too

However, I am not advocating silence. When we don't speak up on the things that matter, we lose our power; we lose our voices entirely. Silence can be toxic. In racial-justice movements, there is a saying: 'White silence is violence'. It speaks to the idea that passive racism – the kind that turns a 'colour-blind' eye to injustice and inequality – is a slow killer. There are far too many good, kind, decent people letting racism prevail.

During the Obama era, sociology professor Margaret A. Hagerman, author of *White Kids: Growing Up with Privilege in a Racially Divided America*, interviewed scores of children and uncovered a worrying new form of racial apathy. She spoke with White kids who believed the presence of a Black president in the White House meant racism was a thing of the past. Years later, the author interviewed children under the Trump presidency and found their apathy had taken a sinister turn. Children were aware of, even participating in racist language and behaviour, but they were far less likely to give two frogs about it. The narrative seemed to have shifted from 'I don't see racism, so I don't care' to 'I see racism, and I still don't care'.

I see racism, and I still don't care. I see people suffering and it makes no difference to me. It's scary to think that rising levels of racism and bigotry can turn kids into apathetic little creatures. The word apathy sounds innocuous. However, it is the antithesis of empathy. And without empathy, we are the lowest form of ourselves.

How many communities worldwide have been devastated by the monstrous swirl of fear and hate, rage and outrage, apathy and silence? As parents, we need to intervene by teaching our kids to challenge what society feeds them, to use their critical thinking skills and to consider the cost not of turning the other cheek, but of turning your face away . . .

Feed Kindness First

Far too many of us are operating in threat mode. We are not just angry, outraged or raging, we are overstimulated. The health fallout from this is intense. Studies show that for people of colour, the constant tension and stress from living in racist environments has devastating effects on wellbeing. It's not only the rising anxiety and depression levels, it's what's known as 'weathering' from micro-traumas that provoke a daily 'fight-or-flight' response. This creates a pile-up of ailments ranging from obesity and hypertension to premature birth. People of all complexions living in racially fractious areas have been shown to have higher mortality rates.[1] Racism harms everyone at every level.

There's an almond-shaped part of your brain that some say is where prejudice begins. Called the amygdala, it has been with us since pre-evolutionary times, helping sort the world and keep us safe. When your body senses danger, your amygdala fires up. It's because of your amygdala that your brain can suss out who's 'in-group' and who's 'out-group' in a fraction of a second. For early humans, this was useful if you came across a wild bear, for instance.

Studies show that one of the most effective ways of calming your amygdala down, and reducing unconscious prejudice, is by developing more empathy.[2] Sociologists refer to the 'contact hypothesis'. In other words, having meaningful and valuable contact with people in an 'out-group' helps build positive feelings about them. It's important to note that 'out-group' fear isn't only racial but can include gender, class, sexuality, sports team or any other characteristic that might create a sense of them vs us.

The beauty of the brain is that it is always changing, rewiring and adapting to its environment. Scientists call this neuroplasticity. I like to think of the brain as PlayDoh. You can help shape it to learn new skills, break old thought patterns and create new habits. This is exciting because it means even the most die-hard bigot can change. And did you know you can actually train your brain to be kinder? Neuroplasticity is most active in the first five years of life, so this is a great time to help your child develop new 'pathways of kindness' too.[3]

We've talked about racism as a socially transmitted disease, but here's the good news. Kindness is contagious too and it has the reverse effect. Not only that but kindness is good for your entire nervous system. The ability to act with empathy and compassion for someone else can switch on your parasympathetic nervous system, aka your 'resting mode'; this increases heart-rate variability, boosts your immune system, lowers high blood pressure.[4] Some doctors even believe it can help slow down the ageing process of our cells. Kindness changes how you respond to events. Just witnessing an act of kindness produces oxytocin, the love hormone, making you feel more connected to other people and boosting your desire to pay it forward. Kindness is the ultimate pick-me-up. And this goes for kids too.

The Art of Holding Space

One concept that has come to my attention lately is what therapists call holding space. This is something you can do when someone is in need, if they are hurting or grieving or need a listening ear. Instead of wading in with your opinions, solutions or experiences, just be a witness. Sit with them in their discomfort, even if it makes you uncomfortable too. Walk alongside them on their journey, but don't try to change their path. Remember, this moment is not about you. Offer support without judgment, resist the urge or the need to identify. Hold space. Sometimes that is all they need to pull through.

I believe every parent – when we are not too frazzled by the day's wear and tear – has practised holding space for their child. Every time we offer a loving face, a soft shoulder, a safe place to land. When we are simply present through their experiences.

We should teach our kids the importance of holding space for each other. Kids are naturally egotistical, so it's not easy, but it is an essential life lesson. It has an alchemic effect, transforming fury to understanding, helplessness to hope. You can even hold space when the monsters are raging because, after all, the monsters are a part of you. Just try not to feed them.

• Talking Points

Q. All this obsession with race and talking to kids about it makes me uncomfortable. Can't we all just move on? If you say feeding things makes them grow, surely we are only feeding racism by focusing on it all the time?
A. I'm not advocating focusing on race all the time. I do encourage having regular talks with your children and loved ones, keeping yourself abreast of what's happening in the wider world and being a lifelong learner in this area. You aren't feeding racism by helping yourself and your children understand and improve race relations through conversation, reading, action and observation. You are feeding change and growing yourself and your children as human beings.

Q. When I think about some of the racism my child and I have experienced, I'm consumed with emotional pain. Should I seek professional support or is that a sign of weakness?

A. One of the most powerful actions you can take for yourself, and for your community, is to raise your voice. Therapy can offer a safe space for you to do this, to speak your truth and feel heard. There is nothing weak about seeking professional counselling; in fact, it's an act of courage to open up and ask for help. Racism is one of the biggest factors affecting the mental health of people of colour, and children of colour often experience higher levels of anxiety, depression and other ailments. Finding racially-sensitive support for yourself and for your child can be an essential step in your healing journey.

Q. My son had a bad experience at a previous school and now he doesn't want to mix with White kids at all. What can I say to change his mind?

A. When I was little, my neighbour's dog bit me. For a while after, I was afraid of dogs even though we grew up with several. Luckily, I had one that I loved very much and so it never occurred to me to avoid dogs altogether. As I grew older, I got over my fear and continue to see most dogs as friendly. My point is that if you help your son to integrate with other White children, outside of the school where he suffered racist abuse, he will grow out of his immediate fear. Hang out with White families that you know and trust, join activity groups and youth clubs, find spaces where he's likely to mingle with a variety of children from different backgrounds. Also, make sure throughout he feels listened to and supported. Try to take things at his pace. You can encourage him, but this is his journey.

CHAPTER 17

Be Cool, Be Kind, Be You

*My wish for you is that you continue. Continue to be who and how you
are, to astonish a mean world with your acts of kindness.*

Maya Angelou, American writer

I talk a lot about coolness on my blog. It's one of my ultimate
values, which might sound strange, as in many ways, I'm the
opposite of cool. You'll find me typing this passage in a baggy
T-shirt and fluffy slippers, hair knotted in an old scarf, kettle
boiling for my hot-water bottle. I wrote a popular post a while
back, titled 'Is Parenthood the death of Cool?' It feels that way
most days. I mean, I remember dancing on tables in nightclubs
in New York, and nowadays, I'm all about the Netflix and
snooze. To be honest, I relish the memories, but I secretly prefer
this version of myself.

When I talk about coolness what springs to mind? Miles
Davis on a trumpet? John Travolta fondling his quiff? Clint
Eastwood in a poncho, spitting out a cigar stub and narrowing
his eyes? Sometimes coolness seems static, a freeze-frame

moment. Something you catch in a half-smile, a pair of Aviators, a stiff collar turned up. Other times, it's more emotive. A band of elderly musicians, jamming on a Havana beach. Frida Kahlo, brimming with too much everything beneath her monobrow.

My definition of cool is much simpler and more expansive than you might imagine. It is about doing your thing and letting others do theirs. Following your own rules without making a performance out of being a rule-breaker. Dancing to the beat of your own orchestra or talking drum or mixtape. It is about starting from a place of grace, while still having a laugh. It's about holding life lightly and enjoying the story because, after all, everything is material.

Be Cool

Let me tell you about two of the coolest people I ever knew. My dad, a child prodigy, so advanced for his years that some mistook him for a midget. A belly laugher and lover of the good life. He hung out with fellow cool cats in libraries and salons, swapping radical plans to remake Africa as a leading force on the planet. On the day he married my mother, he picked her up in his beaten-down Volkswagen, wearing flip-flops. After the registry, he asked if she had money for lunch and she burst into tears. Hardly romantic, but undeniably cool.

From politics to personal, my dad lived life on his own terms. He was ultra-cool after the first stroke, when he was paralysed on one side and gained a new set of wheels. He spent ten years in a wheelchair and, while it wasn't easy for him, he never lost his calm, his integrity, his sense of humour. I'll never forget flying into Enugu airport in the tiniest aeroplane beside my father's coffin. Throngs came out to mourn him and claim him as a son of the soil. An Igbo man and a true Nigerian. A gentleman from start to finish.

What my father taught me: everybody is worth your time, no matter who they are or where they come from. You can be an intellectual giant without making those around you feel small. If you are kind enough, and cool enough, you can get away with almost any form of self-expression. You can strut around in the Lagos heat wearing a Chairman Mao-style jacket, a winter scarf and golf shoes.

You can take a big traditional title and still be detribalised, pushing for a world without barriers, a nation without division. You can be a homebody and a bridge-builder at the same time. You can own your identity and always be ready to meet people where they are, as they are, without judgment.

You can bear the greatest pain with the utmost dignity.

My father always said he didn't care who we brought home – marry anybody, African, Indian, Inuit. It's little wonder that he married someone just as cool.

My mum was born into a prominent Owerri family, the eldest of 22 in a polygamous household. A gifted student, top of her class. When the civil war nearly tore her marriage apart, she stuck by my father. She helped Igbo women get back on their feet. She welcomed countless people to our home. She always fought your corner, always had a word to say in your favour. Nigeria's number-one fan. Like my dad, she could hang with anyone. Her friendships ranged from Heads of State to barely literate village women.

She wasn't just cool at heart – she looked the part. Fashion forward before her time, dark skinned before melanin was #blessed. At a period when smoking and drinking weren't acceptable for women in polite company, she would light up her Marlboros and sink her whisky with the best of them. Chatting up a storm until the early hours of the morning, eyes closed, one leg vibrating with some pent-up energy.

What I learned from my mother: you do not have to sit quietly in the corner; your expressions and opinions count. Especially as a woman of intellect in a male-dominated arena. Make your voice heard and take up space. No matter how bad things might look, you can always find a positive outlook and a kind word to say. Reaching out to people who might not have time for you ordinarily, just to check in on how they're doing, is worth its weight in gold.

You can be a mother figure to many and still be a mother to your own. You can be the sweetest person at heart and dish out the funniest insults.

You can look Death in the eye and tell him, not yet. You can decide to go peacefully in your sleep, with a smile on your face.

When you're a teenager, your parents strike you as anything but cool. Frankly, I thought mine were barmy. Dad in his fez caps and pink leisure suits spending his 'morning jog' on the sofa. Mum in her Rick James wigs and every shiny ornament on the planet beaded onto her top. Yet as you grow and discover who they are as individuals, their coolness shines through.

When I think about coolness, I think about my mum and dad. I also think of my boys who were born utterly cool. They taught me that coolness is innate, but it's also something you can pass on.

Whenever you are bringing up race or other sticky topics, having difficult conversations with children, friends and family, searching for common ground with a stranger ... here's a simple rule: be cool.

Be Kind

Coolness is directly related to kindness. Some say kindness is the new cool. It's everywhere, on movie taglines and social-media quotables. Kindness might seem a bit ineffective, like another word for nice. However, being kind is not the same as being nice. There is a history of nice people – nice women in particular – whose smiles were like razor blades, whose anger scorched their throats. Nice people who look the other way when someone is hurting. Niceness has a blandness to it – because it's a cover-up. There is so much going on behind that nice facade. Niceness is an act, whereas kindness takes action.

Kindness is a choice to go beyond your own and other people's limitations. It goes looking for the best in human beings. Don't confuse kindness with tolerance. In conversations around race, people often bring up that word 'tolerance' and it grates for any person of colour. Tolerance means endurance, suffering, something you bear. We don't want to be tolerated, we want to be treated with fairness, justice and humanity. Kindness does not suffer or cause others to suffer. Kindness means no harm. Kindness is intentional, always. It is bigger than you or me – because we are all in it together.

Kindness does not mean silencing or sitting on your hands. Often the kindest thing to do is to speak your truth and let your heart be known. It is the way you speak that truth, being considerate about the impact of your words. Kindness calls you out without poking at your wounds. It sits with you in all your vulnerability and your human weakness. In every interaction, how you think about people and how you move through the world, putting kindness first serves everybody.

It's not always easy. Sometimes anger without kindness feels right in the heat of the moment. Sometimes criticism and mockery are the easiest responses. I teach my boys to practise doing one kind thing every day, because kindness is a practice, not something that happens overnight. I do believe some people are born with kindness at their essence.

I believe racism is one of the deepest, most destructive forms of self-hatred. It is taking a part of yourself, your own species, and doing whatever you can to debase it because something in you feels lacking. Maybe if you were kinder to yourself, you would be kinder to others. Maybe if we raise our children to treat themselves with the utmost kindness, we can shape a more compassionate world. Because kindness is self-care, and as we've learned, self-care is good for everyone.

Be You

Being kind to yourself and being true to yourself go hand in hand. If you are fully showing up as who you are meant to be in this world, kindness for others flows naturally. You become effortlessly cool. I believe this is who we are at our core.

If there's anything I hope you've taken from this book, it's that we are all part of an incredible, evolving story. And in my opinion, the miracle of diversity is not about race but individuality. It blows my mind that each of us is totally unique; not even twins share the same fingerprints. When I walk down the street, I pay attention to the faces I pass along the way. Each one with a different way of looking at life, a whole history behind them, an entire world spinning in one human being.

When I interviewed people for this book, I finished with the same question each time: what is it you love about your ethnicity? I thought I'd round off with some of my favourite answers. But before I go, this is my invitation to you, dear reader, to keep talking, keep learning, keep engaging with your children on race, culture and identity. Keep walking this journey in the spirit of kindness. Keep holding space for one another – and for your children – however that looks for you. I hope you feel empowered to be braver, cooler and more compassionate with people like you and people who are nothing like you. I hope you raise children who are cool, kind and utterly themselves too.

Final Question: we talk about the challenges, but what is your favourite thing about your ethnicity? What do you think are the advantages of being who you are?

Tinuke: 'I love the richness of Black culture. I love the depth and breadth of what being Black entails. I'm a Dominican Nigerian raised in England. My children are half-Jamaican. Our experiences and understanding of Blackness are all different. I can't really place into words what I love about being Black. It's who I am and I love it entirely. It's a shame that Blackness is still used as a weapon to make people feel "othered" when it's something that should be celebrated.'

Nat: 'I honestly love being a Londoner. I'm so grateful to have been born in this city, because I know where my family comes from – a little Czech village on the Czech border. I'm so glad they chose London. And that I was born in this era. The diversity of the city is what gives so much richness to my life. I came to London as a teenager and I found such a mix of people who felt the same as I did. I'm really grateful to raise my child here. If I think about myself as anything, it's as a Londoner first.'

Timil: 'Race may be a construct, but Blackness is a spiritual experience. Blackness is equal parts creativity, divinity and resilience. Overall, I think our boys look to us to know who they are. We celebrate so much of Black (American) and

Nigerian culture in our home, and our hope is they not only equate Blackness with joy, but also with pride.'

Monica: 'I love being Italian but embracing other cultures and languages – as I have done over the course of my life – has made me lose a bit of my "Italianity" to be more a world person. As a result, I feel a much better, tolerant, warm and mindful individual who is at ease in every environment. On 21 September 2019, I was chosen by the Mayor Sadiq Khan to represent Italy in the first public EU Settlement ceremony at City Hall during the "We are all Londoners" event. As my name and my achievements were read out loud in front of 350 Londoners, I was incredibly emotional. I know that I have belonged to the London DNA even before arriving here.'

Rachel: 'I thank the family I was born into that I have an innate pride in where I come from. And I think that was instilled in me by my grandparents. To feel that my culture and family were important. I grew up surrounded by different generations, uncles and aunties. That for me was the foundation of being a kind, decent human being. I've always wanted to expose my kids to the different age groups in the family. In the West, it's very much about the nuclear family. But the older I get, it really takes a village. I love that I grew up surrounded by so much love from every single auntie and uncle, I don't even know how closely they were related to me. But they were family. They loved us and looked after us.'

Ebele: 'I love EVERYTHING about being Black. I love the community, the different ways of being Black across the

diaspora. I LOVE African-American culture and the defi-
ance and joy of it surviving despite the staggering brutality
of the methods used to try to crush it. I love the arrogance
of Nigeria. I love the food across the diaspora, the music,
the clothing, the art, the culture, the literature, the
STORIES. I love the hair, the SWAGGER. The way there
are millions of ways to be Black. The way you can find
community even in the most random places. The comedy
– there is no one funnier than Black people everywhere. I
love how clothing fits us, and how our men like women with
padding. I love starting a job and seeing another Black
person and doing that thing where you say, "Sis!!! I SEE
you!!" with your eyes and no one else in the room knows
what's going on and then you have their back for ever when
some bullshit goes down (because there will always be
bullshit going down). I love how Black fathers can be with
their children. I love how we find joy and poetry and music
in the midst of unbearable pain and how we can make a
meal out of scraps. I just wish we didn't have to so often.'

Vicki: 'I adore that people think I'm from so many countries,
I think it makes me relatable to so many. I'm stopped in
Paris by tourists asking for directions, asked if I'm South
Asian, Lebanese, Israeli, Brazilian, Spanish, Italian,
Moroccan, Tunisian, Latin American to name just a few.
It's a great conversation starter and has seen me embraced
over the years in many countries on my travels. I've made
great friends through those initial conversations and people
assuming I'm from their own country of origin.'

Shanthi: 'Being so mixed I have a unique vantage point. I know what it's like to be loved at the level of family by many different races. Ultimately, race is one surface aspect of identity. The main thing is to be secure and confident in oneself and to think of identity in a holistic way. True identity is spiritual and beyond race, gender, sexuality and the like.'

Lekia: 'The way I think, the way I see the world, the way I'm raising my daughter. The most important attribute I believe a girl can have in the era we live in now is true self-confidence. The kind of confidence that defies trends and people's opinions, the kind of confidence that is truly comfortable in one's own skin, not the popular skin, not the skin that people fit you in, but your own.'

Natalie: 'Despite everything I've been through, I can't imagine being someone else, nor would I not want to be Black, even with everything that comes with it. I don't know that I have a favourite thing per se about my ethnicity, possibly because I've just not ever really thought about it, but I love my rich culture and history, the Jamaican zest for life and attitude that, incidentally, mixed perfectly with my Irish upbringing as culturally, they have a similar attitude. I wouldn't be who I am and doing what I do without what has come with it. It's brought me deep empathy, compassion, tolerance and sensitivity. After spending a lot of my life feeling bad about these, plus a sense of being an outsider, I've come to recognise that they're part of my superpower. I hope that answers the question!'

• Talking Points

Q. I teach my kids to be kind, but what if they're facing a bully or a racist? Wouldn't kindness just be encouraging the bad behaviour?

A. Don't mistake kindness for weakness. Letting bad behaviour persist is far from kind. It doesn't help the victim or the perpetrator. What is really kind is seeing the human face behind any ugly words or actions and making an effort to empathise with that human. This means first standing up for yourself or someone being bullied as people who are deserving of kindness and humanity. When a child learns to see an attacker – a racist or a bully – as just another human who makes mistakes, it can make them braver in how they respond.

Q. What do you mean by 'be you'? Isn't too much focus on individuals part of the problem? Surely we should teach our kids more about tolerance and cooperation and community?

A. Our first true act of love as humans is learning to love ourselves. If you don't know how to love yourself, how can you truly love anybody else? If you cannot show up fully as yourself in this world, how can you show up for others who might depend on your skills, talents and resources? What the world needs is people who are so happy in their own skin, so delighted with who they are, that they never feel a sense of lack or envy or insecurity around others. Imagine a world in which people didn't hate on each other for resources, looks or abilities. Just imagine.

Q. What about teaching our kids to be brave? Isn't courage the most important thing?

A. Courage is important, absolutely. However, you can't teach a child courage any more than you can teach them hope. Talking a child into bravery is one thing, but true bravery comes from stepping out of your comfort zone and doing things that unsettle you, or downright terrify you. Bravery is also about doing the kind thing even when others don't expect it. It's about keeping your cool when everyone around you is losing their shit. It's about being your whole self in a world that wants to break you down into tiny little parts. These are acts of courage, so that is what I teach my kids and what I hope to pass on to anyone who reads this book. Be cool, be kind, be you. That is the bravest thing you can do.

Further Reading

A selection of books with strong BAME characters and books celebrating diversity and self-acceptance.

Classic Multicultural Books
The Snowy Day by Ezra Jack Keats (Puffin Books) [Ages 2–5]
Handa's Surprise by Eileen Browne (Scholastic/Walker Books) [Ages 4–7]
Roll of Thunder, Hear My Cry by Mildred D. Taylor (Penguin) [Ages 11–16]
Things Fall Apart by Chinua Achebe (Penguin Classics) [Ages 13+]

Multicultural Books for Younger Readers
Everywhere Babies by Susan Meyers (Houghton Mifflin) [Ages 1–4]
Fruits by Valerie Bloom (Macmillan Children's Books) [Ages 1–4]
Baby Goes To Market by Atinuke (Walker Books) [Ages 1–5]
Please, Baby Please by Spike Lee and Tonya Lewis Lee (Little Simon) [Ages 2–5]
Max and the Tagalong Moon by Floyd Cooper (Puffin) [Ages 3–7]

Multicultural Books for Ages 7–12
Jaden Toussaint: The Greatest by Marti Dumas (Plum Street Press) [Ages 6–11]
One Crazy Summer by Rita Williams-Garcia (Harper Collins Children's Books) [Ages 8–12]
The Boy at the Back of the Class by Onjali Rauf (Orion Children's Books) [Ages 8–11]
Ghost by Jason Reynolds (Knights Of) [Ages 10+]
Artichoke Hearts by Sita Brahmachari (Macmillan Children's Books) [Ages 11+]

Multicultural Books for Teens/Young Adults
Children of Blood and Bone by Tomi Adeyemi (Macmillan Children's Books)
Dear Martin by Nic Stone (Simon & Schuster)
Noughts & Crosses by Malorie Blackman (Penguin)
Ghost Boys by Jewell Parker Rhodes (Orion Children's Books)
To All the Boys I've Loved Before by Jenny Han (Scholastic)
The Hate U Give by Angie Thomas (Walker Books)
The Crossover by Kwame Alexander (Andersen Press)

Books Celebrating Diversity
Looking for Lord Ganesh by Mahtab Narsimhan (Lantana Publishing) [Ages 3–7]
Suki's Kimono by Chieri Uegaki (Kids Can Press) [Ages 3–8]
Sesame Street: We're Different, We're the Same by Bobbi Kates (Random House) [Ages 3–8]
Under My Hijab by Hena Khan (Lee & Low Books) [Ages 4–7]
Julian is a Mermaid by Jessica Love (Walker Books) [Ages 4–9]
Amazing Grace by Mary Hoffman (Frances Lincoln) [Ages 5–8]
The Name Jar by Yangsook Choi (Dragonfly Books) [Ages 5–8]

Books Exploring History
The Story of Ruby Bridges by Robert Coles (Scholastic USA) [Ages 4–8]
The Undefeated by Kwame Alexander (Andersen Press) [Ages 5–7]
Little Leaders: Bold Women in Black History by Vashti Harrison (Puffin) [Ages 5–7]
Hidden Figures by Margot Lee Shetterly (William Collins) [Ages 12+]

Books Exploring Mixed Heritage
Mixed: A Colourful Story by Arree Chung (Macmillan Children's Books) [Ages 3–5]
Marisol McDonald Doesn't Match by Monica Brown (Children's Book Press) [Ages 4–7]
Mixed Me by Taye Diggs (Feiwel & Friends) [Ages 4–8]
Wing Jones by Katherine Webber (Walker Books) [Ages 12+]

Books Celebrating Hair
I Love My Hair! by Natasha Anastasia Tarpley (Little Brown and Company) [Ages 2–3]
My Hair by Hannah Lee (Faber & Faber) [Ages 2–5]
The Mega Magic Hair Swap! by Rochelle Humes (Studio Press) [Ages 3–5]
Crown: An Ode to the Fresh Cut by Derrick Barnes (Denene Millner Books) [Ages 3–8]
Hair Love by Matthew Cherry (Puffin) [Ages 5–7]

Books Celebrating Skin Tones
Who Do I See in the Mirror? by Vese Aghoghovbia Aladewolu (Philly & Belle Publishing) [Ages 0–6]
All the Colors We Are by Katie Kissinger (Redleaf Press) [Ages 3–7]
Sulwe by Lupita Nyong'o (Puffin) [Ages 3–7]
The Skin You Live In by Michael Tyler (Chicago Children's Museum) [Ages 4–8]
Genesis Begins Again by Alicia Williams (Simon & Schuster) [Ages 9–13]

Books for Global Citizens
Sleep Well, Siba and Saba by Nansubuga Nagad Isdahl (Lantana Books) [Ages 3–7]
This Is How We Do It: One Day in the Lives of Seven Kids from Around the World by Matt Lamothe (Chronicle Books) [Ages 5–8]
Islandborn by Junot Diaz (Rock the Boat) [Ages 5–8]
Persepolis by Marjane Satrapi (Vintage) [Ages 13+]

Books on Kindness and Self-Acceptance
The Girls by Lauren Ace, illustrator Jenny Lovlie (Caterpillar Books) [Ages 3–6]
I Am Enough by Grace Byers (Harper Collins) [Ages 4–8]
I Can Do Hard Things: Mindful Affirmations for Kids by Gabi Garcia (Skinned Knee Publishing) [Ages 5–11]
Wonder by R.J. Palacio (Corgi Children's) [Ages 9–11]

Multicultural Book Websites
The Brown Bookshelf thebrownbookshelf.com
Knights Of knightsof.media
Lantana Books lantanapublishing.com
Lee and Low Books leeandlow.com
We Need Diverse Books weneeddiversebooks.org

Useful Websites and Organisations
The Conscious Kid theconsciouskid.org
Mixed Up Mama mixedracefamily.com
Teaching Tolerance tolerance.org
Embrace Race embracerace.org
Raising Race Conscious Children raceconscious.org
Kick Racism out of Football kickitout.org
Check out Uju's blog at babesabouttown.com

References

Preface

1 Tatum, Beverly Daniel, *Why Are All the Black Kids Sitting Together in the Cafeteria? And Other Conversations About Race*, Basic Books, Parts I, III & V, 1997.

Introduction

1 Fowler, James H. and Christakis, Nicholas A., 'Dynamic spread of happiness in a large social network: longitudinal analysis over 20 years in the Framingham Heart Study', *British Medical Journal*, 4 December 2008; https://www.sciencedaily.com/releases/2008/12/081205094506.htm

Whose Child Is That?

1 Bressan, Paola, 'Why babies look like their daddies: Paternity uncertainty and the evolution of self-deception in evaluating family resemblance', *Acta Ethologica*, 1 February 2002; https://www.researchgate.net/publication/225624457_Why_babies_look_like_their_daddies_Paternity_uncertainty_and_the_evolution_of_self-deception_in_evaluating_family_resemblance
2 'Children interrupt BBC News interview – BBC News', Professor Robert Kelly interview, YouTube, 10 March 2017; https://youtu.be/Mh4f9AYRCZY

How Kids See Colour

1 Russell, James, Gee, Brioney and Bullard, Christina, 'Why do young children hide by closing their eyes? Self-visibility and the developing concept of self', *Journal of Cognition and Development* 13, no. 4, 2012: 550–76.
2 Kelly, David J., Quinn, Paul C., Slater, Alan M., Lee, Kang, Gibson, Alan, Smith, Michael, Ge, Liezhong and Pascalis, Olivier, 'Three-month-olds, but not newborns, prefer own-race faces', *Developmental Science* 8, no. 6, 2005: 31–6.
3 Vogel, Margaret, Monesson, Alexandra and Scott, Lisa S, 'Building biases in infancy: The influence of race on face and voice emotion matching', *Developmental Science* 15, no. 3, 2012: 359–72.
4 Qian, Miao K., Quinn, Paul C., Heyman, Gail D., Pascalis, Olivier, Fu, Genyue and Lee, Kang, 'A long-term effect of perceptual individuation training on reducing implicit racial bias in preschool children', *Child Development* 90, no. 3, 2019: e290–305.
5 Winship, Lyndsey, ' "That took long enough!" Black ballerinas finally get shoes to match their skin', *Guardian*, 1 April 2019; https://www.theguardian.com/stage/2019/apr/01/pointe-shoes-black-ballet-ballerinas-dancers
6 Neeske, Alexander and Costandius, Elmarie, 'The "human colour" crayon: investigating the attitudes and perceptions of learners regarding race and skin colour', *Education as Change* 21, no. 1, 2017: 113–36.
7 Crawford, Nicholas G., Kelly, Derek E., Hansen, Matthew E. B., Beltrame, Marcia H., Fan, Shaohua, Bowman, Shanna L., Jewett, Ethan, et al., 'Loci associated with skin pigmentation identified in African populations', *Science* 358, no. 6365, 2017: eaan8433 (Sarah Tishkoff study).

Conversations About Race

1 Stats on Black boy exclusions, stop and search, crime and unemployment via Gov.UK Ethnicity Facts and Figures https://www.ethnicity-facts-figures.service.gov.uk/
2 Goff, Phillip Atiba, Jackson, Matthew Christian, Lewis Di Leone, Brooke Allison, Culotta, Carmen Marie and DiTomasso, Natalie Ann, 'The essence of innocence: consequences of dehumanizing Black children', *Journal of Personality and Social Psychology* 106, no. 4, 2014: 526.

The First Time

1 'The only type of bullying schools must record is racist bullying', Asking to See Your Child's Record, Bullying UK/Family Lives https://www.bullying.co.uk/bullying-at-school/asking-to-see-your-child-s-school-record/
2 Marsh, Sarah and Mohdin, Amana, 'Record number of UK children excluded for racist bullying', *Guardian*, 30 November 2018; https://www.theguardian.com/education/2018/nov/30/record-number-of-uk-children-excluded-for-racist-bullying
3 'Children whitening skin to avoid racial hate crime, NSPCC finds', BBC, 30 May 2019; bbc.co.uk/news/uk-48458850
4 Trent, Maria, Dooley, Danielle G. and Dougé, Jacqueline, 'The impact of racism on child and adolescent health', *Pediatrics* 144, no. 2, 2019: e20191765.

Under the Skin

1 Dovidio, Jack, F. and Gaertner, Sam, L., 'Color Blind or Just Plain Blind', *Nonprofit Quarterly*, winter 2005.
2 Sue, Derald Wing, 'Racial Microaggressions in Everyday Life – Implications for Clinical Practice', published in 2007 in the *American Psychologist* (vol. 2, no. 4).
3 West, Keon, 'Testing hypersensitive responses: Ethnic minorities are not more sensitive to microaggressions, they just experience them more frequently', *Personality and Social Psychology Bulletin* 45.11, 2019: 1619–32.
4 Steele, Claude, 'A Threat in the Air: How Stereotypes Shape Intellectual Identity and Performance', *American Psychologist* 52, June 1997: 613–29.
5 McKenzie, Keshia E., full transcript of Toni Morrison's speech 'A Humanist View', https://www.mackenzian.com/wp-content/uploads/2014/07/Transcript_PortlandState_TMorrison.pdf. From Portland State University's Oregon Public Speakers Collection: "Black Studies Center public dialogue. Pt. 2," May 30, 1975 https://soundcloud.com/portland-state-library/portland-state-black-studies-1. Part of the Public Dialogue on the American Dream Theme, via Portland State University Library https://pdxscholar.library.pdx.edu/orspeakers/90/
6 Ellis, Chet, 'The Sound of Silence', https://www.westport-news.com/news/article/You-have-two-choices-being-a-black-person-in-13740290.php

Mixed

1 Livingston, Gretchen, 'The rise of multiracial and multiethnic babies in the US', Pew Research Center, 6 June 2017.
2 Posel, Deborah, 'What's in a name? Racial categorisations under apartheid and their afterlife', *TRANSFORMATION-DURBAN-*, 2001: 50–74.
3 Markle, Meghan, 'I'm More than an "Other"', *Elle* magazine, July 2015, https://www.elle.com/uk/life-and-culture/news/a26855/more-than-an-other/

History Lessons

1 FRONTLINE, *A Class Divided*, 26 March 1985, on PBS website https://www.pbs.org/wgbh/frontline/film/class-divided/
2 Gould, Stephen Jay, 'The geometer of race', *Discover* 15, no. 11, 1994: 65–9.
3 Menand, Louis, 'Morton, Agassiz, and the origins of scientific racism in the United States', *Journal of Blacks in Higher Education* 3, 2001: 110–13.
4 Legacies of British Slave-Ownership, UCL Department of History, https://www.ucl.ac.uk/lbs/
5 Soyei, Sarah, 'The Barriers To Challenging Racism And Promoting Race Equality In Education In England's Schools' – Show Racism the Red Card.
6 Oshiro, Brian, 'Encourage critical thinking with 3 questions', 28 February 2019, TEDxXiguan https://youtu.be/0hoE8mtUS1E
7 LaPlante, Logan, 'Hackschooling makes me happy', 12 February 2013, TEDxUniversity of Nevada https://youtu.be/h1lu3vtcpaY

E Is for Equality

1 'Teach Children about Their Human Rights in Schools, 29 January 2019, BBC Wales; https://www.bbc.co.uk/news/uk-wales-47031262
2 https://downloads.unicef.org.uk/wp-content/uploads/2019/10/UNCRC_summary-1_1.pdf?_ga=2.245427012.154913266.1588279296-1520313033.1588176095
3 Ward, L. Monique, Aubrey, Jennifer Stevens, 'Watching Gender: How Stereotypes in Movies and on TV Impact Kids' Development', 2017, Common Sense Media.

References

Bananas in Public

1 Kandola, Professor Binna, 'Old-Fashioned and Modern Racism in Football', 31 January 2018, Huffington Post, https://www.huffingtonpost.co.uk/entry/old-fashioned-and-modern-racism-in-football_uk_5a6b16fee4b0609b0bf05eb0
2 'Match Football Hate Crime Up by 47%', 19 September 2019, the Professional Footballers' Association, https://www.thepfa.com/news/2019/9/9/match-football-hate-crime-up-by-47
3 'Football Racism: Monkey Chants Aimed at Children', 6 May 2019, BBC News; https://www.bbc.co.uk/news/uk-england-leicestershire-48093032
4 Reijmer, Manju, 'How Disney's new *Jungle Book* corrects for years of troubling racial undertones', *The Week*, 14 April 2016.
5 Hillary Monahan @Hillary Monahan (3 July 2019); https://twitter.com/hillarymonahan/status/1146551030135558145?lang=en
6 Hannah Palframan @HannahPalframan, 4 July 2019; https://twitter.com/HannahPalframan/status/1146710113824194560?ref_src=twsrc%5Etfw
7 'Belgian newspaper faces backlash for picture of the Obamas as apes', 24 March 2014, MSNBC.com, http://www.msnbc.com/the-last-word/belgian-newspaper-depicts-obamas-apes
8 'Race hate crimes against children reach 3 year high', 28 May 2019, NSPCC, https://www.nspcc.org.uk/what-we-do/news-opinion/race-hate-crimes-against-children-reach-3-year-high/
9 Okolosie, Lola, 'Racial abuse in the playground? That's just England in 2019', *Guardian*, 31 May 2019, https://www.theguardian.com/commentisfree/2019/may/31/racial-abuse-playground-schools-racism
10 Griffith, Joanne, 'Josephine Baker: From Exotic Dancer to Activist, 31 December 2014, BBC Culture, http://www.bbc.co.uk/culture/story/20141222-from-exotic-dancer-to-activist

Please, Don't Touch My Hair

1 Sherrow, Victoria, *Encyclopedia of Hair: A Cultural History*, Greenwood Publishing Group, 2006.
2 De Leon, Michelle and Chikwendu, Denese, 'More than just Hair', Hair Equality Report 2019, World Afro Day.
3 'Jamelia: I wanted to look like my idols', 14 September 2018, World Afro Day, BBC News.
4 MacFarlane, Jessica, Tropp, Linda R. and Goff, Phillip Atiba, 'The Good Hair Study: Explicit and implicit attitudes toward Black women's hair', retrieved 13 February (2017): 2018.
5 Holmes, Saxter, 'Update: Yes, A "Redskin" Does, In Fact, Mean the Scalped Head of a Native American, Sold, Like a Pelt, for Cash', *Esquire* magazine, 18 June 2014.

303

What's in a Name?

1 Dickerson, Jessica, 'Why Uzo Aduba Wouldn't Change Her Nigerian Name For Acting', 26 June 2014, HuffPost Black Voices.
2 'David Oyelowo's Dad Mispronounces Oprah's Name', 23 December 2014, *The Tonight Show* with Jimmy Fallon, YouTube https://youtu.be/5A_X2sOR5HA
3 'Emilio Estevez on Why He Didn't Take The Sheen Last Name & "Mighty Ducks" Popularity', 26 April 2019, Talk Stoop, YouTube. https://youtu.be/9D5SHA0fRRY
4 Carneiro, Pedro, Lee, Sokbae and Reis, Hugo, 'Please call me John: Name choice and the assimilation of immigrants in the United States, 1900–1930', *Labour Economics* 62, 2020: 101778.
5 Goldstein, Joshua R. and Stecklov, Guy, 'From Patrick to John F. ethnic names and occupational success in the last era of mass migration', *American Sociological Review* 81, no. 1, 2016: 85–106.
6 Gerdeman, Dina, 'Minorities who "Whiten" job resumes get more interviews', *Harvard Business School: Working Knowledge*, 2017.
7 Carlsson, Magnus and Rooth, Dan-Olof, 'Evidence of ethnic discrimination in the Swedish labor market using experimental data', *Labour Economics* 14, no. 4, 2007: 716–29.
8 Edo, Anthony, Jacquemet, Nicolas and Yannelis, Constantine, 'Language skills and homophilous hiring discrimination: Evidence from gender and racially differentiated applications', *Review of Economics of the Household* 17, no. 1, 2019: 349–76.
9 'Foreign names impact chance of getting an apartment viewing', 9 June 2019, Swiss Info https://www.swissinfo.ch/eng/discrimination_foreign-names-impact-chance-of-getting-an-apartment-viewing/45019430

Different Shades of Beauty

1 Mishra, Neha, 'India and colorism: The finer nuances', *Washington University Global Studies Law Review*, 14, 2015: 725.
2 Nelson, Dean, 'Fair-skinned Indian women paid £1000 extra to be surrogates', New Delhi, 25 October 2012, *Telegraph*, https://www.telegraph.co.uk/news/worldnews/asia/india/9633142/Fair-skinned-Indian-women-paid-1000-extra-to-be-surrogates.html
3 Patel, Ritesh K., 'A conjoint analysis of consumer preferences for fairness creams among small towns located near Ahmedabad city', *Galaxy International Interdisciplinary Research Journal* 2, no. 3, 2014: 12–29.
4 Global Industry Analysts, Inc., 2009b., 'Skin lighteners: A global strategic business report (Report Code MCP-6140)'.

References

5 MaGee, Ny, 'Disturbing Clip of Black Woman Having Skin Peeled (Bleaching) in Bathtub Goes Viral [WATCH]', 26 November 2019, Lee Bailey's EurWeb. com, https://eurweb.com/2019/11/26/disturbing-clip-of-black-woman-having-skin-peeled-bleaching-in-bathtub-goes-viral-watch/

6 Fact Sheet: 'Mercury in Skin Lightening Cosmetics', Mercury Policy Project http://mercurypolicy.org/wp-content/uploads/2010/06/skincreamhg-factsheet_may31_final.pdf

7 Ben-Zeev, Avi, Dennehy, Tara C., Goodrich, Robin I., Kolarik, Branden S. and Geisler, Mark W., 'When an "educated" Black man becomes lighter in the mind's eye: Evidence for a skin tone memory bias', *Sage Open* 4, no. 1, 2014: 2158244013516770.

8 'Children whitening skin to avoid racial hate crime, charity finds', *Guardian* , 30 May 2019, https://www.theguardian.com/society/2019/may/30/children-whitening-skin-to-avoid-racial-hate-charity-finds

9 Bergner, Gwen, 'Black children, White preference: Brown v. Board, the doll tests, and the politics of self-esteem', *American Quarterly* 61, no. 2, 2009: 299–332.

10 *The Doll Test: The Birth of Self Hate,* documentary by Darrel Blake, 2019.

11 Feinman, Saul, 'Trends in Racial Self-Image of Black Children: Psychological Consequences of a Social Movement', *Journal of Negro Education* 48, no. 4, 1979: 488–99.

12 Lupita Nyong'o on Twitter: 'Brown Skin Girl. Thank you @Beyonce for this gift!' 19 July 2019, https://twitter.com/lupita_nyongo/status/1152269165 534707713?lang=en

Books Will Save the World

1 Centre for Literacy in Primary Education, 'Reflecting Realities – Survey of Ethnic Diversity in UK Children's Books', July 2018.

2 Cooperative Children's Book Center, 'Publishing statistics on children's books about people of color and First/Native Nations and by people of color and First/Native Nations authors and illustrators', 2017.

3 Matthews, J. S., Kizzie, K. T., Rowley, S. J. and Cortina, K., 'African Americans and boys: Understanding the literacy gap, tracing academic trajectories, and evaluating the role of learning-related skills', *Journal of Educational Psychology*, *102*(3), 2010, 757.

4 Mar, Raymond A., Oatley, Keith and Peterson, Jordan B., 'Exploring the link between reading fiction and empathy: Ruling out individual differences and examining outcomes', *Communications* 34, no. 4, 2009: 407–28.

Babes in the City

1 Badshah, Nadeem, 'Knife crime hits record high in England and Wales, *Guardian*, 17 October 2019, https://www.theguardian.com/uk-news/2019/oct/17/knife-hits-new-record-high-in-england-and-wales
2 *Last Whites of the East End*, aired on BBC1, 24 May 2016.
3 Easton, S. and Pryce, G. B., 'Not so welcome here? Modelling the impact of ethnic in-movers on the length of stay of home-owners in micro-neighbourhoods', *Urban Studies*, 2019.
4 Nai, Jared, Narayanan, Jayanth, Hernandez, Ivan and Savani, Krishna, 'People in more racially diverse neighborhoods are more prosocial', *Journal of Personality and Social Psychology* 114, no. 4, 2018: 497.

Raising Global Citizens

1 Alexander, Jessica Joelle and Sandahl, Iben, *The Danish Way of Parenting: What the Happiest People in the World Know About Raising Confident, Capable Kids*, Penguin, 2016.

Don't Feed the Monsters

1 Lee, Yeonjin, Muennig, Peter, Kawachi, Ichiro and Hatzenbuehler, Mark L., 'Effects of racial prejudice on the health of communities: A multilevel survival analysis', *American Journal of Public Health* 105, no. 11, 2015: 2349–55.
2 Amodio, David M., 'The neuroscience of prejudice and stereotyping', *Nature Reviews Neuroscience* 15, no. 10, 2014: 670–82.
3 Asby, Dana, 'Why Early Intervention is Important: Neuroplasticity in Early Childhood', *Preuzeto s*, 2018.
4 Kirby, James N., Doty, James R., Petrocchi, Nicola and Gilbert, Paul, 'The current and future role of heart rate variability for assessing and training compassion', *Frontiers in Public Health* 5, 2017: 40.

Acknowledgements

Some say writing a book is like having a child. I'm not sure I'd go that far (ask any mum who's been through labour), however it certainly takes a village to bring a book to life. I would like to thank my village, namely:

Everyone at RML, especially my amazing agent Rachel Mills who made me believe I could change the world in 70,000 words.

Everyone at Yellow Kite, particularly Holly Whitaker, Veronique Norton and Caitriona Horne. Special thanks to Tamsin English who brought me into the fold and Carolyn Thorne, whose kind and steady encouragement steered me to publication. A huge thanks to Anne Newman for your copyediting wizardry.

My brilliant contributors: Andi Oliver, Natalie Lue, Ebele Okobi, Nat Illumine, Vicki Psarias, Nomita Vaish Taylor, Laura Evans, Mirka Moore, Monica Costa, Ivanka Poku, Shanthi Annan, Ruth Kudzi, Mercy Osei-Poku, Professor Sunny Singh, Lekia Lee, Michelle Chai, Timil Ejirika, Tinuke Bernard, Rachel Ezekwugo, Karen Courtenay and others not mentioned by name. Thank you for sharing your views and entrusting me with your stories.

All the people who have supported this book's journey by reading samples, helping me come up with the best title, sharing anecdotes, connecting me with the right people, endorsing my vision or cheerleading when I needed it most. I am most grateful for Gary Belsky, Chika Unigwe, Patrick Dele Cole, Dr Ike Anya, Kadija Sesay, Marc Boothe, Garfield Hackett, Sai Murray, Chanelle Newman, Akala, Courttia Newland, Hollie McNish, Bassey Ikpi, Jenny Arnold, Storm Davison, Nky Iweka, Dr Karen McCarthy Woolf.

Thanks also to Solumna Okongwu, for nagging at me to write the damn book already. Elizabeth Gilbert, whose *Big Magic* was my constant writing companion. Obii and Pax Harry, who opened their home to a teenage scribbler. My Airlie 'inmates' who celebrated me as a writer long before my first byline. My Thornhill mama circle, who kept me going with nights out and coffee mornings. My fellow M-Net writers. Keep creating magic.

Chenna, Brooke, Hannie, Reem, Mona, Jolade, Ronks, Vivi, Kem, Ihuoma, Amaka, Chinwe. Here's to all our stories. Nnenna, for being my first friend, my first reader and my eternal bra.

A warm thanks to my wonderfully wacky family: the Asikas and the Ejiogus. My longtime champions and the best in-laws ever Patrick Dele Cole, Mina Cole, the Cole collective (Tonye, Jolly, Queen, Deinbo, Seun, Boma), lovely Mira and my mother outlaw Helen McLean.

Nkiru, for being there every step of the way and Obi, for being the essence of kindness. Nwando and Seyi and Nuli, you each give me hope for the future. Mayowa, for our deep and dizzy conversations. Isaac, for being the coolest stepson in the world.

Abiye, my love. Thank you for lighting my fire, making me laugh and putting up with my creative wormholes. Ezra and Jed, for being the heart and soul of this book, our blog and our home.

My late parents, Chinyere and Ukpabi, for your wisdom, grace and loving guidance -- then, now and always.

And to you, holding this book in your hand. Thank you for reading it. May it inspire you and your future changemakers.

About the Author

Uju Asika is a multiple award-nominated blogger, screen-writer and creative consultant. She is the founder of the popular parenting blog, *Babes About Town* and influential digital consultancy, Mothers and Shakers. Her writing has appeared in publications such as *The Guardian*, *Time Out*, Salon.com and select literary anthologies. Born in Nigeria, Uju grew up in the UK and has worked in London, New York and Lagos. She lives in north London with her husband and two football-mad boys.